BUILDING ON THE PAST

Visions of housing futures

Edited by Peter Malpass and Liz Cairncross

First published in Great Britain in March 2006 by

The Policy Press
University of Bristol
Fourth Floor
Beacon House
Queen's Road
Bristol BS8 1QU
UK

Tel +44 (0)117 331 4054
Fax +44 (0)117 331 4093
e-mail tpp-info@bristol.ac.uk
www.policypress.org.uk

British Library Cataloguing in Publication Data
A catalogue record for this book is available from the British Library.

Library of Congress Cataloging-in-Publication Data
A catalog record for this book has been requested.

ISBN-10 1 86134 751 0 paperback
ISBN-13 978 1 86134 751 0 paperback
ISBN-10 1 86134 752 9 hardcover
ISBN-13 978 1 86134 752 7 hardcover

Cover design by Qube Design Associates, Bristol
Front cover: photograph supplied by kind permission of Henry Shaftoe
Printed and bound in Great Britain by Hobbs the Printers Ltd, Southampton

This book is dedicated to the memory of
Professor Robina Goodlad, former chair of the Housing Studies
Association, who died in June 2005

Contents

List of tables, figures and photographs

Tables

Figures

Photographs

Foreword

Jon Rouse, Chief Executive of The Housing Corporation

One of the most daunting aspects of my role as Chief Executive of The Housing Corporation is knowing that the decisions we take today about the projects we fund will have a lasting effect on future generations.

At the same time I remind myself that over 90% of the housing stock that we inhabit today will be the same stock we inhabit in over 30 years' time. Thus, the even more daunting task is to make the most of what we've already got.

This publication is designed to help us to face up to both these tasks, in making choices about the new homes we develop and in investing in the welfare of existing communities.

In considering these challenges, I start from a very basic premise, that we should prioritise those who need help the most. Primarily, that means those who are homeless and living in overcrowded conditions, and those who too easily slip through the official definitions of need – the refugee, the older person struggling with financial hardship or the younger single person thrown out of home.

But how will these needs present themselves in 20 years' time, and what will be an appropriate housing response? We only need to consider the changes in expectations since the 1980s in, say, hostel accommodation or sheltered housing, to know how difficult it is to truly build for the future.

Nevertheless, from the excellent contributions in this book I think we can discern certain trends that will help us to plan successfully. The first is that home ownership will continue to be viewed as the tenure of choice for the vast majority of people and that we will have to work very hard to prevent social housing, particularly social rented housing, becoming a residualised form of tenure. This has implications for how we design mixed tenure developments and how we allocate homes. A second trend is that we are becoming a more elderly population and this will require new forms of response both in terms of promoting independent living and also in how we provide care. A third is that affordability will continue to be a problem in many parts of the country for at least the next 10 years as we seek to accelerate the rate of housing supply from its current low base.

Over the next few years we already know that we will see many important changes to the policy landscape as it grapples with these and other issues – Housing Benefit reform, tenure reform, changes to regional planning, changes to local government finance, new environmental standards, to name just a few. The task for The Housing Corporation, as for all parts of government, is to do our best to develop a policy framework that considers the needs of tomorrow's households and not just today's. In order to do that, we need to create and test possible scenarios of what the future could look like. This book will help us face up to the complexities of that challenge.

Acknowledgements

Thanks are due to Lynne Lonsdale and Jane Allen of the Centre for Housing Policy at the University of York for their help in preparing the papers for the conference that preceded this book. Preparation of the chapters for the book was helped by June Nicholls of the Faculty of the Built Environment, University of the West of England, Bristol.

List of contributors

Rowland Atkinson was a lecturer in the Department of Urban Studies, University of Glasgow and is now a senior researcher at the University of Tasmania, Australia.

Richard Best is the Director of the Joseph Rowntree Foundation, York, UK.

Glen Bramley is Professor of Urban Studies at Heriot-Watt University, Edinburgh, UK.

Liz Cairncross was a lecturer in the Department of Planning at Oxford Brookes University, UK, and is now Senior Research Associate at Picker Institute Europe.

Ian Cooper is a partner in Eclipse Research Consultants, Cambridge, UK.

Peter Fletcher is Director of Peter Fletcher Associates, an independent consultancy in the UK working across housing, health, social services and regeneration for older people and other adult groups. He is also Chair of the Board of Housing 21.

Philip Leather is Director of Housing and Urban Renewal at ECOTEC Research & Consulting and Visiting Professor at the Centre for Sustainable Urban and Regional Futures, University of Salford, UK.

Peter Malpass is Professor of Housing Policy and Head of the School of Housing and Urban Studies, University of the West of England, Bristol, UK.

Phil Morgan is Chief Executive of the Tenant Participation Advisory Service (TPAS), UK.

Alan Murie is Professor of Urban and Regional Studies and Head of the School of Public Policy at the University of Birmingham, UK.

Brendan Nevin is Director of Housing at ECOTEC Research & Consulting and Visiting Professor at the Centre for Sustainable Urban and Regional Futures, University of Salford, UK.

Stephen Platt is Chair of Cambridge Architectural Research, an independent consultancy in the UK providing specialist advice and research to the construction industry, design professions and policy-making institutions.

Moyra Riseborough is a lecturer at the Centre for Urban and Regional Studies, University of Birmingham, UK.

Christine M.E. Whitehead is Professor of Housing in the Department of Economics, London School of Economics and Political Science, and Director of Cambridge Housing and Planning Research, University of Cambridge, UK.

ONE

Introduction

Peter Malpass and Liz Cairncross

Building on the past is a title highlighting the way in which modern towns and cities are to a large extent literally built on top of the foundations of earlier structures. As urban populations grow, so governments and planning systems around the world are increasingly emphasising the need to contain physical expansion and to increase residential densities. In Britain, for example, the Report of the Urban Task Force (1999, p 11), called for the development of brownfield land and the recycling of existing buildings to be made more attractive than building on greenfield sites. This was rapidly translated into a government commitment to a target of 60% of new housing on brownfield sites. Our title also refers to the fact that in the case of housing the stock of dwellings inherited from the past represents a valuable resource on which to build a better future; they also constitute an important part of the problem, of course, and the replacement of old and worn-out houses is a major challenge. Governments in Europe and North America have been responding to problems of housing supply and quality for a century or more, and, in principle, it should be possible to use the experience thus accumulated to design smarter policies for the future.

This book is partly about asking what can be learned from the past that may be of value in the future, and it is partly about speculating about how the future might turn out. But the use of the plural in the subtitle is deliberate: the book sets out a series of visions of housing futures, not a programme or manifesto. The various chapters were specially commissioned from housing experts working in both academic and policy settings, and were originally presented as papers at a conference arranged by the Housing Studies Association in April 2005. The majority of chapters draw on and are informed by British research but provide a basis for thinking about housing futures on a wider scale. The intention is to look beyond the immediacy of current concerns and to identify the sorts of issues that will be setting the agenda for housing over the coming 20 or 25 years. Inevitably the problems and solutions will vary to some extent from country to country; echoing Gourevitch (quoted in Harloe, 1995, p 528), we can say that what happens in different countries will reflect the force of epochs, cutting across the particularities of local circumstances, and the force of national trajectories, as different countries react in their own way.

If, as the novelist L.P. Hartley wrote, the past is a foreign country, where they do things differently, then it follows that the same is true of the future. The big difference is, of course, that the future is a country that no one has visited, and there is great uncertainty about which things will be done differently, and about the extent of difference. Thus, while speculating about the future is a popular pastime for many, and a lucrative activity for a few, it is both very difficult to do with confidence and prone to cause embarrassment when outcomes fail to match prophesy. Apparently obvious developments fail to occur, while unforeseen events have a habit of upsetting the most carefully crafted predictions (Holmans, 1991). The intention, therefore, is not to expose a series of housing experts to the risk of subsequent ridicule (or 'the enormous condescension of posterity', to borrow a phrase from E.P. Thompson) by asking them to predict the future, but rather to ask some pertinent questions and to explore key themes that, from the vantage point of 2005, seem likely to demand attention and to influence the way things will turn out over the next 20 years or more.

This opening chapter introduces those themes, but first we want to provide a jumping off point by reflecting on the past and saying something about the housing situation in the present period. In any attempt to write about the future the past is an inescapable point of reference, for it is all we have to draw on. One of the uses of the past in this context is not so much to make accurate predictions but to try to minimise the risk of error. Thinking about the past helps to identify those things that change and those that stay the same; it helps to understand that although housing systems are dynamic, some things change faster than others.

Change and continuity

If you go back far enough it is easy to demonstrate that everything has changed, but even in the relatively short period since the end of the Second World War in 1945 (less than an average lifetime) there is ample evidence of rapid social and economic change, much of it deriving from rising living standards (at least in advanced capitalist economies), the impact of technological innovations and the process known as globalisation. Housing has inevitably been affected by these tides of change, and it is important to remember that patterns of housing provision and consumption have been driven at least as much by these sorts of factors as by conscious policy action. However, housing policy received a considerable boost from the Second World War. Six years of armed conflict cast a long shadow over housing in Britain and other combatant countries, as they struggled to overcome widespread destruction and to catch up with lost investment in both new building and repair and maintenance. When considering the remarkable extent of change in Britain over the period since 1945 it is important to recall that housing was then at a low ebb, with the worst shortage of the 20th century (Holmans, 1987, p 93), a seriously disrupted housing market and building industry, and a virtually bankrupt national economy (Cairncross, 1985, p 90).

The most significant changes in housing in Britain since 1945 are:

- the increase in the overall supply of dwellings;
- the improvements in the quality of living conditions enjoyed by most people;
- the transformation of the pattern of ownership; and
- the rise and decline of housing policy.

The postwar shortages took decades to deal with, by a combination of economic recovery and direct policy action, but it is clear that in most advanced economies housing conditions are now much better than they were in the aftermath of the Second World War. In Britain in 1951 80% of households lived in accommodation that was either unfit, substandard, overcrowded or shared with other families (DoE, 1977, p 10), while in West Germany, for example, things were much worse, with only 10 million dwellings for 16 million households (Harloe, 1995, p 256). Now over 90% of British households have access to not only bathrooms, indoor toilets and hot water systems (features that were absent from a great many dwellings 50 years ago) but also central heating (which was a rare luxury in those days) (Wilcox, 2004, p 104). But, as basic amenity levels have risen over time, so expectations and perceptions of quality have changed and new concerns have emerged, including energy efficiency, security and environmental factors such as the impact of traffic and risk of flooding.

On housing tenure, in 1945 Britain was still largely a nation of renters, with most households renting from private landlords, a tenth renting from local authorities and less than a third owner-occupiers. By 2005 70% were owner-occupiers, 10% were private tenants and the rest were in the social rented sector (although, as will become clear in subsequent chapters, these tenure categories are becoming less well defined and less useful analytically). Academics have debated the drivers of this transformation (Forrest et al, 1990; Saunders, 1990), but it is safe to say that it was a combination of consumer preferences, supply-side interests and government policy, sustained over a long period.

The Second World War led to what later came to be disparagingly referred to as 'big government', and for decades afterwards governments continued to assume greater responsibility for economic management than they had before, and greater than they like to accept now. This had an impact on housing in that the commitment to full employment helped to raise real incomes and the demand for owner-occupation. It also fostered an atmosphere of support for a regulated housing system in which most people, one way or another, paid less than the full market price for their accommodation. Private tenants were protected by rent control (or later by rent regulation), local authority rents were subsidised and homebuyers had access to a sheltered circuit of mortgage finance as well as mortgage interest tax relief. The era of big government saw the construction of unprecedented amounts of social housing, in the British case overwhelmingly built by local authorities (in the 20 years after 1945 local authorities built 60% of all new houses and half of all the local authority houses ever built in Britain were constructed in this period; see Merrett, 1979, pp 320-1).

It was in the context of shortages and interventionist governments that housing policy waxed most strongly, only to wane in the last quarter of the century. It can also be argued that housing policy in Britain has always been based on providing support to the market, even in the postwar period of maximum public sector house building. From the very beginning of housing policy the basic assumption has been that the market would provide for most people most of the time, and that the role of the state was to work with the market rather than against it. In the aftermath of the Second World War the state was drawn into a leading role, but by the mid-1970s the postwar settlement began to collapse and the policy emphasis on achieving high levels of house building gave way to concerns about the volume and distribution of subsidy and the problem of how to contain the growth in public expenditure in a period of high inflation. From the late 1970s policy shifted to a focus on public housing as part of the problem rather than the solution, and the numbers of council houses sold came to exceed the numbers built, in both numerical terms and political importance. Housing seemed to slide down the hierarchy of political issues, and a debate broke out as to whether housing policy was in terminal decline (Kleinman, 1996; Bramley, 1997; Malpass, 1999). However, the end of housing policy has not arrived and renewed concerns about low levels of house building relative to need and demand led the government to issue what it described as a 'step-change' in housing policy (ODPM, 2003a, p 3).

If housing policy has not collapsed it has certainly changed, albeit in directions that are consistent with long-established trajectories. For example, the increased reliance being placed on market forces and on the importance of consumer choice is entirely consistent with trends that have included continued heavy emphasis on the expansion of owner-occupation, on the grounds that it both reflects consumer preferences and is good for the economy. Housing supply issues have returned to the fore, prompting government to commission an inquiry (Barker, 2003, 2004) into the apparent reluctance of builders to respond to price signals in the market. Here is a striking indicator of how the policy atmosphere has changed, because in the early postwar period when high levels of output were needed, successive governments relied heavily on the local authorities, but now the emphasis is overwhelmingly on finding ways to increase private sector production. In addition to reducing public sector investment governments have pursued a policy of eliminating housing subsidies and deregulating the housing market (which has also been considerably affected by the wider deregulation of finance and banking in the 1980s).

In terms of the governance of housing, there are two main developments: first, there has been a shift away from municipal ownership and management towards a social rented sector based on independent not-for-profit housing associations (registered social landlords), and, second, the devolution of housing to the Scottish Parliament and the Welsh Assembly opens up the possibility of divergence within different parts of Britain. Other developments that are potentially significant are the emergence of stronger decision-making bodies at the level of the English regions and the decision to allow private builders to apply for social housing grants (hitherto confined to registered social landlords). The introduction of private finance for housing associations from the mid-1980s began to inculcate a more businesslike approach to this sector of the housing system, and allocation of grant aid directly to builders represents a further step in this direction.

In the early years of the 21st century housing conditions in Britain are, on average, better than ever before: there are more dwellings relative to the population (implying lower levels of overcrowding) and higher levels of amenity. The predominance of owner-occupation accords with popular preference, and there are signs of increasing flexibility in the housing market as a whole, in particular in terms of the levels of investment in private renting. However, there are still significant problems to be resolved before the long-established goal of a decent home for every household at an affordable price can be said to have been reached. These may be listed as follows:

- affordability remains a serious barrier to decent housing for a significant proportion of the population, particularly in London and the South of England;
- there is considerable regional disparity in housing market activity, with some parts of the Midlands and the North of England and parts of South Wales suffering from low levels of demand;
- the supply of new houses has been identified as probably the major policy failure of the past 25 years, and the reluctance of the building industry to increase output in response to rising prices in high-demand areas remains an issue to be resolved; and
- the social rented sector, having been systematically denigrated and starved of investment for a generation, has become increasingly residualised and associated with social exclusion. As a result it poses a severe challenge to the policy community.

What can be said about the future?

The review of housing policy in England in the period 1975-2000 identified four main drivers of change: demographic trends, social change, macro-economic variables (income growth, inflation and economic restructuring) and housing policy itself (ODPM, 2005, p 16). What can be said about the future is that change will continue, and that a focus on the factors driving change is likely to be a fruitful approach. Equally, of course, there will be continuity and it is necessary to think about the constraints on change. The market, for example, is a source of change, but commitment to it is a constraint, placing limits on the sorts of change that are likely to arise.

Housing systems, especially ones based on and exposed to market forces, are dynamic, and change is to be expected. However, profound change takes a long time: the modernisation of the housing market in Britain was a slow process, taking 90 years to move from 90% private renting in 1914 to 70% owner-occupation in 2005; a generation after the introduction of the Right to Buy, two thirds of the stock remains in the social rented sector (if not in local authority ownership), and a decade after large-scale stock transfer was taken up aggressively by government less than half the council stock has been offloaded. Given time, big changes do come about and the question now being debated is not so much whether, but how long, municipal housing will survive in Britain. Thus we can venture beyond the statement that change will continue and we can say something about the kinds of changes that are likely to happen.

The idea of dynamism is important in the context of debates about tenure restructuring, which have perhaps tended to imply a transition to a steady-state situation based on a large owner–occupier sector, a residual social rented sector and relatively small amount of private renting for young and mobile households. Continued change is, however, more likely than an ossified pattern of tenures, and this is an idea taken up in later contributions. It is also important to reflect on what drives change, and to recognise that although continued change is likely it will be driven by different factors. It has been argued above that for 25 years or so after 1945 the Second World War was a major influence on the definition of the housing problem and what to do about it. In more recent decades policy has continued to be influenced by reaction to developments in the earlier postwar period (for example, privatisation can be seen as a reaction to the postwar expansion of the public sector). The further we move from the mid-20th century the more other forces and factors emerge to shape the direction and pace of change.

Looking forward 20 or more years we can make some reasonably confident statements about the housing stock that will then be in use, simply because most of it has already been built. At current rates of construction, around 150,000 dwellings per year, in 20 years houses already in existence would constitute very nearly 90% of the total stock, assuming no losses through demolition or conversion. In fact, however, the age profile of the dwelling stock is one reason why we should expect that there will be renewed emphasis on increasing the rate of replacement: in England alone 40% of the stock in 2003 was more than 60 years old (ODPM, 2003b, p 11). Another reason for clearance of obsolete stock is that in some areas housing market conditions imply that this is the only way to regenerate a healthy market (and this is discussed in Chapter Five by Brendan Nevin and Philip Leather). However, the likelihood is that the majority of older houses will continue to be lived in, almost indefinitely, and that there will be an ongoing process of repair, maintenance, adaptation and modernisation. Most of this will be initiated and funded by individual property owners, and therefore the level of activity and the way that it is financed will tend to reflect the state of the wider economy and individual spending power, as well as changing expectations and aspirations.

In the same way that we can talk about the number of dwellings, we can be confident about the total number of people to be housed in 20 or 25 years' time, because most of them have already been born. However, there is a greater degree of uncertainty about the people, as compared with the dwellings, because of the unpredictability of migration and the risk of epidemic diseases. But the really difficult demographic prediction is the way that people will organise themselves into separate households. From a housing perspective it is households that are important for they hold the key to the level of need and demand. For many years there has been a tendency for the average household size to shrink, as more and more people live in one- and two-person households, but there is clearly a limit to this process.

The changing balance of age groups within their populations is a problem facing a number of advanced capitalist economies over the next few decades. This is a process that has some important housing dimensions. For example, as the age structure changes, with more elderly people and fewer younger people, there will be declining numbers of first-time buyers in the housing market. At the same time there will be record numbers of elderly homeowners, living in family homes that are, in objective terms, under-occupied, and ageing along with their owners. There are questions to be asked about how far these elderly owners will be willing and able to maintain their homes in a good state of repair, a problem that becomes more acute the further we peer into the future, bearing in mind the emergence of concern about the inadequacy of current levels of saving for retirement.

A third area in which it is reasonably safe to risk a prediction is that the market will remain as the dominant mechanism for providing housing. There is simply too much invested in it, both financially and politically, for there to be any chance of a successful challenge to its position. Surveys consistently reveal the popularity of owner-occupation, and the preference for buying over renting has been barely dented by the ups and downs of the housing market (Smith, 2002; CML, 2004, p 41). Owner-occupied houses have become not only where most people live but also their main form of saving, representing the largest single category of privately held wealth. This suggests that not only the maintenance of the market but also property values will be a priority for future governments, barring some dramatic and as yet unforeseen event. It also suggests that market forces will be key drivers of change.

The power of the market can be seen from the way that since the mid-1990s there has been an enormous, unplanned and market-driven growth of investment in so-called 'Buy to Let' activity, in which, according to the Council of Mortgage Lenders, an astonishing £46 billion had been invested between 1998 and 2004 (this refers to individuals buying properties for letting, and is apparently in addition to commercial investment in private renting). Individual investors have poured money into residential property, encouraged by mortgage lenders and perceptions of its relative attractiveness compared with the stock market or pension plans. It seems highly likely that governments will continue to seek ways of encouraging the growth of the private rental market, because of both its investment appeal and its capacity to provide an alternative to social renting.

It seems reasonable to speculate that future governments will want to protect and preserve the housing market and property values because of the potential for converting housing wealth into spending power. Not only is the level of consumer spending important to the wider economy but also housing wealth represents a huge potential resource that homeowners could be required to draw on to pay for services, such as pensions and care in old age, that are currently funded by general taxation. With increasing proportions of housing equity in the ownership of a growing elderly population, governments will almost certainly yield to the temptation to meet the needs of the latter by drawing, one way or another, on the former. Current indications suggest that the most likely strategy will involve some form of means testing, making homeowners responsible for meeting their individual needs. In the context of an apparently emerging consensus about the need to reform the Council Tax, it is important to remember that any move to a local income tax would significantly reduce the already low overall burden of residential property tax, thereby strengthening the argument for requiring homeowners to use their own resources to pay for their welfare needs. This in turn helps to explain the emerging enthusiasm for finding ways to give a wider range of households a share in the equity in their homes.

However, having risked prediction in this area, it is necessary to move quickly on to the point that, when thinking about the future, it is much easier to be confident about the problems than the solutions. Not only are policies more difficult to foresee in any detail, but they come and go with greater rapidity, so in this particular context the safe prediction is to expect the unexpected.

Themes explored in the book

The themes addressed in subsequent chapters cover the main areas of debate about housing futures. The first and inescapable theme is the *dynamism of housing systems*, and all contributors inevitably refer to this idea to a greater or lesser extent. In particular, Alan Murie's chapter (Chapter Two) reviews changes since the 1970s, arguing that many of the certainties that underpinned housing research and policy in the past no longer hold true. Social, economic and demographic changes, combined with new directions in housing policy, have significantly altered the way that different housing tenures work and the operation of the housing market. He sets out key elements in debates about housing policy and research in two eras, referring to changes associated with residential mobility, residualisation and privatisation and reflects on the implications of these changes for how we address questions about the future development of the housing sector. Murie argues that housing research and policy needs to adopt a new perspective on the idea of tenure, which has been so influential, especially in the context of the United Kingdom. In future not only will the established housing tenure categories be different in terms of what they do in the housing system, but they will also be of diminished importance as a basis for both understanding and intervention. Phil Morgan also touches on this idea in his chapter (Chapter Nine), in which he argues that the notion of 'tenant' will become anachronistic as equity sharing becomes more widespread across what is now referred to as social renting.

A second key theme concerns the *problem of supply and demand*. This embraces a whole set of questions, including quantitative issues about how much new building will be needed and how demand for it can be facilitated (what kinds of homes should be built, for whom and at what price?). There are also difficult political questions about where new building should be located – how much agricultural land should be built on and what proportion of new building can be located within existing built-up areas? Building new homes is just one way of responding to demand, and, as has been argued earlier in this chapter, in the foreseeable future existing dwellings will continue to constitute the main source of supply. This raises the question of what can be done to sustain demand for existing residential infrastructure and in particular to prolong the useful life of houses in areas that are old and/ or economically rundown? Richard Best's chapter (Chapter Three) looks at both sustainable new communities and neighbourhood renewal. He considers the key drivers of change in the British housing system, identifying economic, demographic and environmental factors. He develops a critique of policy approaches focusing on sustainable communities and neighbourhood renewal, concluding that more needs to be done to produce adequate amounts of affordable housing than relying on piggybacking private developments. This will find a lot of support among housing specialists.

In Chapter Four, Christine Whitehead also looks at questions of supply and demand. She first looks at the major reasons for increased demand since the 1980s, considering demographics, incomes, finance, the impact of prices and capital gains and government policy. She then looks at supply-side issues: the distinction between gross and net supply; the varying importance of slum clearance, demolitions and conversions; the changing importance of social housing supply; the geographical distribution of housing supply and the match between overall supply and demand. The chapter turns to the geography of inequality and then outlines two visions of the future: the increasing mismatch between regions and areas, leading to the exacerbation of access and affordability differentials; and changing patterns of demand and policy that increase supply and opportunity − the problems of adjustment.

Brendan Nevin and Philip Leather, in Chapter Five, concentrate on the issue of low demand housing, reporting research in the Manchester housing market renewal area. They highlight how some of the primary drivers of multitenure housing abandonment originate from previous public sector interventions, market-driven changes in consumer preferences and the economic restructuring which has been ongoing since the 1960s in older industrial areas. With hindsight the decline of demand for owner-occupied housing in areas of falling population, rapidly changing patterns of land use and declining employment are entirely predictable. The chapter concludes by noting that previous urban policy initiatives have been incapable of addressing the powerful forces which have stimulated housing market decline, because they have focused narrowly on the housing stock rather than the wider processes which make neighbourhoods unattractive as places to live. Furthermore, given the multifaceted nature of the regenerative tasks, the extent of the necessary financial and managerial commitment from government to the process of market renewal may have been underestimated at the outset.

A third key theme of this book is the idea that there is a *strong tendency towards social segregation at the neighbourhood level*, fuelled by market forces and individual preferences, and that increasing inequality will tend to undermine policy attempts to promote mixed sustainable communities. This is explored by Rowland Atkinson in particular (Chapter Seven), but also emerges from a number of other contributions (Murie, for example, suggests that income rather than tenure will become increasingly important as a key neighbourhood characteristic).

A fourth key theme is *affordability*, which has been at the heart of the housing question since the emergence of urban industrialisation in the first half of the 19th century. It connects to debates about supply and demand, and to the link between spending power and housing quality that is implicit in the theme of segregation in market-driven housing systems. Glen Bramley (Chapter Six) looks in detail at the affordability debate, starting from the problem of definition and measurement, and moving on to consider a number of policy approaches, drawing principally on research evidence from England.

A fifth key theme concerns the implications of *demographic change*, in terms of demand and supply as well as cohort effects. The idea of cohort effects is particularly useful in thinking about the future of housing, not least as a warning that the future cannot be simply deduced from the present. This is made clear by Moyra Riseborough and Peter Fletcher (Chapter Eight), who argue that older people in the next 20 or 30 years will be distinctly different from their parents and grandparents. Assumptions about dependency and passivity need to be set aside for a generation that has grown used to affluence and choice. Over the next 15 years the numbers of people over retirement age will begin to increase significantly, especially among the very elderly. Patterns of housing provision will need to respond to both growing numbers and changing expectations. The authors argue that whereas traditionally elderly people have been seen as largely dependent and relatively poor, in future elderly people will be different in terms of their levels of financial independence and their determination to exercise choice. They will also have considerable electoral power, and it remains to be seen how asset-rich elderly homeowners will respond to demands that they draw down their housing wealth in order to alleviate the tax burden on the younger working population.

A sixth theme focuses on housing consumers and the issue of *choice*, in particular the problem of how consumers can make their preferences known, and get them listened to. Phil Morgan (Chapter Nine) looks at the prospects for social housing, suggesting that not only will the landlord organisations change but so too will the tenants. Indeed, he argues that the distinction between tenant and owner will become obsolete as consumers take on more responsibilities in return for a share in the equity in their homes. The consumers' and stakeholders' point of view is also discussed by Stephen Platt and Ian Cooper in their chapter (Chapter Ten) which can also be read as a contribution to a final theme, about *how we can research the future*. They outline three projects designed to find out more about how stakeholders could be involved in useful discussion of neighbourhood futures.

Despite the difficulty of researching the future there are, nevertheless, many interesting areas that can be addressed and much that can be usefully said about what lies ahead and what can be done about it. Detailed prophecy is almost certain to be proved wrong, but at a more general level it is possible to explore the future with some confidence. In the final concluding chapter we return to the themes identified here, and seek to pull together the main conclusions emerging from the various individual contributions.

References

Barker, K. (2003) *Review of housing supply: Securing our future needs. An interim report*, London: HM Treasury and ODPM.

Barker, K. (2004) *Review of housing supply: Delivering stability: Securing our future housing needs, Final report: Recommendations*, London: HM Treasury/ODPM.

Bramley, G. (1997) 'Housing policy: a case of terminal decline?', *Policy & Politics*, vol 25, no 4, pp 387-407.

Cairncross, A. (1985) *Years of recovery: British economic policy 1945-51*, London: Methuen.

CML (Council of Mortgage Lenders) (2004) *The CML mortgage market manifesto: Taking the past into the future*, London: CML.

DoE (Department of the Environment) (1977) *Housing policy, Technical Volume I*, London: HMSO.

Forrest, R., Muric, A. and Williams, P. (1990) *Home ownership: Differentiation and fragmentation*, London: Unwin Hyman.

Harloe, M. (1995) *The people's home? Social rented housing in Europe and America*, Oxford: Blackwell.

Holmans, A. (1987) *Housing policy in Britain: A history*, London: Croom Helm.

Holmans, A. (1991) 'The 1977 national housing policy review in retrospect', *Housing Studies*, vol 6, no 3, pp 206-19.

Kleinman, M. (1996) *Housing, the state and welfare in Europe*, Cheltenham: Edward Elgar.

Malpass, P. (1998) 'Housing policy: does it have a future?', *Policy & Politics*, vol 27, no 2, pp 217-27.

Merrett, S. (1979) *State housing in Britain*, London: Routledge and Kegan Paul.

ODPM (Office of the Deputy Prime Minister) (2003a) *Sustainable communities: Building for the future*, London: ODPM.

ODPM (2003b) *English House Condition Survey 2001, regional report*, London: ODPM Publications.

ODPM (2005) *Lessons from the past, challenges for the future for housing policy: An evaluation of English housing policy, 1975-2000*, London: ODPM.

Saunders, P. (1990) *A nation of home owners*, London: Routledge.

Smith, J. (2002) 'CML market research results 2001', *Housing Finance*, no 53, Spring, pp 13-27.

Urban Task Force (1999) *Towards an urban renaissance*, London: The Stationery Office.

Wilcox, S. (2004) *UK housing review 2003/2004*, Coventry/London: Chartered Institute of Housing/CML.

TWO

Moving with the times: changing frameworks for housing research and policy

Alan Murie

Introduction

This chapter is concerned with the future direction of change in housing, especially in the UK. On the whole we have not been very good in the past at anticipating changes in housing and the intention is to reflect on changes that have taken place since the 1960s and to assess the implications for future change. The starting point is the evidence from housing research over a period of more than 30 years, the frameworks that have dominated the way research evidence has been organised and presented in the UK and Europe, and changes that mean that we need to reassess these frameworks.

In the postwar period a distinctive approach to housing research emerged in the UK and in Europe as part of the challenge to an overarching thesis about embourgeoisement and the redistributive impact of the postwar welfare state. While sociologists had neglected housing (Hole, 1972), economists and urban geographers were satisfied with filtering or trade-off models that focused on land and housing costs, proximity to the city centre or places of work, incomes and travel-to-work costs (see, for example, Evans, 1973). Many of these approaches derived from a literature that assumed state intervention and subsidy were relatively unimportant for housing. The approaches to housing studies were not unchallenged in the US but the dominant paradigm was felt to work in North America, perhaps because public housing was generally insignificant (and access and continued residence in the sector directly related to income) while the private market could be treated as a seamless whole.

From the late 1950s through the 1960s and 1970s a body of work accumulated in the UK that demonstrated that a different paradigm was needed. For example Titmuss's work on the welfare state (Titmuss, 1962, 1963) identified council subsidies and various payments associated with other tenures as potentially important influences on income distribution. Cullingworth's (1963) work on the private rented sector emphasised the significance of public policy, but also the extent to which that part of the housing market in decline did not conform to one version of rational economic behaviour. Nevitt's (1966) work on housing subsidy added to the account of the significance of state intervention, and both Donnison (1961) and Cullingworth (1965, 1967) began to focus on trends and patterns of residential movement that made most sense when explained through the tenure lens. Rather than a seamless market with incomes, housing costs and travel-to-work as key elements, the most effective framework for understanding the way that the housing market operated in Britain began to be based on an understanding of the role and nature of state intervention, and the partitioning of housing finance between different tenures. In a separate tradition Rex and Moore (1967) referred to housing classes that related to housing tenure. Urban managerialist and Marxist accounts of housing also tended to be organised around versions of housing tenure although their emphasis was on production and consumption, exchange professionals and processes that were not so evident from studies of individual household behaviour (see, for example, Bassett and Short, 1980).

What emerged was a framework for housing research that was distinct from the North American approaches, because of different institutional and organisational arrangements and observed patterns of household behaviour. In most of the US it was reasonable to discuss the operation of the market in relation to income, price and other factors irrespective of tenure. In the European context, the significance of large, not-for-profit or state housing sectors, or of a decommodified housing sector, required an alternative approach. There was also a contrast with North American cities where 'race' was a major influence on residential behaviour. In Europe, a housing studies tradition emerged which saw tenure segmentation as fundamental to understanding what happened in the housing sector. The approach adopted in Britain (Murie et al, 1976) used tenure categories in a way that was strongly influenced by the notion of sub-markets (see, for example, Grigsby, 1963), and was influential in the development of housing research in the Netherlands and in Sweden, for example. It drew strength from the political economy approaches that identified different patterns of control and finance associated with different tenures; and from a housing policy approach that identified partitioned housing finance and policy systems.

It fitted with more empirical approaches, seeking to make sense of patterns of residential mobility and trends in the development of the housing market. The legislation relating to different tenures was distinctive and institutional, organisational and financial arrangements were separate. Accounts of what was happening in housing increasingly referred to tenure as the key fault line in the market and this is apparent from Rex and Moore (1967) through Pahl (1975) to Saunders (1990) and others.

Following this we can set out the emerging view of housing tenure that dominated subsequent research approaches and interpretations:

- Private renting was still in rapid decline, affected by significant remnants of rent control, as well as by new patterns of rent regulation but with a non-regulated sector also evident. The dominant picture was of a poor quality housing sector that at best was poorly managed and at worst was characterised by exploitation and discrimination (see, for example, Cullingworth, 1963; Milner Holland Report, 1965; Burney, 1967). It catered for an established immobile tenant population that was ageing in place, and a more transient population with limited rights and no rent allowances or assistance with housing costs. Except for the very low rents paid by households in controlled tenancies, there was little to attract households to private renting. It was the tenure for those already in occupation, for the poorest households and those with least choice. They had least choice both in terms of ability to access owner-occupation (associated with income and access to credit) and ability to access council housing (associated with current housing situation, family structure and residence). The best housing in the private rented sector continued to be transferred to home ownership or the council housing sector, and the numerical decline was speeded by slum clearance and active improvement policies which also speeded the process of tenure transfer and, in some places, gentrification.
- Council housing was a high-quality, high-demand sector; rents were higher than in much of the privately rented sector, and properties were vastly superior. Council housing was also superior to some of the owner-occupied sector, especially those parts that transferred from private renting. The sector was predominantly new, and although there were increasing numbers of flatted properties being added to the stock, these were still new and had not yet attracted the reputation that they often have today. The advantages of council housing in its golden age can be overstated. There is no doubt, however, that it was the aspirational tenure for many households

including affluent working-class households. The quality and condition of the housing stock, the security of tenure and subsidised rents made it the preferred tenure for many households. Rules relating to eligibility and allocation and the preoccupation with rehousing for slum clearance made access to the tenure selective and the way that rationing in a high-demand sector operated was open to challenge (see, for example, Cullingworth, 1969; English, 1979; Henderson and Karn, 1987).

- The owner-occupied sector was smaller and less diverse than it is today. It was a higher- and middle-income tenure, although there was significant development of inner-city owner-occupation, and important regional and local differences which meant that owner-occupation catered for a much wider section of the population in some places. The regulation of building societies and the rationing of mortgage finance as well as redlining and other procedures mean that much of the literature on owner-occupation in this period refers to eligibility and access and gatekeepers in much the same way as it does to eligibility and access to council housing (Murie et al, 1976; Williams, 1976; Boddy, 1980).

Both of the expanding high-demand tenures were subject to systems of bureaucratic rationing as well as processes that were market related. The easy access tenure was private renting. A range of other issues related to regional and local differences, path dependency and gentrification. There was debate about the decline of private renting but most of it referred to the slow goodbye of the landlord, and the likelihood that private renting would continue if only because many landlords did not plan to become landlords and did not operate in an economically rational way. There was little anticipation of a major further change in the respective role of other tenures. The length of waiting lists and popularity of council housing meant that there was little anticipation of the decline of local authority housing. Indeed the importance of housing for local government and the value attached to it by Labour- and Conservative-controlled local administrations was seen as a strong safeguard for the tenure and a guarantee of its success, sustainability and quality. The expansion of owner-occupation was seen to have boundaries related to income and the costs both of house purchase and of maintenance. Government policies continued to favour both council housing and home ownership and the fashionable policy agenda related to a comprehensive housing service with plans and provision related to all tenures and all stages of the family cycle (Cullingworth, 1969). Although distinctive inner-city housing markets, notably those for black and minority ethnic communities, were developing (see, for example, Karn et al, 1985), these were seen as a result of the lack of opportunities in other tenures, rather than evidence that owner-occupation would expand significantly downmarket.

Although there was an active debate about reforming housing finance and increasing the efficiency and fairness of financial arrangements, there was little anticipation of dramatic changes in the nature of tenures, or the respective roles of different tenures. There was little anticipation of changes in the pattern of tenure transfer (those associated in particular with privatisation) and discussions of a change towards greater social tenurial polarisation were not treated with great seriousness. There was a tendency to assume continuity in patterns of housing demand and to refer to demographic change as the key variable likely to shape the future housing market. The neglect of changing aspirations and of changes in housing investment and supply was in spite of the evidence of disinvestment by private landlords, and the emerging debate about council house sales and housing finance.

Transitions

There is a largely unrewarding debate about what were the key turning points in postwar housing policy. In terms of trends or outcomes, however, the 1970s and subsequent decades are marked by a number of departures from the established pattern and mark a transitional phase. There is a substantial literature describing the pattern of change and modernisation of tenures (see, for example, Malpass and Murie, 1982, 1987, 1990, 1994, 1999). In this chapter three elements are referred to in order to develop a discussion of explanations for change and from this to assess the implications for likely future patterns of change. The three elements are considered in turn: residential mobility, privatisation and residualisation of social rented housing.

Residential mobility

More recent discussions about low demand for housing have drawn attention to rising turnover and void rates in the social rented sector in the 1990s (Pawson and Bramley, 2000). For example, Burrows (1999) has shown that, in spite of its decline in size (or perhaps because of it), the number of moves within the social rented sector rose from some 4.2% of the total number of dwellings in 1984 to some 6.9% in 1993/94. Tables 2.1 and 2.2 broaden this agenda and refer to the three main

Table 2.1: Tenure and residential mobility in England: all moving households (ratio of the proportion of households moving into each tenure to the proportion of total stock in each tenure)

Present tenure	1957/58	1960/62	1960-64[a]	1960-64[b]	1984	1994/95	1996/97	1997/98	1998/99	2000/01
Owner-occupation	95	95	88	100	78	58	56	62	60	62
Local authority	85	95	105	93	91	93	109	102	97	95
Housing association					140	178	150	110	150	127
All social rented						95	107	118	104	108	104
Private rented unfurnished	80	81	74	80			296		297	303
Private rented furnished	650	450	243	250			469		466	480
All private rented	114	109	123	107	237	379	284	358	354	356

Notes: [a] Greater London; [b] Rest of England and Wales.

Sources: 1957/58: Donnison (1961); 1960/62: Cullingworth (1965); 1960/64: Woolf (1967); 1984: General Household Survey; 1994 and later: Survey of English Housing

Table 2.2: Tenure and residential mobility in England: new households (ratio of the proportion of households moving into each tenure to the proportion of total stock in each tenure)

Present tenure	1957/58	1960/62	1960-64[a]	1960-64[b]	1984	1994/95	1996/97	1997/98	1998/99	2000/01
Owner-occupation	74	95	80	108	60	49	55	55	49	47
Local authority	40	62	55	46	97	106	115	107	113	126
Housing association					170	154	76	102	136	125
All social rented					103	114	110	106	118	126
Private rented unfurnished	97	94	100	110			274		276	301
Private rented furnished	1150	750	329	400			588		691	703
All private rented	156	130	159	142	318	427	376	397	413	419

Notes: [a] Greater London; [b] Rest of England and Wales.

Sources: 1957/58: Donnison (1961); 1960/62: Cullingworth (1965); 1960/64: Woolf (1967); 1984: General Household Survey; 1994 and later: Survey of English Housing

tenures and a longer time period (1957/58 to 2000/01). The data are presented as ratios to indicate whether tenures play a greater or lesser role in mobility. Where the ratio is 100 the role in mobility is exactly as would be expected from the relative size of the tenure, where it exceeds 100 this implies a greater than proportional role in providing for residential mobility. This approach takes into account the changes in the relative share of the market taken by different tenures over the period involved.

These data highlight major changes in residential mobility affecting each of the major tenures, but the most dramatic changes are in the private rented sector. In each of the sources and years referred to, the changing patterns are affected by changes in the demographic profile but also by deregulation and reputational factors. Earlier surveys distinguished between the furnished and unfurnished private rented sectors because security of tenure and regulation differed between these two parts of the market. In the 1950s and 1960s this accounted for the lower than expected mobility in the regulated, unfurnished sector and the higher than expected rates in the furnished sector. By the 1990s the tenure as a whole had a very prominent role in housing mobile households while the role of the owner-occupied sector had declined in this respect. The private rented sector had become the main entry point for newly forming households. The increasing role of private rented property in residential mobility reflected the progress of decontrol with vacant possession and subsequently the wider deregulation of the 1980s and the availability of Housing Benefit.

The increasing role of social rented housing in housing new households is also significant and reflects a change from slum clearance rehousing. Both council housing and housing associations saw a rise in mobility to the mid-1990s and a subsequent decline – perhaps partly a managed decline with some of the properties being associated with the highest turnover, vacancy and churn being taken out of the stock or refurbished to make them more attractive. The declining role of home ownership in residential mobility is dramatic and partly associated with maturation, with the ageing population of the sector.

The change in the private rented sector has also been associated with a declining role in housing older and retired households. The cohort of controlled tenants has largely left the sector and been replaced by younger households. In this way its profile has been very different from that of the social rented sector that, over the same period, developed an increasingly bipolar distribution with a high proportion of young and elderly tenants with relatively few in the middle age groups. In private renting there was also a growth among both manual and non-manual groups. The private rented sector has become more mixed than the social rented sector but its function and social role is very similar, especially in relation to the under-29 age group. Within the terminology of residualisation the private rented sector has continued to perform a residual function but this has shifted from older people to people below pensionable age. The owner-occupied sector has increasingly included those above pensionable age.

The more important issue emerging relates to churning or turnover. With a much more active sector open to would-be new tenants the sector has a more significant role in catering for households changing address. In 1998/99 the proportion of all private sector tenant households resident for less than 12 months was 41% compared with

25% in 1984. The households moving in were also more mixed. They included more economically active households and households from higher socio-economic groups but they also included, for example, an increasing number of households dependent on Housing Benefit. These patterns reflect the fragmentation of the tenure and its role in different niche markets.

Privatisation

A second key area of change involves policies to reduce the role of the state in housing. A range of policies could be referred to (Murie, 1993), but the focus here is on the sale of state housing. Prior to the introduction of the Right to Buy (RTB) through the Housing Acts of 1980, there had been significant sales of council houses under discretionary policies by local authorities in England, and the characteristics of households and even dwellings sold subsequently under the RTB were established in this period. Council house sales reached high levels despite lower rates of discount than emerged in 1980 under the RTB, the absence of an active central government campaign, the failure of all local authorities to use their discretionary powers and the tendency to exclude significant parts of the housing stock, especially flats (Murie, 1975).

The sale of over two million dwellings since 1980 has been fundamental to the decline in the size of the council sector. The differential pattern of sales changed the spatial as well as social and dwelling type profile of the sector (as well as changing the home ownership sector).

In the debates around RTB in 1979 and 1980, commentators from different ends of the political spectrum tended to argue that its impact would not be dramatic (see, for example, House of Commons, 1980). The evidence that the RTB would speed a move towards welfare housing in Britain was not treated with very much seriousness or it was seen as acceptable or involving more efficient targeting of subsidy. There were different reasons put forward for believing that the RTB would have little impact – related to the nature of the housing stock, and to the low incomes of council tenant households. There was an underestimate both of the latent demand for purchase at highly discounted prices, but also of the cohort effects which would mean a constant recruitment of households into situations where the RTB became more attractive.

For tenants in good quality dwellings the opportunity to purchase at a substantial discount was attractive and the households living in the best properties were often those who qualified for the highest levels of discount (Forrest and Murie, 1990; Jones and Murie, 1999). They were households in the middle of the family life cycle, with the heads of household in their forties and fifties. More affluent tenants qualified for the largest discounts and these applied to the best dwellings. The recipe offered by the RTB generated high levels of sales, especially among more affluent tenants in better quality properties.

The progress of council house sales since 1979 has been uneven. Sales rose dramatically in the early years of the RTB and peaked in 1982. This reflected both the pent-up demand from areas where discretionary sales had not operated and new demand generated by the new terms for sale and the publicity associated with the new legislation. Following this, sales fell to a relatively low figure in 1986 before rising to a new peak in 1989, and fell to their lowest levels in 1995-97. Sales rose again after 1996-97. The fluctuating pattern suggests that rising employment and affluence and the booming home ownership market attracted more tenants to buy properties. In addition, debate about revising the RTB undoubtedly encouraged some people to bring forward plans to buy. They thought – misguidedly – that the policy was about to be revoked. A key element in this was publicity surrounding the change in maximum discount level in 1998 and the statements of ministers in 2002 (Marsh et al, 2002).

The properties sold under the RTB did not represent a cross-section of dwelling types and the progress of sales was uneven regionally and locally. A higher percentage of houses than flats were sold and three-bedroomed, semi-detached houses were heavily over-represented. This pattern of sales considerably changed the council housing stock. In England, for example, the proportion of public sector tenants living in flats increased by 5 percentage points between 1981 and 1993 and the increase was much greater among urban authorities that had large numbers of flats. As a consequence, households seeking council housing were much more likely to be offered a flat than previously and the contrast between dwelling types in home ownership and council housing became more pronounced.

The highest rates of sale in England were in two belts, one across the South and one across the North of England. There were also some strong rates of sale in shire districts in all regions except for Yorkshire and Humberside. The lowest belt of sales was associated with the cross-Pennine route from the Mersey to the Humber and north of that, and there were relatively low rates of sales in the West Midlands conurbation, inner London and Tyneside.

The RTB, in its early years, was particularly attractive to households in the middle of the family cycle. For most households the purchase of the house that they rented from the local authority was not carried out with the intention of moving on. Rather it secured their future and established something that they would be able to pass on to their family. It enabled them to reorganise their finances, especially in retirement, and it gave them more control over repair and maintenance and the management of their own property. These advantages rather than movement to another property are what was sought by the majority of purchasers in the early days of the policy and what has determined the subsequent actions of most purchasers. In more recent years, however, there has been an increase in purchase by younger households. By the late 1990s the proportion of tenants who were in their forties and fifties had declined significantly. The profile of purchasers was bound to change. Increasingly, some tenants benefiting from the RTB were younger, had relatively short periods of tenancy and were less likely to be buying with a view to staying in a house that they regarded as their home. Rather they saw house purchase as an effective way of organising a move on and an exit from their existing house and neighbourhood (Jones and Murie, 2005). This prominence of purchasers with shorter tenancies, along with the reduction of maximum discount after 1998, meant that the deadweight involved in the RTB was reduced. A high rate of sales was being achieved with a lower rate of discount. This made more sense in terms of value-for-money but was less justifiable in terms of the objectives of policy and agendas about targeting long-established tenants who had been paying rent but had nothing to show for it.

Privatisation has transformed the council and social rented sectors and the opportunities they offer have been diminished. At the same time, the RTB has changed the other tenures and the realities of what different tenures offer and where they are located:

• RTB tenure transfers have contributed to the expansion of the home ownership sector and changed the means of access to these properties. The open market purchasers of former council properties have different characteristics from new council tenants. In England just over half of these purchasers were already homeowners. Some 35% of first-time purchaser households were newly formed households. The remainder were established independent households moving from mainly private rented accommodation. A similar pattern applied in Scotland (Jones and Murie, 2005). The choices open to homeowners have increased as those in the social rented sector have diminished.

• RTB tenure transfers have also affected the privately rented sector. Some 8% of properties sold in England under the RTB between 1980 and 1991 had become privately rented (Forrest et al, 1995) and this is likely to have increased subsequently, especially in the more unpopular estates and lower demand markets. In some cases this adds to the problems of managing and regenerating estates.

Residualisation of social rented housing

The discussion of the residualisation of social housing in Britain is part of a wider debate about socio-tenurial polarisation. Discussions of trends in the British housing market in the late 1970s and early 1980s increasingly referred to tenure polarisation and drew attention to the significance of a changing tenure structure in the context of higher unemployment and greater inequality of incomes (Forrest and Murie, 1983; Hamnett, 1984; Bentham, 1986). This served to draw attention to differences between the two dominant tenures that had emerged with the decline of private renting. However, with some exceptions (Stephens et al, 2005), there has been a tendency to walk away from representing this as social polarisation. Lee and Murie (2002) argue that the sale of council houses and other developments in the council housing sector have reduced the social mix in that tenure (but not in council housing neighbourhoods). Consequently, it is more accurate to talk of a residualised council housing sector with a predominant role in housing lower-income groups. However, at the same time as this pattern has been developing, the owner-occupied sector has not experienced a reduction in social mix and has not become more exclusively a tenure for the rich. The owner-occupied sector has become more differentiated. Its role in housing lower-income groups has expanded and it is its role in housing the middle-income groups rather than the highest-income groups that has expanded most. Thus, rather than a bipolar tenure structure with one tenure catering for the poor and the other for the rich, we have an increasingly residualised council housing sector and an owner-occupied sector which has expanded to embrace a wide range of incomes. Van Kempen (2002, pp 48-9) argues more fundamentally that discussion of polarisation and suggestions of dualism or a dual society are more generally difficult to sustain. He states that the most important arguments against the formulation of the dual city are the large numbers of households with a middle income that occupy positions at neither end of the dual spectrum. These households are neither rich, nor very poor. An approach that refers to the very poor and the rest also neglects the differences within these groups. In this context it seems more appropriate to engage with notions of stratification than the dualism associated with social or tenure polarisation. It is better to talk about residualisation of social rented housing and differentiation or stratification within the owner-occupied sector rather than tenure polarisation.

The changing role of social rented housing has become a major element in discussion of inequality and polarisation in cities in the UK. Pahl writing in 1974 commented positively on the record of council housing in Britain:

> To a large extent Britain has got a more humane and generous approach to housing than other, ostensibly richer, societies. This is largely due to the size and quality of its local authority housing, which despite what its critics would say, is probably the best-managed, publicly-owned housing stock in the world. (p x)

This high-quality housing, had it been in the market, would have commanded higher rents and been accessible only to those with higher incomes and secure employment. The organisation and finance of housing meant, however, that it was accessible to others and formed an important element in the redistributive welfare state – and an element with a stronger spatial impact resulting in planned decentralisation of the population and greater social mix in suburban and new town contexts than was associated with the older areas of cities segregated by income and property value.

At the time that Pahl was writing, it was already apparent that the nature and role of council housing was changing. The sustained decline of the privately rented sector was reducing the alternatives for lower-income households and increasingly funnelling them into the council sector. At the same time, the increased supply of property for sale and the financial, political and status advantages seen to be associated with home ownership meant that an increasing proportion of those that could afford to buy did so, rather than wait in unsatisfactory housing until the higher-quality local authority housing became available. Residential mobility generated a selective pattern of redistribution of population between tenures and increasing differentiation between tenures (Murie et al, 1976). The pattern was clear well before the introduction of the RTB in Britain. Family Expenditure Survey data showed that in 1963 26% of households in the bottom three income deciles were council tenants but by 1979 the comparable figure was

47%. In 1967 45% of the recipients of supplementary benefit (the means-tested assistance benefit designed as a social safety net) were council tenants, and in 1979 61% were (Murie, 1983).

The term 'residualisation' first appeared in the literature concerned with the social rented sector in England in the late 1970s and early 1980s. It largely grew out of examination of national data related to the changing social profile of different tenures, and referred to the narrowing social profile of the tenure and more targeted nature of policy. Residualisation was represented variously as the unplanned consequence of the decline of private renting and privileging of owner-occupation and an incremental process associated with differential cohort responses to the changed structure of the housing market; as the direct result of national level housing finance and other policies which treated council housing as residual and designed for those unable to buy; and as the decline in the relative quality of housing in the sector as a result of lack of investment in new housing and in maintenance and improvement (see, for example, Forrest and Murie, 1983; Murie, 1983; Malpass, 1990). These accounts argued that the environment in which council housing was operating had changed. In a period of increasing social inequality there were fewer alternatives for lower-income groups as private renting declined in size. At the same time, council housing was becoming attractive to a narrower section of the community and the advantages associated with owner-occupation meant that demand from the higher-income and social class groups among younger households was drawn away. The data used to establish that residualisation was occurring included that relating to the changing household profile (age, income, social class, gender, economic status), the structure of the housing stock and the characteristics of movers into council housing (Forrest and Murie, 1988; Prescott-Clarke et al, 1988, 1994). At the same time, a number of policy changes speeded up the process of residualisation, and it was evident that government and other key stakeholders were not concerned about the trend. Policy changes included the introduction of the RTB in 1980, increased rents in real terms and reorientation of council housing subsidies, placing more emphasis on income-related assistance. These changes speeded up the departure of more affluent tenants from council housing.

It is important to consider whether the residualisation trend has continued, and Tables 2.3 and 2.4 provide data related to this. Table 2.3 shows that between 1980 and 1990 the proportion of social rented sector households in the lowest three income deciles increased. The past trend continued and was associated with a declining representation

Table 2.3: Percentage of households in major tenures in different income categories

	1980	1990	2000
The lowest three income deciles			
Social rented	44.6	63.9	64.3
Owner-occupied	18.2	15.4	18.3
Private rented	42.0	41.7	39.5
The middle four income deciles			
Social rented	39.6	29.8	31.1
Owner-occupied	39.9	43.7	43.7
Private rented	42.1	42.0	41.5
The highest three income deciles			
Social rented	15.9	6.3	4.5
Owner-occupied	41.9	40.9	38.1
Private rented	16.0	16.3	19.0

Source: Family Expenditure Survey, Family Spending

Table 2.4: Percentage of households in different income categories by tenure

	1980	1990	2000
The lowest three income deciles			
Social rented	51.8	54.4	47.9
Owner-occupied	33.0	34.0	38.8
Private rented	15.3	11.6	13.3
The middle four income deciles			
Social rented	34.4	19.1	17.8
Owner-occupied	54.1	72.2	71.5
Private rented	11.5	8.7	10.7
The highest three income deciles			
Social Rented	18.4	5.3	3.7
Owner-occupied	75.8	90.1	89.3
Private rented	5.8	4.5	7.0

Source: Family Expenditure Survey, Family Spending

in social renting of both middle- and higher-income categories. Between 1990 and 2000, however, the change was very small, and might suggest that the trend had in fact bottomed out.

Table 2.4 refers to the same data, but presents the tenure profile of different income categories. When presented this way, the move towards residualisation of social renting appears less convincing than that indicated in Table 2.3. Households in the lowest three income deciles were increasingly likely to be owner-occupiers but the probability of their being in the social rented sector rose only slightly between 1980 and 1990 and declined after 1990. The middle- and higher-income groups show a marked fall in the probability of being social rented tenants between 1980 and 1990 and, although this continued after

1990, it was much less marked. The increase in low-income home ownership is not compatible with a polarisation model that suggests the affluent moving to home ownership and the less affluent to social renting.

Other data can also be used in this context. The Survey of English Housing shows a continuing decline of multiple earner households in the social rented sector and a growth in households with no earners. There has also been a continuing growth in one-person households (from 22% in 1977, to 35% in 1987, 41% in 1998/99 and 43% in 2003); and a decline in large adult households (18% in 1977, 14% in 1987 and 8% in 2003 (ODPM, 2004a)). At the same time, the age structure has been changing. The period in which the social rented sector was becoming increasingly elderly seems to have passed. In the council housing sector the proportion of tenants aged 65 or over increased from 30% in 1977 to 40% in 1987. By 1999 this had fallen back to 35% and in 2003 it was 34%.

Because the social rented sector has declined, its capacity to continue to house even more of the lowest-income groups has been reduced; some of the inertia in patterns is likely to relate to the relative immobility of older households; both of these factors bring forward the point when there is limited scope for further residualisation. This notion of a saturation level does not imply that a greater concentration of lower-income groups in social housing is not possible but rather that there is little scope for such change, and the pace and extent of any further change will be affected by developments in other tenures and by cohort effects.

These data suggest that the UK housing system has moved beyond an active residualisation phase into a phase in which the trend associated with residualisation is no longer progressing rapidly. One view would be that the late residual phase is associated with rejection of social housing, and the sector has graduated to a point where it has a different role in the housing market as well as a different social profile. In the next phase of development, the demographic profile is likely to change as the older cohort of tenants departs and the new tenant population are younger and less likely to remain as tenants. This change in demography may mean a more transient role but not a more residual role in terms of income or economic status.

Accounting for change

The three dimensions of change referred to above take us beyond the simple statistics of tenure change. These statistics demonstrate that, over a period of 30 years, the UK housing market has seen a quantitative adjustment in the share of different tenures, the pattern of new building and the scale of housing problems. But when we look at residential mobility, privatisation and residualisation, a qualitative change in housing is apparent. The meanings and reputations of different tenures, and household behaviour, have changed. The housing market has been highly dynamic and passed through a series of crises, phases of policy and market fluctuations. A number of observations grow out of the discussion above:

- Some of the key changes highlighted have derived from supply-side changes: decisions about disinvestment by private and social landlords have been critical in determining patterns of change.
- Each of the major tenures experiences a life cycle or maturation process and dominant household and dwelling characteristics change.
- There are important cohort effects associated with tenure growth and transfer: the passing of the cohort of private tenants affected by rent control has been as important as deregulation for changes in the private rented sector, and the RTB has affected a specific cohort in the right place at the right time.
- These cohort effects have left all tenures with highly skewed social and demographic profiles that affect the next phase of response to a policy (the changed demographic profile of council tenants made it probable that there would be a change in the characteristics of who takes up the RTB) and the next phase of development of the housing situation.
- Policy changes have been important in changing tenures but their impact is determined through interaction with demographic, social and economic changes, and attitudes and aspirations related to housing are not simply determined by policy.
- There are spatial effects associated with uneven tenure patterns of new building and tenure transfer: these are apparent at a regional level where the share of different tenures has remained very different, and at a more local level.
- The changes affecting any one tenure impact on others: the residualisation of the social rented sector is affected by attitudes to and opportunities in other tenures as well as what happened within the social rented sector; the RTB has transformed the social rented and home ownership sectors but also affected private renting.

This list of implications begins to establish a set of questions related to explanations of change and these in turn suggest the likely pattern of future change.

In a discussion of residualisation in European social housing van der Heijden (2002) seeks explanation in contributions by Harloe (1995) and Kemeny (1992, 1995). Both of these contributions come from international comparisons of housing and housing policy but neither is mainly concerned with the social role of the social rented sector. Harloe identifies the driving influences on the role of social housing as economic development and state policies associated with this. He refers to a convergence towards a residual model from the mid-1970s because of a common economic driver. Kemeny emphasises the embeddedness of the role of housing in the social structure and argues that different national systems reflect ideological and cultural factors. Kemeny's explanation, superficially, is not compatible with convergence evidence and would have suggested that the more tenure-neutral traditions, for example in Scandinavia, were inconsistent with residualisation. Both accounts provide general overarching perspectives and are more effective at explaining the origins and structures of social housing provision than recent changes. They place particular emphasis on the legal, organisational, financial and housing policy arrangements that institutionalise economic and cultural regimes. This leads to a tendency to seek explanations for change in the same arrangements – with a continuing focus, for example, on housing policy and tenure-neutral financial arrangements.

Discussions of residualisation for example, have tended to explain why this was occurring in the UK, without reference to other countries. Some commentators argued that it was not occurring throughout the UK or was unimportant because of the size of the social rented sector. Others argued that the location of social rented housing within more generous welfare states, as well as the size and organisation of the sector, explained why similar underlying processes did not generate the same outcomes (see, for example, Murie and Priemus, 1994). But most of the commentaries essentially took the view that residualisation was evident in the UK because of its peculiar political tenure strategies, the development of a residual approach to housing policy from the 1960s onwards, privatisation, the ideological as well as financial support for home ownership and the increasingly less generous welfare regime of the UK. In all of these respects it was argued that the UK, especially after 1980, was out of step with the other European countries with large social rented sectors and reflected a residual, liberal or Anglo-

Saxon approach to welfare (see, for example, Esping-Andersen, 1990; Kemeny, 1992, 1995).

It is important if we are to engage with explanations of change at this level to consider what has happened outside the UK. If the direction of change related to social and public rented housing has continued to differ between the UK and other European countries, then the explanation for residualisation is reasonably associated with the idiosyncracies of the management, ownership and finance of the British system. But if residualisation has also been experienced in other key European comparators, the drivers of change would seem to rest in other factors that are more common across these countries.

There is not room in this chapter to discuss this fully but van der Heijden (2002) presents data for six Western European countries in the 1990s (the Netherlands, Germany, Britain, France, Belgium and Sweden), and refers to income distributions within tenures. His data show that within Belgium, Germany and France there are similar proportions of households in different income deciles in the social rented sector. In France the lowest two income deciles are less likely to be in social rented housing than the two deciles above them, and there is a limited decline in the probability of being in the social rented sector among successive higher-income groups. The three countries with the largest social rented sectors – the Netherlands, Britain and Sweden – show a much higher proportion of lower-income deciles in the social rented sector and a much steeper decline in the proportion of households in social rented housing as income rises. In these three countries social rented housing plays a distinctive and differential role in disproportionately providing housing for lower-income groups. There are differences between these three 'low-income skewed' systems, with Britain showing the most regular and steepest decline in the role of social rented housing as income rises and the Netherlands (with the largest sector) having a higher proportion of all but the lowest-income decile in the social rented sector. In Sweden the lowest three income deciles are less likely to be in social rented housing than they are in Britain, but the decline in the proportion in social renting as income rises presents a similar pattern.

Van der Heijden also presents data showing changes (over the 1980s and 1990s) in the distribution of households in the social rented sector according to income. While Britain showed the strongest association between income and social renting throughout this period, all of the countries considered, except Belgium (with its very small sector), showed the same trend. The most rapid changes were apparent in Germany and Sweden, where the percentage of social rented tenants in lower-income groups rose most markedly and the proportion in the higher-income groups fell. Van der Heijden is careful to account for the changes both in terms of changes in rents, subsidies and other housing policies, and in wider economic and social policy developments, and argues against any automatic assumption of convergence towards a residual model. Borgegard and Dawidson (2000), referring to Sweden, account for the decline of some areas of municipal housing into distressed areas by referring to differentiation of location and type of property (multifamily housing) and increasing income inequality. These factors affected the hierarchy of preference and distinguished between areas and properties in a way that the finance system did not. In a similar vein, Kristensen (2002) has explained the changing social composition of social housing in Denmark in terms of the attractiveness of owner-occupied housing from the 1970s onwards.

This evidence goes against the view that attitudes to tenure in the unitary systems associated with social democratic welfare regimes were embedded in welfare regimes and cultures. Two initial possibilities emerge. First, accounts of unitary systems may have exaggerated the significance of tenure-neutral finance and underestimated the significance of other differences (in dwelling type, size, location) between tenures. Alternatively, the unitary system has begun to fracture because of increasing affluence and inequality, cohort effects and changes in policy. In either case the cultural explanation for differences in housing systems appears difficult to sustain. While it is no doubt an important continuing element in differences it should not bear the whole weight of explanation such that we would have to interpret the evidence as demonstrating a Europe-wide adoption of 'Anglo-Saxon' attitudes.

The evidence referred to above does not alter the view that the UK has gone further along the residualisation road, or that its social rented sector is more residual than in other European countries referred to. However, it does suggest that the other countries are on the same route and may be catching up. The gap may also have narrowed because the pace and nature of residualisation in the UK has changed. European social housing is undergoing a similar pattern of change with respect to residualisation in spite of different financial and organisational arrangements.

This kind of discussion suggests that a different explanatory framework is needed than is considered by van der Heijden. Understanding origins and institutional structures is critical to understanding the path that change takes but is not sufficient. If we are to understand the contemporary influences on social housing in different countries we should also look elsewhere and embrace dimensions related to social and demographic changes and other factors.

These observations also cast some doubt on the value of some alternative perspectives. For example, there are accounts that attribute patterns of change to the internal dynamics of single tenures or neighbourhoods. Prak and Priemus (1986) suggest that processes on social housing estates are similar and generate similar situations and a common spiral of decline that accounts for the transition from mixed to residualised estates. In this account, what happens at an estate level across the social rented sector affects tenure-level statistics. The drivers for change in the tenure are developments at the estate level and incremental failure has undermined and delegitimated the sector. This approach emerges from research focusing on estates with problems, but there is a danger in assuming that it represents the inevitable progression of social housing and therefore an explanation for a common experience of residualisation. Various other contributions follow this broad approach, focusing on processes within estates and on the management of social rented housing (Power, 1987, 1997; Taylor, 1995). This reductionism in the analysis is unhelpful and, especially if it is extended to the tenure as a whole, neglects important common external influences and estate-level sources of difference.

Some of the literature that emphasises the local and managerial and the intrinsic attributes of tenures does not consider alternative explanations behind the similarities and differences between these estates. The accounts at times appear to buttress a previously held view and suggest that management is the key to an explanation of what has gone wrong in these areas. Power (1993), for example, provides an account of a group of estates in France, Germany, Britain, Denmark and Ireland. These estates were selected because they exhibited a range of problems and had been included in government rescue programmes involving new resources and approaches. Power emphasises the importance of local policy and issues of ownership and control and gives in to the temptation to rewrite history to fit the argument being advanced – that different organisational arrangements have intrinsic strengths and weaknesses.

This chapter suggests that differences in organisation do not prevent a common trend towards residualisation across Europe. The drivers of change are at least partly external to the tenure and the neighbourhood being examined. Other research does not confirm the neighbourhood dynamics perspective. Recent research in six different European countries and 11 cities and two neighbourhoods in each city (see, for example, Musterd and Murie, 2002; Murie and Musterd, 2004). The neighbourhoods dominated by social rented housing in different cities and countries do not have the same role and function within housing markets; nor are they experiencing the same problems. Peripheral estates in different cities are not all isolated and badly connected through public transport. Some have strong communities and others weak. Some are largely dependent on state services and others have strong private and community-based activity. More fundamentally, the processes associated with different estates reflect differences in local economies and the nature and functioning of welfare state systems that remain very different within Europe. Estates have very different resources in terms of their populations and their cohesion, and this is both a product of who lives there and affects who lives there.

The alternative explanation for change, compatible with the key points highlighted above, would not neglect changes within tenures or neighbourhoods but would refer to supply-side changes as well as the interaction between what happens at an estate or tenure level and wider social and economic developments at different spatial scales. The starting point for this type of approach would be that, rather than having intrinsic attributes as suggested, for example, by Saunders (1990), the characteristics, reputation and status of tenures shift with a number of contingent factors. The expectations and aspirations associated with successive cohorts of the population have changed: from cohorts brought up in poor quality private rented housing and regarding council housing as a privileged tenure to cohorts brought up in owner-occupation and expecting to be homeowners and regarding council housing as associated with failure, poor quality housing and homelessness. Increasing affluence associated with increased employment, and a growth in women's employment after the mid-1990s, have strengthened this effect. The changing structure of the housing market has resulted in a change in the relative attractiveness and advantages associated with different tenures and parts of tenures. Hierarchies of choice between and within tenures have changed. Associated with this is a long-standing decline of private renting and a long-standing pattern in which national housing policy has privileged home ownership in financial and ideological terms.

A combination of other factors contribute to changing patterns of housing market behaviour:

- greater uncertainties in household arrangements with changes in marriage, the family, household structures and the age structure of the population;

- weakening welfare state ambitions and widening income inequality and social polarisation;
- the end of the postwar pattern of full employment and the commencement of a new pattern of economic restructuring and deindustrialisation;
- professionalisation of employment alongside the growth of multiple earner households, atypical working and insecure employment;
- the continuing contraction of the easy access private rented sector and the growth of homelessness;
- the maturation of council housing and the loss of early attributes associated with a stock of modern high-quality housing (with a comparative advantage over other tenures) and a niche market for young families and affluent workers (as these increasingly chose home ownership and the early cohort of tenants aged);
- the ending of a 60-year trend of growth of council housing and the beginning of numerical as well as proportional decline;
- the ending of slum clearance and improvement policies affecting the development of inner city neighbourhoods;
- the reduction in public expenditure on housing and the shift from object to subject subsidies reducing the privileged position of council housing and creating a new portable Housing Benefit subsidy – but one that was determined directly by income;
- the emergence of home ownership as the sole tenure of choice by government and among households and the development of new financial arrangements for home ownership;
- the passing away of rent control and at the same time deregulation of private renting – with both of these factors contributing to changes in the dynamics of the sector; and
- a policy of general privatisation with different elements from asset sales and stock transfers to new approaches to rents, regulation and management.

All of these factors have contributed to changes in urban management, housing tenures and patterns of residential behaviour. The combination of the RTB, the termination of new building and under-investment in management and maintenance involved a significant restructuring of the council housing sector. The RTB would not have had the same impact on the composition of the council housing stock had it been accompanied by an active new build programme, as it was, say, in the 1960s and 1970s. It also contributed to a significant restructuring of home ownership. This, as well as changes in the regulation of Building Societies and other financial institutions, ended the era of rationing of mortgages and replaced it with one of a market responding to the demands for borrowing. This is not to say that there are no longer gatekeeping functions in this market, but they are more subtle and less categorical. They may mean that people with different credit records or in different occupational situations, or wanting to borrow higher proportions of income, pay premium rates of interest, but they are less likely than in the past to be unable to obtain a formal loan at all. Different forms of insurance have developed and different practices to manage risk by financial institutions mean that the language is less about access and eligibility and much more about costs and affordability.

Finally, in relation to the privately rented sector, the period of decline has appeared to have bottomed out. The rent controlled element has almost vanished – not simply because of deregulation through legislative process, but through household dissolution and death. What has emerged is a more differentiated privately rented sector, with segments catering for students, higher-income professionals, Housing Benefit dependent households, asylum seekers and refugees. And, with the development of a Buy to Let market, the supply side has also changed, and the future of the sector may be increasingly affected by the financial plans of landlords related to the weaknesses of pension schemes rather than the direct returns from letting. The portability of Housing Benefit has meant that, in some parts of the country, lower-income households can exercise some degree of choice. It may not be a vertical choice between qualities or prices of properties, but it is a horizontal choice between locations, and, in some cases, between similar properties in different tenures.

Changing frameworks for analysis

The changes identified above essentially involve a realignment of stratification in different spheres. This links to the changing spatial patterns of British cities and regions, with decentralisation of the population and a layering of housing form and tenure in zones of cities associated with different phases of development; and with patterns of gentrification and its opposite (devalorisation? proletarianisation?) as the economy of the city changes. Residualisation is associated with a strengthening correlation between social stratification (income, place and status) and housing stratification (hierarchies of preference and status related to quality and tenure). This is associated with the commodification of housing and the consequent reduction in the extent to which households are in housing (sizes, qualities and locations) that they could not have accessed through the market. This is a pattern of change which links with debates about political influence and power. It is also a pattern associated with the changing economy of cities, changing patterns of employment and occupation – for example, with issues addressed elsewhere in relation to patterns of migration, social polarisation and professionalisation in cities (for example, Hamnett, 1994). In this way it is not simply a housing process but relates to the new economies of cities, whether as global cities or cities of consumption, and away from their previous organisation around the process of production. Rather than demand being related to proximity to workplaces and the role in the reproduction of labour, it is increasingly related to its qualities in consumption (and accumulation). This change has occurred in Britain at the same time as processes of obsolescence and dilapidation are affecting social housing more severely, and as a more diverse population has developed. Attributes that are associated with difference and 'cosmetic' quality and elite status are reflected in demand and price – and these are associated with private housing.

Aspirations and choices

The shifting balance of tenures in the UK means that an increasing proportion of newly forming households assume that owner-occupation is a normal and natural tenure. They are the sons and daughters of owner-occupiers rather than of tenants, and their housing practices are more likely to be affected by this. Households which entered the social rented sector when it was an aspirational tenure are more likely to see their days out in that dwelling (and tenure unless they exercise the RTB). They dampen the impact of changing reputation and the changing aspirations of new households, but increasingly the social rented sector will be exposed to its current reputation or the one founded in a period after its golden age. At this point it is much more likely that it will become a transitional, residual tenure. At the same time, part of the privately rented sector will continue to be transitional, and parts of the owner-occupied sector will also have this role. The unevenness of the owner-occupied sector in terms of quality, condition and price has become more apparent.

Fault lines

When we come to look at future patterns we need to modify our view of a segmented housing market with the key fault lines associated with tenure. Rather than a segmented market with gatekeepers and eligibility criteria and a complete lack of choice and access to different tenures, we need to conceptualise the housing market as a highly stratified market. We need to introduce active competition between tenures rather than the assumption of different rules of access. We need to recognise that investment and disinvestment decisions affecting supply may have little direct articulation with demand – but rather be influenced by electoral or fiscal calculations or by considerations related to pensions and the stock market. We need to recognise time lags and cohort effects. We need to introduce a stronger spatial dimension (regional, sub-regional and local), and we need to introduce fault lines within tenures.

The portability of Housing Benefit means that households with limited resources can exercise choices and can move between tenures that in the past would have been regarded as representing different housing classes and having different eligibility rules. While there are differences in tenants' rights, and the processes of access continue to have to be negotiated, they are less difficult lines to cross than in the past. The RTB and other routes into owner-occupation also mean that there are more households that cross between the rented sectors and owner-occupation. In some parts of the country, the costs of owner-occupation have also not been significantly higher than the costs of renting. This is partly because of the rent regimes that have been introduced by the government.

What has emerged varies between region and city and the key fault lines may not be the same in each case. The contention is, however, that they will cross tenure boundaries rather than coincide with them. For example in some areas the key divisions in the market may be between:

- a high-priced, high-income positional market that may be uniformly owner-occupied although it may have private rented property within it (sometimes temporary lets while owners are away). It may be helpful to typify this in terms of Council Tax band or dwelling type (detached houses), and there is often a spatial dimension to this part of the market. These are exclusive zones often but not always in rural or urban–rural fringe areas where employment and commuting affect lifestyles and housing choices, and housing investment is part of wider wealth creation strategies for households; and
- parts of the housing market that embrace much of the social rented sector, parts of the private rented sector and the bottom end of the owner-occupied sector. It may also be helpful to identify this in

association with Council Tax band or dwelling type. These are the mixed tenure, inner-city areas and council estates which feature strongly in debates about deprivation and the restricted choices of black and minority ethnic communities as well as in neighbourhood renewal areas. They are the new melting pot in the housing market where which tenure you are in may no longer be as important as which neighbourhood you are in and issues about neighbourhood management are more important than tenure itself. While the progress of the RTB has been unequal, and there are very great differences in the degree of tenure mix existing within particular council housing estates, it is only very small enclaves that have no tenure mix. It is not clear that owner-occupiers in these areas have a distinctly different housing experience than the council or private tenant in these areas. These older inner-city neighbourhoods in cities such as Birmingham have equally become mixed tenure with Buy to Let properties and family housing which, rather than being sold, is retained for letting, existing alongside social rented and owner-occupied property. Recent research on homeowners in the worst parts of the housing market in Housing Market Pathfinder areas (ODPM, 2004b) suggests that these areas function as low-income neighbourhoods rather than single tenure neighbourhoods. Their characteristics are associated with their place in the urban hierarchy and the housing and neighbourhood hierarchy rather than a tenure hierarchy.

Rethinking home ownership

This kind of division has fundamental implications for debates about home ownership. The home ownership category that has dominated housing analysis since the 1960s has no longer much meaning in analytical terms. It embraces a wide variety of very different circumstances and situations. Saunders (1990) identified home ownership as a key 'consumption sector cleavage', representing a vertical division in society and delivering ontological security. In this perspective homeowners have common interests irrespective of social class and the consumption sector cleavage cross-cuts traditional conceptions of class, 'race' and inequality. The argument against this is that the common category 'home ownership' embraces enormous variation and inequality in circumstances. This means that homeowners do not have a common interest, but that their interests as homeowners, in the part of the home ownership market that they are in, are more likely to coincide with their interests in relation to work and other aspects of their lives.

As the divisions within home ownership have become more pronounced, it is less tenable to argue that any common interest between homeowners is greater than the differences between them. Some homeowners are seriously indebted while others own outright; some experience massive increases in the value of their property sustained over a long period, while others experience much lower rates of appreciation and occasional periods of loss. With the development of the RTB and new City Living strategies involving the construction of high-density city centre housing, an increasing number of homeowners own leasehold apartments and their rights and responsibilities diverge from the conventional image of the homeowner. Homeowners own properties in different neighbourhoods and environments, and the image of home ownership as a tenure that confers status and relative affluence does not apply to the same degree or in the same way to every homeowner. One view would be that if home ownership in the past was a measure of social position and position in the labour market, as it expands beyond a certain point it can no longer be a positional good in that sense. What begins to happen is that parts of the home ownership market become associated with social position (Hirsch, 1977). Gentrification, which has in the past been associated with tenure transfer and an older working-class population being displaced by younger professionals, will take different forms in a predominantly owner-occupied market.

There are areas that consist wholly of owner-occupied property, where this property is exclusive and comes close to the definition of positional good. This is one stratum within the home ownership market. In contrast council and social rented housing is less differentiated than in the past, and so form a stronger analytic category. There is less differentiation of occupation, income and household circumstances than there was in the 1960s and 1970s, but households in this tenure category are more likely to be living in mixed tenure neighbourhoods. And the nature of the property and place has an impact on the desirability of their housing and the reputation associated with their place of residence. If we only look through a tenure lens we could have a distorted picture.

The next phase of development of the housing sector will be affected by the stronger commitment of government to home ownership and the stronger alignment of a variety of interests behind the private market in housing. The comprehensive housing policy associated with a previous era has given way to a comprehensive home ownership strategy to develop a range of products and routes into home ownership to match almost the complete range of housing needs. This environment narrows down the range of possibilities.

Against this background it is appropriate to consider how the home ownership sector is likely to develop. The divisions within the home ownership sector are likely to become clearer with the exclusive, positional market at one extreme and, at the other, home ownership, which is largely indistinguishable from other tenures. The top end of the market will continue to recruit upwardly mobile, high-income households and to retain its current attributes. Other strata within the home ownership market are likely to experience differing futures. As with the social rented sector and private renting in the past, there will be a demographic and economic effect in some neighbourhoods of owner-occupation. These areas with predominantly elderly populations may see a decline in property and condition, and may see surges in the properties coming on to the market for sale. The changing flow of properties on the market will affect how exclusive or desirable they are seen to be. In some places the difficulties associated with selling properties will mean tenure transfers to private renting or, depending on the policies of social landlords, to the social rented sector. This is the pattern that we have seen in some areas since the mid-1990s.

Neighbourhood effects associated with such transfers and with mixed tenure will mean that owner-occupation delivers very different things in such areas than elsewhere. If the social rented sector becomes significantly smaller, and if the variety of routes into home ownership sponsored by government increases, we may find that there are parts of the home ownership market that show a considerable amount of churning of population and of tenure status. These kinds of developments lend themselves much more to an analysis that will categorise the areas in terms of their social and economic status rather than their housing tenure.

Reviving private renting

One of the products of the sustained expansion of home ownership and of the low taxation, low-interest economy and wide income inequality has been (especially in the environment of faltering pension provision) to generate a demand for second home ownership. One possibility is that a continuing and even expanding enthusiasm for investment in the private rented sector is generated by the view of property as a secure investment for older age among asset-rich, income-rich, low-taxed, affluent, middle-aged, owner-occupier households.

There is a potential cohort effect here that could contribute to the expansion of the private rented sector unless alternative investments emerge that are more attractive. The possibility that historical patterns and contemporary opportunities mean that the promotion of home ownership actually generates a supply of privately rented housing should not be discounted. The other side of this coin is that such an expansion would have a supply-side effect on opportunities for house purchase among lower-income households and first-time buyers. The affordability problem would be exacerbated by the actions of existing owners wanting to buy additional properties rather than by the planning system.

Since the early 1980s investment in private renting has switched from its traditional role towards a role for Housing Benefit recipients, then to the student housing market and then to asylum seekers and refugees. The results have been influenced by the development of the Buy to Let market. All of these switches relate to a market and landlords who have sufficient flexibility to follow finance or policy opportunities. The logic of this is that in the longer term, and depending on the continued attractiveness of investment in this sector for individuals' long-term financial plans and pensions, the private rented sector will consist of a number of different sub-sectors addressing demand from particular groups. Changes in the Buy to Let market or similar factors may affect the overall size of the sector but the orientation will reflect opportunities in the market and its ability to compete with social renting and with the lower end of the home ownership market. This is likely to vary significantly by region and within regions. Some privately rented housing is likely to continue to be former RTB properties on council estates, but in other areas the transfer may be from home ownership in suburban and older, inner-city neighbourhoods with mixed housing and with less attractive housing in general.

Renewing public sector housing?

Changes in the RTB since 1998 may mean that it has largely run its course. However, as long as the RTB remains, and as long as there is a financial advantage associated with purchase in that market, it would be unwise to assume that there will be no continuing trickle of tenure transfers through this route. More importantly a future government may reintroduce a more active privatisation policy. There are still enough tenants in the social rented sector for the government to see this as an electorally popular step, and there are still enough advantages to the Exchequer to see the sale of properties as desirable.

Whether council housing offers an attractive or superior alternative to the lower strata of private renting and home ownership will depend on the scale of investment and quality of council housing. In the UK we have become used to a debate about the declining quality and reducing relative attractiveness of social rented housing, but it is feasible to reverse that and the new investment taking place under Decent Homes and regeneration actions (perhaps involving demolition and urban renewal – including providing high-quality new social rented housing) may have this effect in some areas. Some of the issues here are about land and finance and the extent to which investment in housing is ring-fenced. If the capital receipts associated with sales of land and social rented housing are reinvested in the housing sector and used in a strategic way with recycling of receipts, there is a significantly different prospect than otherwise. It could be possible to renew the sector through the addition of high-quality housing that would meet aspirations. This implies a priority for housing investment when an alternative view is that regional development agendas will increasingly draw public expenditure towards transport and other regeneration initiatives rather than housing. It also implies a priority for investing in quality housing when the preoccupation of government and agencies such as The Housing Corporation is with keeping costs to a minimum.

The households that will be in the social rented sector in the future are more likely to be younger and at early stages in their housing careers. Unless there is sufficient recruitment to social rented housing from the owner-occupied sector in middle age and later, the sector will establish a clearer role associated with newly forming and younger households. How far this develops and whether there is also a niche associated with people moving out of home ownership at a later stage in their housing career may depend on the strategies pursued regionally and by social landlords as well as on the nature of the home ownership and private rented sectors in the same market. The implication of this is that we are unlikely to see further residualisation of social rented housing but a shift towards a more transient residual role associated with a changed demographic profile. Policy interventions related to privatisation and investment will also be crucial in the pattern and pace of change. These patterns are likely to be uneven regionally and locally. Regional differences that have increased – with the London market most distinctive – are likely to become stronger and differences within regions and segregation within cities will grow, especially if the pattern of out-migration from older urban areas continues.

Conclusion

If we are to anticipate the way the housing market will change in the future, we need to start from a different baseline set of assumptions than was the case in the 1960s and 1970s. We need to continue to be aware of the significance of tenure but to emphasise that tenures are differentiated, dynamic and in competition with each other; and we need to take much more account of wider demographic, social and economic influences on change, and to give more attention to neighbourhood and place as well as to diversity within the population. If the aspirations and behaviour of different communities defined in terms of age or class or 'race' differ significantly, then these categories merit more direct analysis rather than assuming common patterns of behaviour related principally to tenure.

This does not suggest abandoning reference to housing tenures in analysis of housing markets, nor does it suggest reverting to the North American trade-off models in which price, income and location are the dominant issues. What it implies is treating tenure categories as insufficient and obscuring difference. It implies introducing other factors that are fundamental to the meaning of the home and not assuming that the fault lines relate simply to tenure rights. Property type and neighbourhood and the status associated with property and place among different age, class and ethnic groups merit much more attention and particularly in relation to divisions of home ownership.

Having said this, it is important to recognise that it is not easy to follow such an approach at a national level and there are limitations to our ability to develop the account without reference to regional and sub-regional analysis. The temptation to stick to a simpler tenure framework will remain strong.

The argument presented in this chapter emphasises the importance of decisions about investment and disinvestment by private and social landlords. It also emphasises cohort effects that are likely to impact on home ownership and social rented housing. Increasingly the social and private rented sectors are likely to house younger and more mobile households – and to compete with parts of the home ownership sector also providing for this market. The outcome of this competition will depend on policy interventions but is unlikely to be the same everywhere – partly because the unevenness of the previous development of tenures and tenure transfers means that the degree of age and income mix in much of the market is limited. We are likely to see a continuation of a fragmented private rented sector, but with the pattern of switching of investment changing over time and place and influenced by developments in home ownership and new patterns of property ownership.

Demographic and cohort effects which have worked through the private rented sector and are working through the social rented sector will continue to impact on home ownership and mixed tenure areas. Patterns of stratification in the housing market will be linked with parts of tenures and associated with a wider range of neighbourhood characteristics. Residualisation will become even less associated with single tenure areas and the association with mixed tenure areas will be more pronounced – with factors other than tenure contributing to this effect. One implication of this is that the current assumption that mixing tenures mixes incomes will be further challenged. What happens in the housing sector will have wider implications for the attractiveness of neighbourhoods, cities and regions and will contribute to the pattern of economic development of these. Housing will continue to be shaped by economic patterns but will also contribute to the way the economy develops and to stratification and status associated with wealth and location.

References

Bassett, K. and Short, J. (1980) *Housing and residential structure: Alternative approaches*, London: Routledge and Kegan Paul.

Bentham, G. (1986) 'Socio-tenurial polarisation in the United Kingdom, 1953-83: the income evidence', *Urban Studies*, vol 23, pp 157-62.

Boddy, M. (1980) *The Building Societies*, London: Macmillan.

Borgegard, L.E. and Dawidson, K. (2000) 'The development of and prospects for Swedish housing policy', Paper for ENHR Conference, Gavle.

Burney, E. (1967) *Housing on trial*, London: Oxford University Press and IRR.

Burrows, R. (1999) 'Residential mobility and residualisation in social housing in England', *Journal of Social Policy*, vol 28, no 1, pp 27-52.

Cullingworth, J.B. (1963) *Housing in transition*, London: Heinemann.

Cullingworth, J.B. (1965) *English housing trends*, London: Bell.

Cullingworth, J.B. (1967) *Scottish housing in 1965*, Edinburgh: Scottish Development Department.

Cullingworth, J.B. (1969) *Council housing purposes, procedures and priorities*, London: HMSO.

Donnison, D.V. (1961) 'The movement of households in England', *Journal of the Royal Statistical Society*, Series A, Part 1, pp 60-80.

English, J. (1979) 'Access and deprivation in local authority housing', in C. Jones (ed) *Urban deprivation and the inner city*, London: Croom Helm.

Esping-Andersen, G. (1990) *The three worlds of welfare capitalism*, Cambridge: Polity Press.

Evans, A. (1973) *The economics of residential location*, London: Macmillan.

Forrest, R. and Murie, A. (1983) 'Residualisation and council housing: aspects of the changing social relations of housing tenure', *Journal of Social Policy*, vol 12, no 4, pp 453-68.

Forrest, R. and Murie, A. (1988) *Selling the welfare state*, London: Routledge.

Forrest, R. and Murie, A. (1990) *Selling the welfare state* (2nd edn), London: Routledge.

Forrest, R., Murie, A. and Gordon, D. (1995) *The resale of former council dwellings in England*, London: HMSO.

Grigsby, W.G. (1963) *Housing markets and public policy*, Philadelphia, PA: University of Pennsylvania Press.

Hamnett, C. (1984) 'Housing the two nations: socio-tenurial polarisation in England and Wales 1961-81', *Urban Studies*, vol 43, pp 387-405.

Hamnett, C. (1994) 'Social polarization in global cities: theory and evidence', *Urban Studies*, vol 31, pp 401-25.

Harloe, M. (1995) *The people's home? Social rented housing in Europe and America*, Oxford: Blackwell.

Henderson, J. and Karn, V. (1987) *Race, class and state housing: Inequality and the allocation of public housing*, Aldershot: Gower.

Hirsch, F. (1977) *The social limits to growth*, London: Routledge and Kegan Paul.

Hole, V. (1972) 'Housing in social research', in E. Gittus (ed) *Key variables in social research Vol 1, Religion, housing, locality*, London: Heinemann.

House of Commons (1980) *Second Report of the Environment Committee, Council House Sales, Vol I Report*, HC 366- 1/1980-1, London: HMSO.

Jones, C. and Murie, A. (1999) *Reviewing the RTB*, Birmingham: University of Birmingham.

Jones, C. and Murie, A. (2005) *The Right to Buy*, Oxford: Blackwell.

Karn, V., Kemeny, J. and Williams, P. (1985) *Home ownership in the inner city: Salvation or despair?*, Aldershot: Gower.

Kemeny, J. (1992) *Housing and social theory*, London: Routledge.

Kemeny, J. (1995) *From public housing to the social market*, London: Routledge.

Kristensen, H. (2002) 'Social housing policy and the welfare state: a Danish perspective', *Urban Studies*, vol 39, no 2, pp 255-63.

Lee, P. and Murie, A. (2002) 'The poor city: national and local perspectives on changes in residential patterns in the British city', in P. Marcuse and R. van Kempen, *Of states and cities – The partitioning of urban space*, Oxford: Oxford University Press, pp 59-87.

Malpass, P. (1990) *Reshaping housing policy: Subsidies, rents and residualisation*, London: Routledge.

Malpass, P. and Murie, A. (1982, 1987, 1990, 1994, 1999) *Housing policy and practice*, London: Macmillan.

Marsh, A. et al (2003) *The impact of the 1999 changes to the right to buy discount*, London: The Stationery Office.

Milner Holland Report (1965) *Report of the Committee on Housing in Greater London*, London: HMSO.

Murie, A. (1975) *The sale of council housing*, Birmingham: University of Birmingham.

Murie, A. (1983) *Housing inequality and deprivation*, London: Heinemann.

Murie, A. (1993) 'Privatization and restructuring public involvement in housing provision in Britain', *Scandinavian Housing and Planning Research*, vol 10, pp 145-57.

Murie, A. and Musterd, S. (2004) 'Social exclusion and opportunity structures in European cities and neighbourhoods', *Urban Studies*, vol 41, no 8, pp 1441-59.

Murie, A. and Priemus, H. (1994) 'Social rented housing in Britain and the Netherlands: trends, trajectories and divergence', *Netherlands Journal of Housing and the Built Environment*, vol 9, no 2, pp 107-26.

Murie, A., Niner, P. and Watson, C. (1976) *Housing policy and the housing system*, London: Allen and Unwin.

Musterd, S. and Murie, A. (2002) *A comparative report on social exclusion and integration in neighbourhoods in 11 cities in 6 European countries*, Amsterdam, the Netherlands: AME.

Nevitt, A.A. (1966) *Housing taxation and subsidies*, Edinburgh: Nelson.

ODPM (Office of the Deputy Prime Minister) (2004a) *Housing in England 2002/3*, London: ODPM.

ODPM (2004b) *Home ownership solutions for low demand areas*, London: ODPM.

Pahl, R. (1974) 'Foreword', in M. Harloe, R. Issacharoff and R. Minns, *The organization of housing*, London: Heinemann.

Pahl, R. (1975) *Whose city?*, Harmondsworth: Penguin.

Pawson, H. and Bramley, G. (2000) 'Understanding recent trends in residential mobility in council housing in England', *Urban Studies*, vol 37, no 8, pp 1231-59.

Power, A. (1987) *Property before people: The management of twentieth century council housing*, London: Allen and Unwin.

Power, A. (1993) *Hovels to high rise: State housing in Europe since 1850*, London: Routledge.

Power, A. (1997) *Estates on the edge*, London: Macmillan.

Prak, N.L. and Priemus, H. (1986) 'A model for the analysis of the decline of post-war housing', *International Journal of Urban and Regional Research*, vol 10, no 1, pp 1-7.

Prescott-Clarke, P., Allen, P. and Morrissey, C. (1988) *Queuing for housing: A study of council housing waiting lists*, London: HMSO.

Prescott-Clarke, P., Clemens, S. and Park, A. (1994) *Routes into local authority housing*, London: HMSO.

Rex, J. and Moore, R. (1967) *Race, community and conflict: A study of Sparkbrook*, Oxford: Oxford University Press.

Saunders, P. (1990) *A nation of home owners*, London: Routledge.

Stephens, M., Whitehead, C. and Munro, M. (2005) *Lessons from the past, challenges for the future for housing policy: An evaluation of English housing policy 1975-2000*, London: ODPM.

Taylor, M. (1995) *Unleashing the potential*, York: Joseph Rowntree Foundation.

Titmuss, R.M. (1963) *Essays on the welfare state* (2nd edn), London: George Allen and Unwin.

Titmuss, R.M. (1962) *Income distribution and social change*, London: George Allen and Unwin.

van der Heijden, H. (2002) 'Social rented housing in Western Europe: developments and expectations', *Urban Studies*, vol 39, no 2, pp 327-40.

van Kempen, R. (2002) 'The academic formulations: explanations for the partitioned city', in P. Marcuse and R. van Kempen (eds) *Of states and cities: The partitioning of urban space*, Oxford: Oxford University Press, pp 35-56.

Williams, P. (1976) 'The role of institutions in the inner London housing market: the case of Islington', *Transactions of the Institute of British Geographers*, New Series, vol 1, no 1, pp 72-82.

Woolf, M. (1967) *The Housing Survey in England and Wales 1964*, Government Social Survey, London: HMSO.

THREE

A new vision for UK housing?

Richard Best

"Initiatives for housing and regeneration? This government has more visions than Mother Theresa and more pilots than British Airways." (Professor Alan McGregor, University of Glasgow)

This chapter considers the government's twin visions of 'sustainable new communities' and 'neighbourhood renewal'. It notes the economic, social and environmental drivers for increasing housing supply within sustainable communities, and it touches on the importance for northern urban areas of the housing market renewal initiatives. It concludes that these twin approaches to easing housing problems are justified by the evidence, but that the desired outcomes will be hard to achieve.

The chapter notes how political factors moderate the prospects for progress, and how delivery of these housing visions will also be difficult if underlying truths about land, about the costs of implementation and about dependency on the private sector are not faced. In particular, additional resources will be needed to acquire land and boost the supply of subsidised housing and this is best done through regulated, non-profit bodies where the subsidies are locked in for public benefit in perpetuity. The medicine is fine, but the dose is too weak, and it needs to be administered by people with social goals.

Economic drivers

The report commissioned by the Chancellor of the Exchequer from Kate Barker of the Bank of England spelt out the economic drivers for housing to move up the political agenda (Barker, 2004). If supply and demand get out of kilter, and the market does not correct that imbalance, economic consequences follow. Competitive success and a global economy depend on a nation's ability to attract and retain mobile, talented people: if such people are deterred from contributing to the

UK economy because of shortages of accommodation – at all levels of society – competitiveness will suffer. London may stake a valid claim as the world's capital, and the prosperity it generates from its international business makes us the fourth strongest economy in the world, but if there is insufficient satisfactory housing then the workforce – whether they are bankers or cleaners – will go elsewhere, thus threatening the world position of the UK.

Housing shortages reduce the mobility of labour and deny public and private sectors the workers they need. Shortages lead to housing costs absorbing disproportionate levels of earnings, distorting other parts of the economy. They lead to long-distance commuting that is both wasteful and costly. And, combined with easy access to borrowing, shortages add to economic volatility and instability with dangers of boom and bust in the housing market creating inflationary and recessionary pressures.

Broadly, the Barker Review (2004) spells out the imbalance between rising demand – that is, the number of new households looking for a home – and restricted supply of housing – that is, the number of homes actually built (Barker, 2004). Analysis of the official figures – by Alan Holmans, based on the 2001 Census – spells out population growth projections for the decade 2001-11 at 1.9 million people in England. (This means the population in England would rise from 49.4 million to 51.3 million.) Meanwhile, the number of households is expected to go up over this decade, proportionately, by twice as much: an increase of 1.8 million households from 20.6 million to 22.4 million (Holmans et al, 2004).

Despite the UK's historically low birth rate, the number of households looks set to rise steadily over the next 20 years (see Figure 3.1). It is not the number of babies born today that will put pressure on the housing market in the next decade, rather it is the number born 15-25 years ago (who will form new households in the next 10 years) that counts, together with the rate at which people die. When demographic change is leading to more households and this combines with increased affluence, extra households mean demand for extra homes.

Increased affluence means we can now afford not to stay at home until our thirties or forties and not to live with our children in retirement. The cottage in the village that once housed the farm worker, his wife, four children and their grandparents, now contains one childless couple, or one retired professional, because so many of us can afford to acquire the space we want.

Figure 3.1: More households (projected number of households in England) (2001-21)

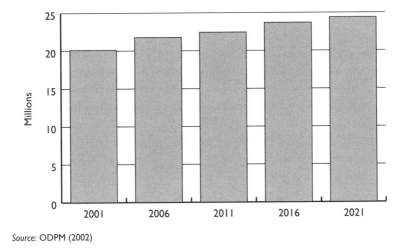

Source: ODPM (2002)

Demographic trends are generating more house-hunting single-person households. Figure 3.2 shows the biggest increase in household numbers is coming from among single people under 65 (while there is a substantial reduction in the number of couples with children). Some of these young singles never marry/settle into a permanent partnership; those who do, tend to leave it until 10 years later than their parents, postponing settling down and having a family until their

Figure 3.2: More single-person households (projected change in household make-up) (1996-2021)

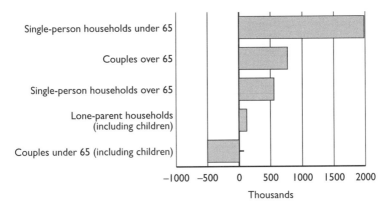

Note: Data apply to England.
Source: ODPM (1999)

mid-thirties instead of their mid-twenties; and a high proportion of marriages/partnerships break down and are not followed by a new marriage/partnership.

Affluence also combines with increased longevity to impact on household numbers. Half the small households of tomorrow will be occupied by pensioners. And because we live longer, we do not pass on our home to the next generation as quickly as we used to. Roughly speaking, the extension of our life expectancy over the last century means the UK must now accommodate one more generation. Grandparents are more plentiful and great-grandparents are becoming commonplace (see Figure 3.3). Those with parents who are owner-occupiers are not likely to inherit their properties until they are over 50. While it is good news that we can all expect to live longer – and about half our extra years will be years of good health – this makes a very big difference to the requirements for building additional homes.

The next important factor in increasing numbers of households comes from the net inflow of immigration over emigration: the Government Actuary's Department estimates that an extra 130,000 people will be added to the population each year up to 2021 (Figure 3.4). But because poorer immigrants share (often overcrowded) accommodation, this translates into rather fewer households than for the indigenous population: nevertheless, immigration probably adds over 30,000 to the UK's annual requirements for new homes.

Figure 3.3: More older people (projected increase of population aged 60-74 and 75+) (2003-26)

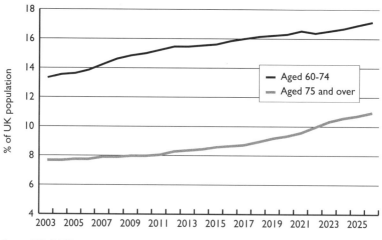

Source: GAD (2005)

Figure 3.4: More people moving in than out (projected annual net inward migration) (1998-2021)

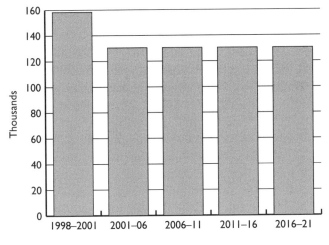

Source: GAD

It should be noted that the much reviled asylum seekers contribute the very least to increased housing pressures. Those who wish to receive assistance with their housing are dispersed to areas of low demand where there are no problems of shortages, and, indeed, where there is a surplus of (empty and sometimes abandoned) housing. Those who opt to stay in London – and forfeit entitlement to housing support – move in with friends and relations in overcrowded conditions that do not impact on the housing market. At the other extreme, of course, those people attracted to London by the financial and business services sector have a significant impact on the housing market because they can afford to out-price local people. Some 40% of the workforce at KPMG's London office (their largest in the world) comprises people from overseas who can pay lots of money for their homes, whether rented or owned. Few people would argue for more curbs on the immigration of these contributors to national wealth.

In so far as we demolish housing we need to replace it, although not always in the same place. Demolition went out of favour in a big way after the 1970s, not least because of a general view that much of the housing of the 1960s and 1970s was less satisfactory than the old Victorian terraces that were pulled down. Until quite recently, demolition was an almost insignificant part of the housing statistics. But this is beginning to change as local authorities in the areas of low demand – particularly in the nine housing market renewal pathfinder areas – look to more extensive demolition of unpopular, often 1960s and 1970s, council-owned stock.

People have moved away from many of the northern industrial towns, and if their housing is demolished behind them, new homes are needed in the places to which they have gone. Over the next decade, about 20,000 homes each year will be needed to replace those that are demolished.

The final reason why it is not enough simply to build the same number of new homes as there are new households emerging relates to the backlog of unmet need. People whose housing needs are not yet met can claim as much priority as new households. This has been a neglected priority for decades.

As the Chief Economic Adviser to the Treasury said last June: "Since 1960, the UK has invested a lower proportion of its national income in housing than any other EU country – private and public. Over that period, the number of housing completions has halved from their peak of 400,000 (for the UK) in the mid-1960s to under 200,000 in the mid-1990s while the percentage of major planning applications granted has also fallen" (Balls, 2004). In theory, we need over 900,000 more homes to accommodate all those who are homeless or in overcrowded accommodation or in properties unfit for human habitation. But in practice the pundits regard a figure of 650,000 as sufficient. How quickly this could be reduced is a matter for political judgement and depends on the availability of resources. Shelter has called for the backlog to be gradually reduced to 50% of its current level, over a 15-year period – this seems a very balanced approach; and will require an additional 22,000 new homes each year (Shelter, 2004).

Overall, as shown in Figure 3.5, house building in England has hovered between 145,000 and 155,000 homes each year for well over a decade. In 2002, it reached its lowest point since the mid-1920s. When we bring together the impact of 20,000 demolitions and the target of 22,000 homes to halve the backlog of unmet need, and we add these to the number of homes required to meet the needs of the extra 180,000 households forming each year, we reach the grand total of over 220,000 extra homes each year for the period 2001-21.

Building this number of extra homes does not look too daunting when we consider what has been achieved in the past. Harold Macmillan set the target of 300,000 extra homes for the UK as a whole and achieved this at the end of the 1950s. During Harold Wilson's time in the late 1960s, exceeding 400,000 homes across the UK in a year did not prove impossible: so surely 220,000 homes sounds

Figure 3.5: Falling house building in England

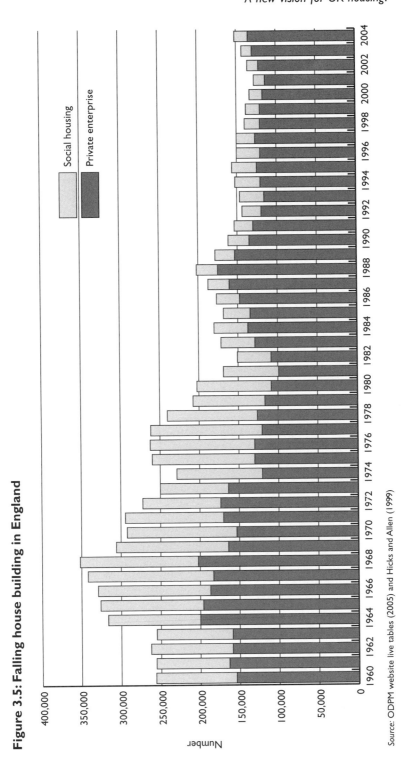

Source: ODPM website live tables (2005) and Hicks and Allen (1999)

manageable. If the UK achieved this, Kate Barker's analysis concludes that we would still fail to bring down the annual rate of increase in house prices from the 3.3% which it has scored over the past three decades, to the European average of 1.1% per annum over general inflation. But this level of house building would reduce price rises to around 1.8% over inflation and that would help the economy – and the home seekers.

The Barker Review (2004) explains that the shortfall in supply is not attributable to a significant decline in the output of private sector house builders. What has changed – and this gives a hint for the conclusions later in this chapter – is that the other half of the house building pipeline – the production of subsidised homes, previously by local authorities and now by housing associations – has dwindled away. From its peak of over 200,000 extra homes a year, the subsidised sector has fallen to about 20,000 homes (as Figure 3.5 makes clear).

The mismatch between demand and supply is of particular significance to those living in the South. As Figure 3.6 indicates, the gap between population increases and new house building over the five years to 2003 was most evident in the southern regions. And, as Figure 3.7 shows clearly, these disparities are set to get appreciably worse in those same regions, year by year, if housing completions do not rise very significantly and very soon. The paramount considerations

Figure 3.6: Homes shortfall in the South

Regional disparities between population increases and new house building (1988-2003)

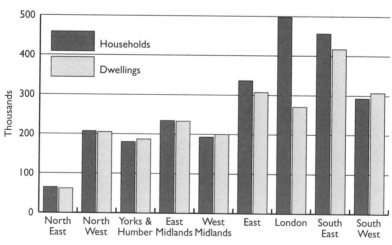

Source: ODPM website live tables (2005)

Figure 3.7: Future demand versus supply

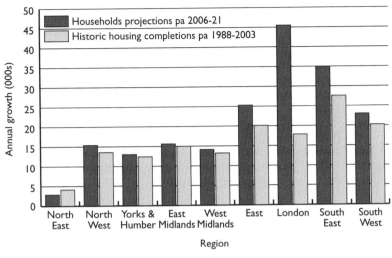

Source: ODPM website live tables (2005)

for the Treasury may well be the constraints on the areas of wealth generation, held back by housing shortages. But the painful social consequences will intensify for more and more people in these regions and beyond.

Social justice drivers

Of course, policy is not driven by economics alone. Major pledges such as to abolish child poverty over 20 years spell out the parallel social justice agenda. In the context of housing shortages, it is the rise of homelessness that has the most dire effects on those afflicted – and children in particular.

Since the late 1990s there has been an inexorable rise in the number of homeless households in temporary accommodation (Figure 3.8). These are the households in priority need for whom no permanent accommodation is available. The good news is that these are very much less likely than in the past to be found in bed and breakfast hotels or even hostels for homeless people, and much more likely to be in the private rented sector on a temporary basis (but not always in housing that is suitable).

Homelessness is, of course, the tip of the iceberg of problems caused by housing shortages. There are an estimated 500,000 overcrowded households, forced to share: young couples living with their parents

Figure 3.8: Homeless households in temporary accommodation

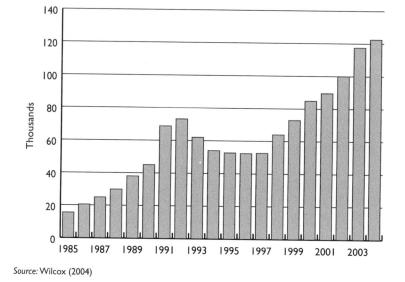

Source: Wilcox (2004)

and in-laws, single people sleeping on the floors of friends, or adults continuing to live with their parents into middle age. Enforced sharing and overcrowding brings serious tensions, makes home life impossible for many and is particularly unfair to children who need space to play and study. Most of these will never have had a home of their own; some will have been forced to leave previous accommodation, for example because of repossession when job loss has led to a failure to keep up mortgage payments.

Then there are the households who are managing to pay their own housing costs, but whose rents or mortgages absorb a much higher proportion of their income than for their European or North American counterparts. Also included are those who cannot afford to live near their place of work and must commute for long distances that take such a toll on family life, sometimes with both parents barely seeing their children between dawn and bedtime.

Shortages drive up prices and cause problems of affordability that have now reached an acute pitch. Investors who Buy to Let but who purchase properties in the same market – increasing demand but not adding to supply – may well contribute to the inflationary pressures. While the number of Buy to Let mortgages has risen by over 200,000 per annum in recent years, the number of first-time buyers has fallen by a similar number – to the lowest level as a proportion of homes bought since records began.

Problems of affordability are disproportionately significant, of course, in the South of England. Work for the Joseph Rowntree Foundation by Steve Wilcox, *Can work – can't buy* (2003), analysed house prices and incomes, looking at the cheapest houses and looking at actual local incomes, for every local authority area. This sophisticated exercise produces a much more sensible picture than simply comparing average incomes with average house prices in different places. It shows that some of the areas with very high house prices are actually more affordable than those where prices are lower because incomes in the expensive areas are also much higher. Professor Wilcox's work shows how new households in the West Country fare particularly badly because incomes are appreciably lower than in London or the South East, although house prices are not so far behind (Wilcox, 2003).

In the hierarchy of problems created by supply failing to keep up with demand, next comes the problems for the delivery of the services we all need. Employers cannot attract the workforce they need and all of us face the consequences. This is most obvious in relation to the recruitment of so-called 'key workers' – nurses, police, teachers – whose support we all miss so badly if their posts are unfilled because of local housing costs. But an absence of housing affordable to those needing to fill job vacancies in the voluntary sector can be just as damaging, and in the private sector it can mean businesses are constrained and the local economy suffers.

Next on the list of problems from housing shortages comes the burden on parents of those seeking to break into the housing market: these will, increasingly, have to make bigger sacrifices for their children. In 2004, the Joseph Rowntree Foundation asked MORI to conduct a poll on this theme. It showed that most parents expected to have to help their children with housing costs. On average, these parents believed they would need to find £17,000 in financial assistance – £24,000 in the South – per child. For more and more people this will mean taking out a mortgage in later life (MORI, 2004). So, while many of us homeowners may feel a warm glow when we note that the value of our home has risen, parents – and grandparents – must increasingly realise that they may also be the victims of rising values if the next generation is to be able to afford a home.

Breaking into home ownership looks an increasingly remote possibility for households without parents who can assist. The average deposit for a first-time buyer in 2003 was £26,800. The divide between owners and tenants has grown wider, and bridging it will become less and less likely. This polarises society between those who build up equity in their property – a long-term investment, not least to draw down in older age – and those who are cut off from this form of wealth creation. This is a major barrier to 'social mobility', the opportunities for people to progress in society.

The government now talks in terms of the need for new homes to be in mixed communities. The segregation of social housing in separate estates where residents can become labelled and stigmatised is recognised as a key housing policy issue. If all the lowest income households are congregated in identifiably different social housing, this can diminish life chances by cutting people off from the networks of those in employment and from role models of people in work, and by concentrating those with difficulties to the point where good neighbourliness and good parenting can be overwhelmed.

In the March 2005 Budget Gordon Brown announced plans to increase new building of housing for sale amidst existing council housing to rebalance tenure and income mix. The model advocated by the Joseph Rowntree Foundation differs somewhat from the Chancellor's in recommending that some of the new homes be allocated to those transferring from existing rented accommodation, with the vacancies sold on the open market to create income and tenure mix within the existing stock as well.

Meanwhile, a lot of existing council housing is of poor quality and the government has set out its plans for local authorities and housing associations to achieve the Decent Homes standards by 2010. Existing neighbourhoods and estates will need a blend of demolition, upgrading and tenure mix.

But the logical route to achieving social justice ambitions in housing is to increase the supply of social and affordable housing, directly, by providing the necessary resources to social housing providers – which, today, means housing associations and arm's length management organisations annexed to local authorities. This straightforward path to raising the numbers, however, is entirely contrary to the trends since the mid-1990s.

As Figure 3.9 demonstrates, from over 200,000 homes each year in the late 1960s, council housing was already little more than half this level by 1980. Thereafter new municipal house building disappeared over a 20-year stretch, and while housing associations did better in the middle of the 1990s, they too have since halved their output.

Environmental drivers

Environmental factors are now of national and international importance. The Prime Minister has targeted these concerns, alongside his hopes

Figure 3.9: Declining output of social housing (local authority and housing association new build homes completed in the UK)

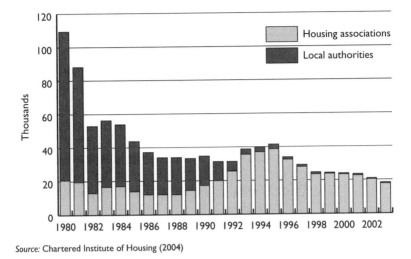

Source: Chartered Institute of Housing (2004)

for Africa, for his term at the head of the G8 countries and the UK's EU presidency. House building consumes resources and new homes emit CO^2. House building, therefore, is inherently bad for the environment. However, the answer is not to seize on the environmental arguments as the grounds for opposing all new development. Economic, social and environmental concerns must be reconciled. Economic growth pays for improvements to the environment. Social justice demands that basic human needs be satisfied as well as environmental considerations being met.

Urban sprawl increases traffic pollution and congestion. New housing needs to go in built-up areas or as urban extensions that plug into the existing urban infrastructure. Densities need to be such that public transport can pay its way, hopefully with proximity to workplaces, schools and shops being close enough to encourage walking and cycling.

If we are going to build whole new settlements that are free-standing from existing urban areas, these need to be on a sufficient scale to avoid most of the population having to travel elsewhere for all their business and personal needs. Because that means new settlements of 10,000 homes or more, very little of tomorrow's new housing will be found in these places.

About two thirds of new development is now on recycled land, or 'brownfield' sites. And increasingly it is built to higher densities, with more apartments and fewer houses. These trends help the environment but there are dangers of them being taken too far: some brownfield land might be better as green space in urban areas – 'pocket parks' – and, if we are not to see families with young children condemned to living in high-density flats, we need to recognise the continuing value of homes with gardens. Aspirations for the suburban home can still be fulfilled by sustainable communities of relatively high-density family housing.

In York the Joseph Rowntree Foundation is planning a model new community that meets these different requirements. A sustainable urban drainage system, cycle paths, pedestrian-friendly Home Zones – and a car club so not everyone needs their own car – protection of the natural environment: all these features can be combined in a fully mixed tenure urban extension, as it is planned to demonstrate in the Derwenthorpe Project of 540 new homes.

Meanwhile, the energy saving within individual homes needs year-on-year improvement and changes to Part L of the Building Regulations will seek to achieve these. The UK does, indeed, need to lead the way now that global warming is recognised as a reality. The homes of tomorrow need to give much more prominence to environmental issues. The message is about how we deliver the homes we need in environmentally friendly ways, not why environmental concerns make it impossible to do what has to be done.

So is there another vision?

My conclusion is that the two visions of sustainable new communities to meet current and growing shortages, and neighbourhood renewal to revive housing markets in the low-demand areas, are highly commendable. The problem lies not in conjuring up these visions of the future but of delivering them in practice.

Where politics dims the vision

Housing featured in the 2005 General Election in somewhat arbitrary – and often negative – ways. First, new house building is almost universally unpopular among those who live next door to the planned development. In particular, those who enjoy views across countryside, or the opportunity to walk dogs on open land, naturally object vehemently to the loss of amenity (and the possibility of lower house prices). More broadly, although meeting all housing need for decades ahead will only absorb a small percentage of undeveloped land, there is a general view that new housing inevitably 'concretes over rural

England'. Poor design by house builders can contribute to this distaste and – often with spurious environmental grounds as the excuse – politicians can capitalise on the sentiments. At the local level, councillors get few votes for supporting a new development in their ward: few of those who will benefit are likely to live nearby, while all who believe they may be adversely affected can exert their electoral power (and the local media) to stop new homes being built.

In particular, the idea of social housing in the locality can produce fierce opposition. Images of drug addicts and 'ASBO (Anti-Social Behaviour Order) teenagers' are conjured up, even though mixed-income, mixed tenure new developments, in which the social housing is indistinguishable from the housing for sale, should diminish these fears.

A further level of confusion is added by those who oppose immigration for reasons unconnected with house building. Their misconceptions are summarised by: 'A third of the current housing is being built to cope with the consequences of net inward migration, and a third of all homes are being built on greenfield sites: so it follows that if immigration was halted, no more new housing on greenfield land would be needed'. These figures are entirely fallacious. To meet the requirements from immigration would absorb about 15% of the total housing supply needed in the UK. And the pressure for building in the suburbs does not come from new migrants: it comes from new household formation within the indigenous population there, and from the strong desire for suburban living by those leaving older urban areas. The greatest exodus from the conurbations is out of the places in which few migrants have settled, for example, the North East, Hull, and so on. And those coming to live in this country – with 70% going to London – are much more likely to favour inner-city lifestyles at high densities. (In the unlikely event that the UK population would be willing to live in the densities of, say, Singapore, all of us could be accommodated on the Isle of Wight!) In terms of where new homes are most sought, therefore, pressures on the 'countryside' are home-grown.

As Margaret Thatcher proved, there are votes in extending home ownership. Today's politicians have vowed to extend home ownership through shared ownership schemes and through equity-based loans (Homebuy). Since there is a sub-market between those able to buy a home of their own and those who can afford no more than a subsidised rent, and since the number of first-time buyers has fallen so dramatically, meeting the needs of this middle market seems an important policy objective. But, on the one hand, this must not be at the expense of resources for social renting. And, on the other hand, the safety net available for tenants through Housing Benefit needs some corresponding protection for those with mortgages: these people are currently at risk of homelessness, as a result of unemployment or of interest rate rises, if their family circumstances change suddenly.

Meanwhile, both the Labour and Conservative Parties are looking again at extensions of the Right to Buy: where these involve compelling landlords to diminish their own assets, for the benefit of those who happen to live in their homes at a particular time, the net result is a loss of much-needed social housing. But if the government compensates for the discounts provided to tenants, enabling homes lost to be replaced, this can support the move to more mixed-income housing estates (except in those places – like some rural areas – where there is no chance of building new housing to replace the sold stock).

In the quest for votes from the mythical 'Middle England', politicians steer clear of setting bold targets for reducing housing shortages or increasing housing investment in 'social', subsidised rented homes. But must we wait for a dire crisis before these national priorities are addressed by whoever is in power?

Where the vision is blurred

To succeed in stepping up production and achieving affordability across housing markets, any future government needs to grasp several nettles. House builders, through accumulating land banks, purchasing options and good local intelligence, secure the key resource for new house building – land. But while they may complain that the planners are responsible for the slow rate of land release for building – and the planning system is in urgent need of the streamlining and reforming which is now getting underway – is it wise for society to allow one sector to control this crucial ingredient? If other players are to participate and boost overall supply, there has to be direct intervention in the marketplace by statutory agencies like English Partnerships, the sale of publicly owned land to the non-profit providers, and the opportunity for registered social landlords to acquire land (or land options) before planning consent is given.

The source of profit for house builders is principally the gap between the cost of producing the homes and the price paid for the land. If construction costs are reduced, for example, through the use of modern methods, this can increase profits without necessarily having any impact on house prices. Conversely, it is through using the increase in land values for public benefit that affordability can be locked in and gains for the communities secured: this is how the garden cities and later the New Towns (and the model communities of New Earswick in York and Bourneville in Birmingham) have funded their social components and achieved their affordable housing.

Important steps have been taken to cap some of the gains from land value appreciation through Section 106 Agreements. The new Joseph Rowntree Foundation report (2005), from Sarah Monk and Christine Whitehead at Cambridge and Tony Crook and colleagues at Sheffield, shows how important these Section 106 Agreements have become to social housing provision. They have made it possible to incorporate non-market housing within developments on high-priced land, avoiding the segregation of social housing on separate – low-value – sites. But planning gain is not a substitute for the direct provision of additional, affordable homes (Monk et al, 2005).

Over recent decades, production by house builders has been fairly constant, as Figure 3.10 shows. It is the public/voluntary/social sector that has declined so dramatically. There is little reason to expect the private sector to step up production dramatically: it is not in the interests of house builders to increase output to the level at which demand wanes. And there seems little reason to believe the sector has much desire to produce more homes than it has done, in a relatively steady way, decade by decade for 50 years.

Piggybacking on private developers' output through planning gains may not increase the total number of homes built, even though it could increase the amount of affordable housing in unstigmatised,

Figure 3.10: Average annual house building by decade and tenure

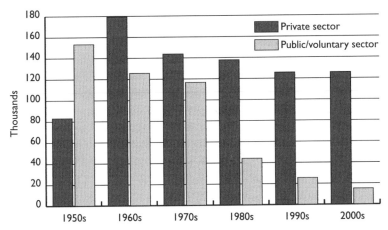

Source: ODPM website live tables (2005) and Hicks and Allen (1999)

mixed tenure developments. The danger is that relying on percentages of private developments will mean declining levels of affordable housing if the housing market falters and private sector production drops. Meanwhile, the government wants to go a stage further in reliance on house builders by opening up access to Social Housing Grants to the private sector. Some £1.67 billion will be available over the next two years – even before an initial £200 million pilot has started – for house builders and developers (and, with more justification, to arm's length management organisations of local authorities). It seems odd to turn to the house builders to boost the stock of social housing when this group have little or no experience of rented provision and, indeed, have often opposed the inclusion of rented housing within their developments.

Under a number of headings, not least in relation to the subsidies for affordable housing, achieving the vision of sufficient and affordable housing will be costly.

Whoever receives the Social Housing Grant – the capital subsidies that enable homes to be let at rents that do not require dependency on Housing Benefit for those on less than average earnings – a step-change in production will require a hike in public funding. There may be apparent economies in providing the Grant to house builders, not housing associations, but these are likely to be short-lived. The house builders may build more cheaply when they do not have to satisfy a partner housing association – a partner who knows that rented accommodation must be more robust since its occupants will not engage in DIY from day one, who knows that it is a travesty to increase profits from the site by confining the social housing to the worst corner, and who knows they will have responsibility for decades to come for the management and maintenance of this stock. And house builders do not have the expense of a regulatory system that has protected the social sector from abuse, scandals and mismanagement for 30 years but which makes heavy demands on registered social landlords.

Unfortunately there will be other, substantial calls on the public purse if the government's visions are to be accomplished. Housing market renewal will not come cheap and the initial tranche of £500 million represents little more than £1,000 per property in the low-demand areas covered by the nine pathfinders. Meeting the environmental requirements and infrastructure needs for the growth areas, and the Thames Gateway in particular, will need big resources and much ingenuity. Bonds redeemed by the capital gains from rising land values may help. But new transport systems, investment in water supply and prevention of flooding, will all require big investment. And if the challenge of achieving greater public control over how major sites are to be developed is accepted, and, through English Partnerships or other agencies, land acquisition proceeds on some scale, then upfront costs – although the sums may come right in the longer term – will be significant.

Building tomorrow's sustainable communities requires commitment not just to the provision of extra housing, or even to the provision of affordable housing in mixed communities. It also demands attention to the public realm, to the provision of amenities, and to the long-term, stable management of a new community. The skills to provide these key components are not the stock in trade of private sector house builders. These tasks require the continued nurturing of a strong non-profit sector – the third way between public and private – committed to social goals. Instead of diverting resources away from the registered social landlords, future success in achieving the important vision of ending housing problems points to greater backing for this independent sector.

Another major disadvantage in shifting public subsidies to house builders is that the capital gains from the rented homes will be largely captured by the companies concerned. As properties become vacant, perhaps 25 years into the future, profits will be made when underlying values increase and the homes are sold.

Subsidies given to regulated non-profit organisations are locked in for social purposes in perpetuity. This has meant that registered social landlords have accumulated the resources that today can be recycled to produce more homes or can underpin important social provision for tenants and others in the neighbourhood. If, instead of providing grants to the housing associations over the last 30 years, the government had pursued their new policy of funds for house builders, we would today be watching the stock of social housing diminish as vacant homes were sold, capital gains taken and the receipts to government only sufficient to cover a fraction of the cost of replacement.

Conclusion

This chapter argues that the government's visions for UK housing – for sustainable communities and for neighbourhood renewal – point in the right direction. The medicine is fine. But the implementation of this two-part vision will not be achieved unless it is pursued by both a bolder approach to planning and direct intervention in land acquisition, and by an increase in supply-side subsidies for social/affordable housing and investment in infrastructure. A new vision for UK housing requires a stronger dose if the medicine is to work.

Three components, therefore, are identified for a vision of satisfactory and affordable homes for all to become a reality.

First, leadership is needed to increase *public awareness* and shift public attitudes from outright hostility to new development – born of disenchantment with the past products of the public sector and the recent offerings of the private sector – to a greater understanding that, as this chapter spells out, addressing housing shortages has to be a national priority.

Second, politicians must accept that it will require *public action* to achieve the outcomes of wholesome, sustainable new communities and revitalised older neighbourhoods. The free market is not equipped to resolve deep-seated housing problems. This means proactive, positive planning, with local planners once again engaged in the task of assisting or executing real planning for new settlements and existing areas in need of regeneration. Planning is not just about protection of existing environments or the passive processing of proposals from the private sector: it must be about setting out and actively pursuing plans for the long term which will require the backing of much larger infrastructure support and housing subsidies.

Third, in accomplishing the vision, and seeing neighbourly communities for all income groups, it is misguided to expect house builders – through the 'carrot' of allocating them Social Housing Grants and the 'stick' of placing planning obligations on them – to accomplish the social functions required for quality provision and long-term management. These jobs have never been achieved by the 'for-profit' sector. Social or *public agencies* – today, most often the registered social landlords – are needed to take the vision forward. The value – and the values – of committed practitioners cannot be underestimated: a strong, regulated, non-profit sector that locks in the capital gains from rising property values for the long term, and has an underlying motivation of service to the community, is the vital third ingredient in achieving the two-part housing vision for the UK.

Legislative and administrative arrangements are in place to turn the dream into a practical reality. But without attention to these three components – public attitudes, public action and public agencies – housing inequalities will grow: the haves – the owner-occupiers, mostly in under-occupied property – will move further apart from the have-nots. While talk of a new vision can sound trite and hackneyed, the UK needs the inspiration of a picture of this country freed from acute housing shortages and the damning impact of degrading neighbourhoods.

References

Balls, E. (2004) 'Prospects for the economy: housing and the Treasury', Speech to the Chartered Institute of Housing Annual Conference, London: HM Treasury (available from: http://www.hm-treasury.gov.uk/ newsroom_and_speeches/speeches/chief_economic_advisor_ to_the_treasury_speeches/CEA_speeches_ 150604.cfm).

Barker, K. (2004) *Review of housing supply: Delivering stability: Securing our future housing needs, Final report: Recommendations*, London: HM Treasury/ODPM.

CIH (Chartered Institute of Housing) (2004) *UK housing review 2004/ 2005*, London: CIH.

GAD (Government Actuary's Department) (2002) *2002 based population projections for the United Kingdom and constituent countries*, London: GAD.

GAD (2005) *2003 based population projections for the United Kingdom*, London: GAD.

Hicks, J. and Allen, G. (1999) *A century of change: Trends in UK statistics since 1900*, House of Commons Library Research Paper 99/111.

Holmans, A.E., Monk, S. and Whitehead, C.M.E. (2004) *Building for the future – 2004 update*, A report of the Shelter Housing Investment Project, London: Shelter.

Monk, S., Crook, T., Lister, D., Rowley, S., Short, C. and Whitehead, C. (2005) *Land and finance for affordable housing: The complementary roles of Social Housing Grant and the provision of affordable housing through the planning system*, York: Joseph Rowntree Foundation.

MORI Social Research Institute (2004) *Homeowners: Sons and daughters*, London: MORI.

ODPM (Office of the Deputy Prime Minister) (1999) *Projections of households in England to 2021*, London: ODPM.

ODPM (2002) *Projections of households in England to 2021*, London: ODPM.

Shelter (2004) *Policy statement*, London: Shelter.

Wilcox, S. (2003) *Can work – can't buy: Local measures of the ability of working households to become homeowners*, York: Joseph Rowntree Foundation.

FOUR

Housing demand, supply and the geography of inequality

Christine M.E. Whitehead

The issues

Housing outcomes are the result of a range of choices and constraints that help to determine demand and supply as modified by government policy. In spatial terms two of the most important attributes of housing are its locational specificity and its longevity. To state the obvious, but an important obvious, housing is built in a particular location which cannot be changed without incurring very significant costs; a particular dwelling is located in a relatively well-defined and only slowly changing physical environment in terms of other housing, infrastructure, accessibility to employment and local services; and what is built initially can only be modified by investing in repair and improvements which rarely change the essential nature of the building except when full-scale regeneration occurs. The vast majority of the housing stock is therefore relatively immutable; what changes is people's attitude to that stock and their preparedness to live there, and thus the factors which affect relative demand for different attributes and locations (Charles, 1977; Whitehead, 1984; Balchin et al, 1995). Given these fundamental determinants and the different histories of demand and supply across regions, it is hardly surprising that housing outcomes vary enormously in geographic as well as personal terms.

One objective of the government is to develop policies that modify demand, the existing stock and new supply in order to help ensure "a decent home for every household at a price within their means" (Department of Environment, 1971). This objective is defined in terms of meeting households' needs; spatial patterns are not an inherent element of this policy except to the extent that outcomes vary not only because of household and dwelling attributes but because of their location (Department of Environment, 1977; Smith, 1999). Clearly the spatial relationships between dwellings, different activities and regions do affect these outcomes, and geography is therefore a relevant factor to be addressed. Whether these problems have to be dealt with by spatially specific policies, however, depends on both the fundamentals of demand and supply and the relative costs of different types of policy to achieve basic objectives.

In this context the aims of this chapter are threefold:

- to clarify the factors which will tend to generate geographic inequalities in housing outcomes;
- concentrating at the regional spatial level (rather than on intra-regional/intra-urban issues), to provide some evidence on the extent of regional housing inequalities in England; and
- to raise questions about the implications of these inequalities for the future and for the types of housing policies which might best achieve fundamental housing objectives.

The principles: what generates geographic inequalities?

Demand, supply and price determination

Housing outcomes in market systems are the result of the interaction of demand and supply which help determine the quality, quantity and price of available housing and who lives in the dwellings. These outcomes therefore bring together the individual decisions made by consumers, producers and providers of the existing dwellings.

Individual household decisions about the *demand* for housing can be described using basic economic models: consumers maximise utility across all goods and services subject to their income, the relative price of goods and services and their own preferences (Maclennan, 1982; Muth and Goodman, 1988; Turnbull, 1995). Thus households with the same income and facing the same house prices may choose very different dwellings in different locations and spend different proportions of their income on housing as compared to other goods and services because they have different preferences. More realistically, different households will face different opportunities. However, in general, as incomes rise they will consume more housing, while as the price of housing increases they will change both their overall consumption of housing and the mix of attributes they choose (including, in particular, location).

The market demand for housing can be determined by taking all the consumers' decisions together, and will thus be dependent on these individual choices, the number of households in the market and the ways that government policy affects demand by modifying prices and incomes (through taxation and subsidy), as well as through regulations and direct provision, both of which modify the choices available. Thus, on the demand side, to understand the pressures that generate geographic inequality one must provide evidence on demographics, on the distribution of income and on the relative real prices of housing as compared to general prices in the economy and between different types and locations of dwellings.

Supply responds to changes in house prices because these modify the relative profitability of housing and of different types and locations of housing (Maclennan, 1982; Muth and Goodman, 1988). Individual suppliers are generally assumed to be attempting to maximise profit – that is, to achieve the best net value possible from the resources they have available. Changes in the costs of production, improvement and management of the existing stock all affect the incentives to supply. So, for instance, increases in land, building and finance costs all impact on individual supplier decisions because they modify relative profitability. Equally, government policy, with respect to taxation, subsidy, regulation and its own direct involvement, modifies the choices available to suppliers.

What is particularly important about the supply side, however, is the fact that new supply, whether in the form of additional dwellings or in terms of improvements to the existing stock, is a very small proportion of the total housing available. As a result it is almost impossible to make rapid large-scale changes to supply (either increases or decreases) in response to modifications in housing demand – so when there are changes in demand this is addressed mainly by price rather than quantity and quality adjustments (Barr, 1998; Evans, 2004). The resultant variations in prices both over time and between areas provide the most immediate evidence of differential housing pressure and geographic inequalities (Meen, 2001; Baker, 2003, 2004).

The complexities of housing

The interpretation of evidence on demand, supply and prices and their relation to inequality is made more difficult by a range of issues relating to the complex nature of housing. First, measuring the amount of housing available is not straightforward (Muth, 1960, 1969). The usual starting point is the number of dwellings – but it is clear that this is not like measuring tons of steel or kilograms of apples. One dwelling is very different from another in terms of size, space, services provided within the dwelling and location – variations in any of these affect the supply and value of housing available. Of particular importance in this context is that most households only demand one dwelling – but as their incomes increase they want more from that dwelling. As a result, a better measure of housing supply, once there is some element of balance between households and dwellings, may be space, or a set of housing attributes, or indeed housing value (Rosen, 1974; Whitehead, cited in Cheshire and Mills, 1999). This is particularly important in the context of inequality as both housing standards and housing wealth are of relevance to inequality in addition to simple access to a home.

A second important issue is the extent to which house prices themselves impact on household formation, in that if a person cannot afford to pay for housing they may stay living within another household, leave home later in life or have to enter an institution. The number of households may therefore be a poor estimate of the number of potential households in need of accommodation – and the extent of the discrepancy varies in relation to housing pressure (Peterson et al, 1998; Meen et al, 2005).

Third, the impact of house prices and rents on affordability and the capacity to pay for adequate housing depends heavily on the stage in the person's housing career, because housing expenditures can be spread over people's lifetimes in many different ways (Scanlon and Whitehead, 2004). Thus, someone just starting out will actually have very different outgoings than someone in the same value home, with the same income, who purchased their dwelling some time ago. Therefore affordability problems are not usually best measured by simple means such as price or rent to income ratios but by more complex approaches which take account of residual incomes (that available for other necessities) and housing wealth as well as current expenditure (Hancock, 1993; Freeman and Whitehead, 1996).

Fourth, on the supply side, the costs of housing are to some extent endogenous to the housing market because land prices are heavily determined by expected profitability in that market. In other words price increases in the housing market provide an incentive to provide more housing. But because land is in relatively short and inelastic supply, this results in higher land prices, which then build into the costs of providing more housing (Evans, 2004). Increasing demand for housing and land may therefore mainly generate increases in land prices rather than in output. The impact of these constraints is likely to be heavily dependent on the extent of pressure on land in different areas and therefore contributes heavily to geographic inequality.

Finally, government policies themselves – through regulation (notably of land uses), taxation, subsidies and the provision and allocation of housing to lower-income households – both directly affect who is able to obtain what housing as well as affecting prices and capacity to pay for those obtaining market-provided housing (Stephens et al, 2005). As the impact of government policy varies greatly between areas, it is itself a major factor in determining the geography of housing inequality.

Definitions and measurement of inequality

Inequality, at its simplest, means households have different opportunities and outcomes. It can be defined in terms of *horizontal* equity – that households with similar attributes should have similar opportunities and outcomes; or in terms of *vertical* equity – that households with fewer resources should be compensated and income and wealth should be redistributed until equal opportunities and outcomes occur (Le Grand et al, 1992). In the context of geographic inequality both types of equity are relevant – because households who are similar in all respects except location may have very dissimilar opportunities and outcomes; and because the distribution of incomes and wealth vary spatially as well as between household groups.

Of particular relevance is whether housing inequality should be regarded as a distinct issue separate from that of general income inequality – especially as much of the evidence finds it hard to distinguish housing-specific problems from problems associated with poverty (Wilkinson, 1996). The most important reason from the point of view of welfare is that access, house prices and value for money vary so greatly across regions that the problems cannot simply be addressed by reallocating incomes.

As with efficiency, applying the principles relating to inequality to housing is quite complex. This is partly because of the extent to which both choice and constraint enter into individual decisions, so that inequality in outcomes does not necessarily imply inequality of opportunity. Other factors include the problems in measuring housing outcomes (as discussed above), and the extent to which government itself determines the criteria by which inequality might be defined (Department of Environment, 1977; Whitehead, 1998; Stephens et al, 2005).

Given the importance of choice in housing it can be argued that the most relevant definition is in terms of equality of access – that everyone should be in a position to make similar choices for similar costs. In this case equality comes down simply to the distribution of income. More usually inequality is defined by housing outcomes, notably the quantity and quality of housing obtained, the affordability of that housing to different households, and the extent of choice available. Of particular relevance in the context of this chapter is whether the definition of inequality should be wholly person- and household-specific (for example, is one type of household able to gain access to adequate housing more easily than another?) or whether spatial and locational factors should be taken directly into account when assessing the nature and extent of inequality (Harrison and Whitehead, 1978).

The answer has to involve at least three distinct elements: is the value of the housing that people obtain affected by other factors than the dwellings themselves, in which case a similar dwelling for a similar price may not reflect the true nature of housing inequality (this will mainly relate to neighbourhood and services)? Are the opportunities available constrained by location (for example, the range of dwelling types or tenure may be more limited in some areas than in others, restricting the housing options for those less able to move)? And, in policy terms, do the costs of addressing inequalities vary depending on location and the concentration of households with particular problems (so, for instance, if certain regions have much higher unemployment than others the range of policy options may be constrained; if poverty is concentrated in particular areas it may cost more to achieve given housing standards)?

All of these three elements are probably present in determining the extent of housing inequality – but practically the most important issue is whether problems are more easily and effectively addressed by government if they use specific locationally based instruments.

Important in this context is exactly what the government is aiming to achieve. The classic distinction lies between policies to ensure that households are able to achieve government-defined minimum standards with respect to housing and other necessities of life, and policies that aim to increase equality of opportunity and outcomes in housing or more general terms. In the main, especially in the context of housing, the first approach dominates – so that appropriate measures of success in reducing inequality are based on achieving defined standards of access, quality and affordability. More general issues of spatial differences in price, availability, costs of living and housing opportunities are often of less immediate importance.

A final issue in evaluating the extent and importance of regional inequalities relates to how the overall price and availability of housing affects inequality outcomes. If there were no national housing problem, regional inequalities would not have such a significant impact on welfare. However, almost all of the housing market failures, for example, monopolistic pressures, financial constraints, risk and even externalities, tend to suggest that markets will produce less housing than would be socially desirable (Whitehead, 1998, 2003; Whitehead and Monk, forthcoming). In addition there are clear incentives on the part of owner-occupiers, landowners, social providers and indeed the government to maintain values at the expense of constraining supply (Whitehead, forthcoming). These problems are clearly reflected in the empirical analysis that shows important constraints on housing supply (Barker, 2003, 2004; Bramley et al, 2005).

As a result there are general problems of housing availability and value for money which have different impacts across the country, resulting in very different types of problems in areas of housing pressure as compared to those where supply is more able to adjust. Current government policy recognises this distinction through its emphasis, on the one hand, on growth areas and, on the other, on regeneration (Bramley et al, 2005; ODPM, 2005a).

To summarise the argument so far:

* spatial inequalities in housing would be of far less importance if housing markets and government policy worked better to achieve higher overall levels of supply;
* housing inequalities are only one element in the overall picture of the uneven distribution of opportunity, income and wealth. However, they are particularly important because of the significance of housing in both household welfare and household expenditure;
* the geographical pattern of housing inequalities is of relevance both because households do not have the capacity to move around the country without cost and because market imperfections generate different spatial outcomes; and
* the government needs to understand the nature of these spatial variations in order to implement policies to improve both the operation of the housing market and its capacity to meet housing demand more effectively across the country and to offset spatial inequalities through their own actions and by their impact on housing markets.

Regional housing inequalities: the evidence

The framework set out above helps us to understand both the factors that we should be examining when looking at spatial inequalities in housing and their relative importance in different types of housing market. Using this framework as a basis, the rest of this chapter focuses on an empirical analysis of regional housing market inequalities in England.

In examining the geography of housing demand, supply and inequality there are three main groups of variables:

- demographics, supply and the balance of households and dwellings – that is, the geography of demand and supply;
- incomes, house prices and affordability; and
- measures of housing outcomes in terms of access, quality and tenure choice.

In looking at these indicators we can often divide England into four main regional groupings: the North, the Midlands, the South and London. In other contexts it may be more relevant to compare London and the rest of the country, and in still others looking at smaller areas may be important.

The geography of demand and supply

Table 4.1 shows how the numbers of households and dwellings have changed since 1981 and, as a result, what has happened to the balance between the two. Over the period between 1981 and 2001, the overall numbers of dwellings and households have both increased by some 19% – implying a slight increase in the absolute crude surplus but a decline in the proportionate surplus from 3.4% to 3.3%. Both proportions are below the usually accepted requirement for flexibility in the housing system of around 4%, so this decline is of relevance to overall accessibility to housing (Holmans, 2005).

What is also clear is that this balance varies very considerably between regions. In London the crude surplus is only around half of one per cent, a figure which, especially given spatially differentiated problems with the Census, is well within the confidence interval for a zero surplus or even a deficit. In the North the surplus is well over 4%. Moreover that differential has been increasing quite rapidly, especially in the 1990s. In itself these data suggest that there are considerable differences in basic availability of housing across regions, with the major problems concentrated in London.

Figure 4.1 helps to explain the reasons for the growing problems of access in London – it shows how net international migration has increased from roughly zero in 1981 to more than 100,000 per annum at the beginning of the 21st century. At the same time, net migration

Table 4.1: Households and dwellings in 1981, 1991 and 2001: analysis by region

	1981	1991	2001	Changes 1981-1991	1991-2001
North					
Dwellings	5561	5898	6270	337	372
Households	5356	5722	6006	366	284
Crude surplus	+205	+176	+264	−29	+88
Midlands					
Dwellings	3404	3727	4022	323	295
Households	3270	3620	3899	350	279
Crude surplus	+134	+107	+123	−27	+16
South					
Dwellings	6287	7213	7881	926	668
Households	6046	6938	7617	892	679
Crude surplus	+241	+275	+264	+34	-11
London					
Dwellings	2661	2914	3110	253	196
Households	2635	2811	3094	176	283
Crude surplus	+26	+103	+16	+77	−87
England					
Dwellings	17912	19753	21282	1841	1529
Households	17306	19090	20614	1784	1524
Crude surplus	+606	+663	+698	+57	+5

Source: Holmans (2005)

Figure 4.1: Net migration to/from Greater London (1981-2003)

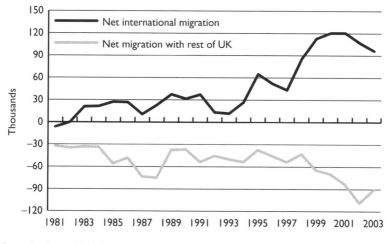

Source: Gordon et al (2004)

Table 4.2: Housing completions in England

	1992/93 (000s)	%	2002/03 (000s)	%	% house-holds	% change in numbers of households	
						1991-2001	2001-21
North	38.7	27	37.2	27	29	19	17
Midlands	30.6	21	28.8	21	19	18	17
South	59.0	41	56.2	41	37	45	43
London	14.4	10	15.8	11	15	19	23
England	142.5	100	137.9	100	100	100	100

Source: Housing and Construction Statistics; Holmans (2005)

to the rest of the UK has also increased, impacting on the demand for housing in the rest of the South. Thus the mix of households in London has changed at the same time as indigenous growth has outpaced that observed in the rest of the country. It is not surprising therefore that the propensity to form separate households has slowed in the face of decreasing availability of housing (Gordon et al, 2002, 2004).

This problem is also reflected in the evidence on how housing completions have varied across the country over the last decade – the period when differential housing pressures have built up most obviously (Table 4.2) (Urban Task Force, 1999; Bramley et al, 2005; Holmans, 2005).

This shows first that, on average, output levels overall have tended to decline rather than expand in the face of increasing demand. Second, general output levels are more in line with the regional distribution of households overall than with the distribution of *changes* in the number of households, which concentrates demand in the South and in London in particular. On this basis completion levels in London are under 60% of additional requirements. Moreover the expected changes over the 20 years from 2001 to 2021 suggest that this imbalance will worsen – with over 3.5 million more households, two thirds of which will be in London and the South and nearly 25% will be concentrated in London (Holmans et al, 2004, 2005). Thus all the evidence on the changing balance between households and dwellings suggests that the problems are concentrated in the South, and in London in particular.

Incomes, house prices and affordability

The evidence on incomes, prices and affordability is rather more difficult to interpret as the issues with respect to access and opportunity among households newly entering the market are very different from those related to inequality across the full range of households (Holmans, 2001).

Figure 4.2 shows how earnings of both men and women have risen relatively in London as compared to the rest of the country. The differential has increased consistently since 1980, although that for women has risen more slowly during the 1990s. Relative capacity to pay in London has on average therefore increased considerably. However, house prices in London have also generally been more volatile and have been increasing very much faster than average during much of the 1990s (Figure 4.3) (Gordon et al, 2004).

Table 4.3 provides rather more detail on how relativities have changed between regions. It shows that the divergence between regions has increased considerably over the past few years. In 1999 only London and the South East had average house prices more than 50% above those in the North. Five years later this was true for all four southern regions. Regional differentials overall had also increased. The result of this pattern of price increases is that house prices in London were over 2.5 times those in the North in 2004, and nearly twice as high as in the Midlands. Prices in the South were twice those in the North

Figure 4.2: Average weekly earnings of full-time men and women workers: Greater London relative to Britain (1970-2003)

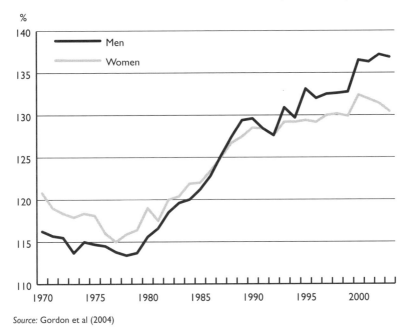

Source: Gordon et al (2004)

Figure 4.3: Mix-adjusted house price indices (1990-2001)

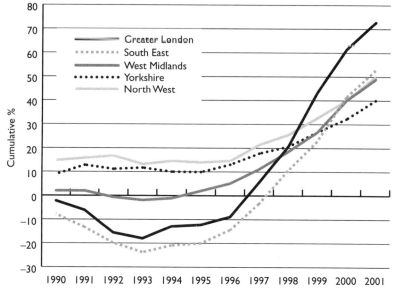

Source: Housing and Construction Statistics; Council of Mortgage Lenders

and more than 50% above those in the Midlands. As a result, access problems in the South have been growing rapidly, generating concerns about the impact of house prices on the competitiveness of the UK and more directly on the capacity to attract key workers to London and the pressure areas in the South.

In the rental sectors rents are also higher in the South, and especially in London, than elsewhere, although the differentials are not so large.

**Table 4.3: Relative house prices across regions (1994-2004)
(North = 100)**

	1994	1999	2003	2004
East Anglia	119	130	167	152
East Midlands	110	113	136	129
Greater London	174	237	287	257
North	100	100	100	100
North West	114	106	112	108
South East	161	182	228	200
South West	129	136	193	175
Wales	106	102	112	113
West Midlands	118	123	145	135
Yorkshire and Humberside	108	104	114	111

Source: Council of Mortgage Lenders, *Housing Finance*, table 9 (various years)

Moreover, as will be evidenced below, access to social rented housing is far more difficult in these high pressure areas.

So, if it is minimum standards of access and affordability which are the relevant criteria for evaluating equality those in the South and particularly in London do far worse than elsewhere in the country, facing greater difficulties in obtaining social housing, higher rents in the private rented sector and much higher price to income ratios and weekly costs of entering owner-occupation.

On the other hand, the evidence on standards of living points to a very different picture and shows that the average Londoner still does considerably better than workers elsewhere, even allowing for the higher costs of housing (Gordon et al, 2002, 2003). Moreover, this position has improved in relative terms especially since 2002, as incomes have continued to increase more rapidly than elsewhere, but house price increases have slowed in relative terms. In this context it should be noted that the rate of change in house prices has peaked in London and the South while prices elsewhere have continued to rise rapidly. As a result, in 2004 London ranked ninth and the South East tenth out of the ten regions in terms of the year-on-year percentage change and indeed only seventh and fifth for the five-year period from 1999 to 2004 (Gordon et al, 2004). There are thus signs that the traditional ripple effect of the housing price cycle is operating as predicted, which is resulting in worsening access and affordability across the country (Wilcox, 2003).

On the issue of housing wealth inequalities, although the rate of change of house prices may 'ripple' out to other regions, the absolute capital gains enjoyed by the vast majority of those already in the owner-occupied sector in London and the South means that households in these regions are far better off than those elsewhere in the country. Moreover, this increasing differential is supported by government taxation policy that allows owner-occupied housing capital gains to remain tax free until death. In equality terms, therefore, the 'average' owning household is considerably better off in the South of England than elsewhere in the country. Moreover, a similar analysis can be applied to the social rented sector. Rents are higher in London and the South, but in residual income terms it is those in the Midlands and the North who are worse off (Chaplin et al, 1995; Freeman and Whitehead, 1996). Despite high rents, the extent of rental subsidy is on average far higher in London and the South (Solomou and Wright, forthcoming).

Overall, therefore, if the relevant measure of inequality is in terms of meeting immediate goals of access and affordability among lower-income households, London and, to a lesser degree, the rest of the South are significantly worse off than elsewhere. With respect to overall equality, measured in traditional terms of average incomes and wealth, taking account of housing costs, the situation is reversed.

Access, quality and tenure choice

Turning to the issues of what households actually obtain we find similar patterns. Table 4.4 provides a range of indicators of housing access and the quantity of housing available. It is in this context that the relative inequality of London shows up most clearly. First, the problem of concealed households – that is, couples or single people with one or more children living within another household – is heavily concentrated in London, even though the proportions of these types of households are disproportionately low in London (Holmans et al, 2004).

Second, although London accounts for only around 15% of England's households, almost 30% of homeless acceptances are in the capital, reflecting the extent to which households are unable either to achieve social housing or to find private rented sector housing for themselves, even with the help of Housing Benefit (Burrows et al, 1997; Gordon et al, 2004).

Third, overcrowding measured either by the bedroom standard or by persons per room is fundamentally a London problem – with a third or more of the households affected located in the capital. Moreover, while space standards have been improving across the country overall, they have been falling in London – to the point where almost 40% of households living with more than one person per room are located in London (Reynolds, 2004).

Table 4.4: Measures of pressure

	London	Rest of England	London as % of England
Concealed households 2001 (000s)	35.4	125.6	22
Homelessness Acceptances 2003/04 (000s)	31.5	105.5	30
Crowding Below bedroom standard (000s) % of households 1999-2001	171 5.1	341 1.9	33 –
More than 1 person per room (000s) 1991 2001 % change 1991-2001	113.5 150.0 +32	275.0 236.8 –13.9	29 39

Sources: Census (1991, 2001); Survey of England Housing (2000, 2001); Housing Statistics (2004)

If the evidence on availability and quantity of housing obtained is put together with that on prices and rents it is very clear that, in value for money terms, households in London do far worse than households anywhere else in the country. They find it harder to access housing; they obtain less housing per person when they do; and they pay more for this lower quantity.

However, there are other measures of what people obtain, notably with respect to housing quality, where the story is somewhat different – although London still generally stands out as facing some of the worst conditions. For instance, if we look at housing quality as measured by unfitness, we find that these problems are indeed still concentrated in London but that the other regions suffering relatively poor conditions are in the North (where the housing stock is somewhat older than average and households are poorer) (Table 4.5). On the other hand, in the relatively well-off South of England the amount of unfit housing is disproportionately low (ODPM, 2005b).

This pattern is even clearer when we look at the proportions of households with central heating. There are 11 authorities where more than 20% of households are without central heating, and they are heavily concentrated in large metropolitan areas in the Midlands and the North (Table 4.6). Among the seven authorities with fewer than

Table 4.5: Measures of quality: unfit dwellings (2003) (England)

	Numbers	% of unfit dwellings	% of total dwellings
North	426,219	35	29
Midlands	222,772	19	19
South	331,068	28	37
London	225,850	19	15
England	1,205,909	100	100

Source: HIP Housing Strategy Statistical Appendix (2004)

Table 4.6: Measures of quality: no central heating

Highest >20%	%	Lowest <3%	%
Liverpool	27.0	Wycombe	2.7
Barrow in Furness	26.4	Basingstoke	2.8
Penwith	24.7	Waverley	2.8
Knowlsley	23.7	St Albans	2.8
Kirklees	23.4	Cambridge	2.8
Bradford	22.9	NE Derbyshire	2.9
Kingston-upon-Hull	21.3	Aylesbury	2.9
Leeds	20.7		
Birmingham	20.5		
Exeter	20.4		
Poole	20.3		

Source: Census (2001)

3% without central heating, six are in the South and the seventh is a high-income area in the Midlands. On this measure, therefore, inequality appears to be related to two main variables – the wealth and income of households on the demand side and the age of the existing stock on the other.

A final indicator of inequality relates to tenure choice and access. Table 4.7 shows clearly how heavily private rented housing is concentrated in London. This provides flexibility but it is also the sector where problems of quality, crowding and affordability are particularly concentrated. Further, the proportion of owner-occupation is positively correlated with regional incomes except with respect to London, where the proportion lags far behind that found in other less affluent regions. In part this is an outcome of the particularly important role played by social renting in London. However, as we have already seen, that proportion is nowhere near large enough to address the issues raised by homelessness.

To summarise: it is clear that the fundamentals of income distribution measured both spatially and with respect to households, the nature of the existing stock and the capacity to expand supply are the most important factors determining housing inequalities. But it is also clear that housing itself is helping to worsen that inequality, notably through the effect that house prices have on wealth on the one hand and opportunity on the other.

At a regional level, the stylised facts of housing conditions can be summarised in terms of the basic government objective of a decent home for every household at a price they can afford (Table 4.8). The Midlands comes closest to the national average. Obviously overall objectives are not fully achieved. However, on average problems are reasonably limited in terms of the balance of households and dwellings, new output, affordability and quality. The difficulties faced in the North mainly relate to 'a decent home' defined broadly to include the problems of neighbourhood and investment that go with low incomes and general lack of opportunity. In the South the major emphasis is on 'at a price they can afford' – in other words, housing standards are on

Table 4.7: Choice: tenure by region (dwellings) (%)

	Owner-occupied	Private rented	Social rented
London	59.4	15.7	24.9
North East	65.6	7.1	27.1
West Midlands	71.4	7.7	20.9
South East	75.9	10.6	13.4

Source: ODPM Housing and Construction Statistics (2004)

Table 4.8: A typology of the geography of inequality

1. The Midlands	'The national average' Reasonably available, reasonably affordable, reasonable quality housing
2. The North	'A decent home' Poor-quality housing and neighbourhoods, low demands and low investment
3. The South	'At a price they can afford' High price income ratios Inadequate supply response Limited social and private rented sectors
4. London	'For every household' Homelessness and concealed households Overcrowding but also affordability and quality problems

Source: Gordon et al (2004)

average relatively high but supply simply cannot keep pace with demand – making existing owner-occupiers richer, but worsening affordability among younger and lower-income households. Further, those at the bottom of the income scale have little or no choice with respect to either social or private rented housing.

The most important housing issue still remains that of having secure shelter for every household – and it is in this context that London stands out as the region where we as a society fail most obviously to meet basic requirements. More generally, London comes out worst across almost all measures of housing problems – including unfitness which is often seen as being fundamentally a northern problem.

Yet it is worth reiterating that on a broader definition of inequality London comes out as having the highest levels of housing wealth and the highest overall standards of living in the country. Under this definition the ordering is reversed, with the North facing the greatest problems of inequality; the Midlands being fairly average; and the South and particularly London doing well. In simple terms, those who are excluded either because of low incomes or because they are new to the market, do far worse in London but those further upmarket on average do far better than elsewhere in the country.

Implications for the future

How might geographic inequalities change?

How the situation will change in the future depends on what happens to the main variables that have been discussed above. First on demographics: the current projections suggest that the growth in households will, if anything, be more concentrated in the South. Post-Census estimates put 80% of household growth to 2011 in the South, with 27% in London and 53% in the rest of the South. The Midlands will be disproportionately low, with only 12% – as compared to 19% over the period from 1991 to 2001 – and the North expects around 8% – almost all from household fission – which implies little growth in income associated with what expansion of households there is (Holmans, 2005).

What are the uncertainties relating to these projections? The first is in terms of longevity: if people live longer than projected there will be relatively more households in the areas with older populations – that is, the Midlands and the North – but not enough to impact greatly on the overall picture. The second area of uncertainty is in the context of international migration: this is concentrated in London and any decline would reduce the growth in London but also modify the extent of outward migration into the rest of the country. The likely outcome is both the result of changes in policy, notably with respect to refugees and asylum seekers, and the economy – where structural changes in labour availability point to higher levels of immigration notably from the expanded European Union.

A final, and particularly important, issue, with implications for housing demand, is the impact of broader government policy. The potential for young people to form new households may be affected by the growth of debt derived from their increasing propensity to go on to higher education and changes in the funding of that education. And at the other end of housing careers there are the costs of supporting people to remain in their own homes as they get older and the extent to which the government will modify policy to help ensure that housing wealth supplements pensions. In addition, there are more general issues relating to eligibility for Housing Benefit and the effect of the restructuring of that benefit on household formation.

The second area of importance for the future is incomes and house prices. Income elasticity of demand is measured at around unity – so if incomes rise by around 2% per annum over the next decade the demand for housing can be expected to rise by not much short of 25%. To the extent that supply is not able to adjust, house price increases will offset this increase in demand – and again this will concentrate the adverse impact on affordability in the South of England. However, the impact of worsening income and wealth distribution may be even more important in terms of both household and geographic inequalities. All the evidence points to increasing concentrations of wealth and income in artificial intelligence, technology and network-based industries that are again disproportionately in the South. Similarly the proportions of non-participant households are likely to grow in regions with older age profiles – that is, particularly in the North. Thus income and price projections would point to worsening inequalities – both in terms of access and the position of lower-income households in the South and especially in London and in terms of increasing differentials in average wealth and income favouring these same regions.

How might government respond?

The three areas of policy which might help to offset these pressures towards increasing inequality relate to:

- changing incentives mainly through taxation although also perhaps through regulatory change;
- improving supply responsiveness thereby increasing access and reducing prices; and
- modifying allocation procedures to address problems of exclusion and lack of choice.

One of the most fundamental issues is the extent to which house prices are expected to appreciate and how far the tax benefits related to that appreciation are expected to be maintained. If instead government was to introduce some form of capital gains taxation – perhaps with rollover possibilities – the incentive to invest in high priced/high appreciation areas would be reduced. In addition – or alternatively – local government taxation could be modified better to reflect the value of property – resulting in lower incentives to purchase additional housing and acting as a surrogate for a wealth tax (Muellbauer, 2004). Both of these measures would reduce geographic inequalities and limit the benefits of investing in housing in pressure areas – thus helping to release supply and improve access. On the other hand, both would be highly unpopular with voters and could lead to cash flow problems, especially for older households.

Getting the supply right by increasing responsiveness of supply to increasing demands is the subject of the Barker reports (Barker, 2003, 2004). At the present time there is considerable optimism about the likely outcomes – yet it is likely to prove much harder to generate large-scale increases in provision than is currently suggested. Moreover, were supply to expand it could well lead to greater immigration – or less out-migration from the currently pressured areas – which would lessen the regional equalisation effects of expanding supply.

In many ways the equally important issue is whether evidence of expansion and responsiveness would lead to changing expectations about future house price increases, thus reducing the incentive to invest in housing and reducing prices. An expectational effect of this sort would be at least initially concentrated in pressure areas and could reduce geographic inequality.

Finally, administrative allocation of housing has often helped to worsen geographic inequality because of the lack of opportunity to move to areas where jobs and more appropriate housing might be located (Cho and Whitehead, 2004; Cho et al, 2005). Moving more to a system where problems are not necessarily solved where they are located could help to reduce pressure on social housing in the highest demand areas. This, taken together with improved choice-based letting schemes, area-based Housing Benefit and maybe social rents more related to differential values across regions, could provide greater equity both between households and between regions (DETR/DSS, 2000).

Overall, therefore, there is much that government policy could do to improve equality between regions while at the same time helping to maintain competitiveness in the economy and to ensure better housing outcomes. However, many of the policies are inherently unpopular, not least because they cannot be achieved without taking away from those who have built up housing wealth. Given the high levels of owner-occupation and the ageing population it is difficult to be optimistic about the potential for very significant improvements in geographical equalities with respect to housing except to the extent that these emerge out of macro-economic change.

Conclusion

There are a number of very clear conclusions with respect to current inequalities and their sources as well as the potential for change.

First, it is impossible to generate adequate housing investment and to meet aspirations without income growth, economic activity and a strong demand base. Unless these issues can be addressed in many parts of the North and maybe the West Midlands – as well as some areas in the South – inequalities will be maintained.

Second, areas of high pressure are inherently areas of high demand, relatively high house prices and lower housing quality except for those in the upper income range. Government policy cannot offset these effects – and people who live in these areas obtain other benefits which make it worth their while to remain. However, there is no reason for the government to worsen this situation by maintaining tax benefits for existing owners, thus worsening access still further.

Third, areas of lower pressure are made more desirable and attractive by lower house prices and higher standards. However, adjustment does not occur if households feel they are losing too much by moving away from pressure areas. Generating lower increases in house prices and lower expectations of further increases helps both types of area and improves welfare overall.

At the present time the most likely scenario is increasing inequalities for both households and regions. Yet there is much that government can do both directly and in terms of helping market adjustment to modify these outcomes and to increase both equality and opportunity.

References

Balchin, P., Bull, G. and Kieve, J. (1995) *Urban land economics and public policy* (5th edn), London: Macmillan.

Barker, K. (2003) *Review of housing supply: Securing our future needs. An interim report*, London: HM Treasury and ODPM.

Barker, K. (2004) *Review of housing supply: Delivering stability: Securing our housing needs, Final report: Recommendations*, London: HM Treasury/ ODPM.

Barr, N. (1998) *The economics of the welfare state*, Oxford: Oxford University Press.

Bramley, G., Fitzpatrick, S., Karley, N., Monk, S. and Pleace, N. (2005) *Evaluation of English housing policy 1975-2000, Theme 1, Supply, need and access*, London: ODPM.

Burrows, R., Pleace, N. and Quilgars, D. (1997) *Homelessness and social policy*, London: Routledge.

Chaplin, R., Jones, M., Martin, S., Pryke, M., Royce, C., Saw, P., Whitehead, C. and Yang, J. (1995) *Rents and risks*, York: Joseph Rowntree Foundation.

Charles, S. (1977) *Housing economics*, London: Macmillan.

Cheshire, P. and Mills, E.S. (eds)(1999) *Handbook of regional and urban economics*, North-Holland: Elsevier Science.

Cho, Y. and Whitehead, C. (2004) *Who moves and where? A comparison of housing association tenants in London and the Northern Regions*, Sector Study No 40, London: The Housing Corporation.

Cho, Y., Lyall Grant, F. and Whitehead, C. (2005) *Affordable housing in London: Who expects to move and where?*, Sector Study No 39, London: The Housing Corporation.

DETR (Department of the Environment, Transport and the Regions)/ DSS (Department of Social Security) (2000) *Quality and choice – A decent home for all: The Housing Green Paper*, London: DETR/DSS.

Department of Environment (1971) *Fair deal for housing*, Cmnd 4728, London: HMSO.

Department of the Environment (1977) *Housing policy: A consultative document*, Cmnd 6851, London: HMSO.

Evans, A.W. (2004) *Economics and land use planning*, Oxford: Blackwell.

Freeman, A. and Whitehead, C.M.E. (1996) *Halifax affordability report III: Spatial patterns of housing association rents and affordability*, Halifax: The Halifax.

Gordon, I., Travers, A. and Whitehead, C. (2002) *London's place in the UK economy*, London: Corporation of London.

Gordon, I., Travers, A. and Whitehead, C. (2003) *London's place in the UK economy*, London: Corporation of London.

Gordon, I., Travers, A. and Whitehead, C. (2004) *London's place in the UK economy*, London: Corporation of London.

Hancock, K.E. (1993) '"Can pay? Won't pay?" or economic principles of "affordability"', *Urban Studies*, vol 30, no 1, pp 127-45.

Harrison, A.J. and Whitehead, C.M.E. (1978) 'Is there an inner city problem?', *Three Banks Review*, September.

Holmans, A.E. (2001) *Past and current trends in house prices and incomes and access to home ownership*, Research Report IV, Cambridge: Cambridge Centre for Housing and Planning Research.

Holmans, A.E. (2005) *Households and dwellings in England in 1991 and 2001: A post 2001 Census analysis*, Research Report X, Cambridge: Cambridge Centre for Housing and Planning Research.

Holmans, A.E., Monk, S. and Whitehead, C.M.E. (2004) *Building for the future – 2004 update*, A report of the Shelter Housing Investment Project, London: Shelter.

Holmans, A.E., Monk, S., Ni Luanaigh, A. and Whitehead, C.M.E. (2005) *Building to meet housing need and demand: Assessment of the prospects in 2005*, London: Shelter.

Le Grand, J., Propper, C. and Robinson, R. (1992) *The economics of social problems*, Basingtoke: Palgrave.

Maclennan, D. (1982) *Housing economics*, Harlow: Longmans.

Meen, G. (2001) *Modelling spatial housing markets*, Dordrecht: Kluwer Academic Publishers.

Meen, G. et al (2005) *Affordability targets: Implications for housing supply*, London: ODPM.

Muellbauer J. (2004) *Property and land, taxation and the economy after the Barker Review,*York: Joseph Rowntree Foundation.

Muth, R.F. (1960) 'The demand for non-farm housing', in A. Harberger (ed) *The demand for durable goods,* Chicago, IL: University of Chicago Press.

Muth, R.F. (1969) *Cities and housing,* Chicago, IL: University of Chicago Press.

Muth, R.F. and Goodman, A.C. (1988) *The economics of the housing market,* New York, NY: Harwood Academic Publishers.

ODPM (Office of the Deputy Prime Minister) (2005a) *Sustainable communities: People, places and prosperity,* London: ODPM.

ODPM (2005b) *English House Condition Survey, Key findings for 2003: Decent homes and decent places,* London: ODPM.

Peterson, W.G., Pratten, C. and Tatch, J. (1998) *An economic model of the demand and need for social housing,* London: DETR.

Reynolds, L. (2004) *Crowded house – Cramped living in England's housing,* London: Shelter.

Rosen, S. (1974) 'Hedonic prices and implicit markets: product differentiation in pure competition', *Journal of Political Economy,* vol 82, pp 34-55.

Scanlon, K. and Whitehead, C. (2004) *International trends in housing tenure and mortgage finance,* London: Council of Mortgage Lenders.

Smith, G.R. (1999) *Area-based initiatives: The rationale for and options for area targeting,* CASEPaper no 25, London: Centre for the Study of Social Exclusion, London School of Economics and Political Science.

Solomou, W. and Wright, P. (2005) *Understanding the rent restructuring formula for housing association target rents,* Cambridge: Cambridge Centre for Housing and Planning Research.

Stephens, M., Munro, M. and Whitehead, C.M.E. (2005) *Evaluation of English housing policy 1975-2000: Overview,* London: ODPM.

Turnbull, G.K. (1995) *Urban consumer theory,* Washington: Urban Institute.

Urban Task Force (1999) *Towards an urban renaissance,* London: Spon.

Whitehead, C.M.E. (1984) 'Privatisation and housing', in J. Le Grand and R. Robinson (eds) *Privatisation and the welfare state,* London: George Allen & Unwin, Chapter 8.

Whitehead, C.M.E. (1998) *The benefits of better homes,* London: Shelter.

Whitehead, C.M.E. (1999) 'Urban housing markets: theory and policy', in P. Cheshire and E.S. Mills (eds) *Handbook of regional and urban economics,* North-Holland: Elsevier Science.

Whitehead, C.M.E. (2003) 'The economics of social housing', in A. O'Sullivan and K. Gibb (eds) *Housing economics and public policy*, Oxford: Blackwell.

Whitehead, C.M.E. (forthcoming) 'Planning policy and affordable housing: the UK as a successful case study?', *Housing Studies*.

Whitehead, C.M.E. and Monk, S. (forthcoming) *Does spatial planning increase value and welfare?*, London: Royal Town Planning Institute.

Wilcox, S. (2003) *Can't work – can't buy: Local measures of the ability of working households to become homeowners*, York: Joseph Rowntree Foundation.

Wilkinson, R. (1996) *Unhealthy societies: Afflictions of inequality*, London: Routledge.

FIVE

Understanding the drivers of housing market change in Britain's postindustrial cities

Brendan Nevin and Philip Leather

Introduction

One of the striking features of the present period is that it is no longer reasonable (if it ever was) to refer to the housing market in the singular: demand varies considerably from place to place. This is unlikely to be an ephemeral characteristic, since it reflects deep-seated developments in the wider economic base of different regions and sub-regions. The issue of low-demand housing raises important questions about the role of government and the extent to which market forces can be, and should be, interfered with in an era of rhetorical emphasis on deregulation and small government. This chapter suggests that the form and function of cities have been determined by past and current market forces and a legacy of public sector intervention that has on occasion been misguided. It emphasises the importance of understanding the historical drivers of change that have shaped our older industrial cities.

Low demand has been at the centre of the debate about housing, regeneration and planning in the North of England and parts of the industrial Midlands since 1998, when evidence of falling prices and the localised abandonment of housing began to emerge in the public domain. As a result of considerable lobbying by local authorities, registered social landlords (RSLs) and Members of Parliament, the government established a Housing Market Renewal Fund that was targeted initially at nine pathfinder areas[1]. These were not small neighbourhoods or estates like many previous housing programmes, but larger areas containing, in total, 784,000 households and a population of 1.9 million (Leather et al, 2004). The pathfinder areas contain between 60,000 and 140,000 properties.

All of the areas chosen to be Housing Market Renewal Pathfinders exhibited net out-migration, falling populations, high dwelling vacancy rates in particular neighbourhoods, and high levels of residential turnover, as well as areas of chronic deprivation (Audit Commission, 2005). The housing market renewal initiative has a number of distinctive features, which include:

- the requirement for local authorities to work together across boundaries. All of the pathfinder areas[2] cover parts of at least two local authorities and one covers parts of five;
- an intended 15- to 20-year implementation period (although it remains to be seen whether the programme can survive this long);
- a tenure-blind approach, with pathfinder areas covering all tenures and no tenure-based restrictions on activities which the Housing Market Renewal Fund can support;
- a recognition of the importance of local differences in problems and solutions, reflected in high levels of local autonomy in the development and implementation of programmes;
- a declared emphasis on influencing housing markets (supply and demand) rather than the housing stock; and
- an explicit requirement to link housing interventions which are eligible for support from the Fund with action to influence wider programmes impacting on the sustainability of the pathfinder areas (such as economic development or education) and to attempt to influence wider local, sub-regional and regional strategies (such as Regional Spatial Strategies or City Region Development Plans) to achieve alignment with pathfinder objectives.

These features are reflected in the complex and wide-ranging objectives associated with the programme. In the early stages these focused on the symptoms of falling prices and high void levels, but as the programme has developed, they have become more concerned with restructuring or balancing housing markets and delivering sustainable communities.

The costs of the programme across the North and Midlands will be significant. The government has allocated around £1.5 billion for the programme from 2003 to 2008, with additional funding being available from The Housing Corporation, English Partnerships and recycled land receipts. The initial bid to the government's Comprehensive Spending Review identified that expenditure of up to £8 billion would be required from a Housing Market Renewal Fund over a 15-year period to secure a sustainable housing market in each of the target areas (see Nevin, 2002). The largest cost within this programme relates to the clearance of private sector housing, where an initial review of approved plans suggested that up to 100,000 dwellings would be cleared during the 15-year programme (Cole and Nevin, 2004). However, this has proved a controversial element and it is likely that the emphasis will shift towards site assembly and new building, at least in the short term.

The speed with which the national body of research on the problems of low-demand housing was incorporated into political lobbying and then translated into official government policy is unprecedented in modern urban policy. The impacts are already evident in the pathfinders, where the worst areas of housing abandonment in inner Merseyside, Manchester/Salford and Newcastle upon Tyne are being addressed through clearance. However, in some respects the programme has moved faster than the ability of academics and practitioners to transfer their knowledge into appropriate strategies, and some early interventions represent a continuation of earlier initiatives of stock renovation. As a result of this, 2005 will be a defining moment for this programme as the pathfinders are required by the government to review their strategies prior to allocation of the available resources for the 2006-08 period (Cole and Nevin, 2004; Audit Commission, 2005).

The body of evidence that supported the concept of housing market renewal was generated in a fragmented manner and was responding to a perceived crisis in the northern conurbations. The rate of residential turnover and void levels in the social rented sector in parts of the North rose dramatically during the 1990s (Pawson and Bramley, 2000), waiting lists for council housing were declining (Nevin et al, 2001), and prices were low and falling in a number of neighbourhoods in northern cities (Murie et al, 1998). These research findings coincided with an emerging concern about the effectiveness of public sector investment in the older industrial cities, exemplified by Dr Henry Russell Court, a Housing Corporation-financed development in Newcastle upon Tyne, which was demolished only three years after completion because of a lack of demand (Weaver, 1999). In Merseyside, The Housing Corporation told local authorities that a rigorous analysis of future demand was essential if any further RSL investment was to be provided in the area.

The concern about these changing housing conditions in the North were subsequently amplified by government-sponsored research which identified around one million homes that were affected by low demand, of which approximately 50% were privately owned (DETR, 2000). Research in Liverpool suggested that once certain critical thresholds for vacancies and residential turnover were surpassed, vulnerable neighbourhoods were likely to experience abandonment where they were located in weak city or sub-regional housing markets (Lee and Nevin, 2003). There was therefore considerable evidence describing the nature of the problem by the time the Housing Market Renewal Fund was approved. However, there was also a wide range of potential explanations for these changes in demand, all of which had a degree of plausibility. For example, Webster (1998) noted a high degree of correlation between the loss of blue-collar employment and subsequent problems of low demand. Murie et al (1998) highlighted a number of societal, economic and aspirational changes which had affected housing demand, while Cole et al (2003) found that changing demand for social housing was still the dominant factor (in Leeds) underpinning neighbourhood trajectories, despite the multitenure nature of the issue at the city level.

The broad social and economic shifts that occurred across the cities undergoing deindustrialisation did not translate into a uniform pattern of change in working-class neighbourhoods. Lee and Nevin (2002) identified a series of neighbourhood characteristics, which, when located within weaker housing markets, were associated with lower prices, vacancies and potential abandonment. These characteristics included monolithic provision of certain types of property, a predominance of rented housing, poor quality stock in owner-occupation, and a concentration of households that were economically inactive or unemployed. This method of quantifying the potential spatial location of areas 'at risk' of low demand produced maps illustrating the way in which these neighbourhoods were clustered in highly specific locations in the cores and in some peripheral estates around the older industrial conurbations. However, this did not explain why some neighbourhoods were experiencing profound difficulties while others were often deprived but not in crisis in terms of house prices, demand or void rates. The ability to explain how neighbourhood collapse is triggered in weak sub-regional markets is a key question for policy makers, who appear to have been struggling with three interconnected housing issues. These issues can be summarised as: a widespread change in the demand for social rented housing which has impacted severely in some council estates; a localised but significant deterioration of the relative performance of parts of the pre-1919 terraced sector within some conurbations; and a comparatively small-scale collapse of multitenure neighbourhoods (see Leather et al, 2004).

A simple maxim to follow when devising a solution to a problem is to ensure that the causes are understood and that the responses are sufficient to produce the desired outcomes. A review of the eight completed market renewal prospectuses[3] by Cole and Nevin (2004) has shown that policy makers have struggled to interpret the causes of change within their local housing markets. This is not surprising given the disparate or inadequate information available to them and the large number of unanswered questions that the body of research, however influential, had exposed. A second issue that arises when reviewing the literature is the extent to which the academic debate has focused on the housing dimension to urban change in postindustrial cities. To a certain extent this is understandable given the physical manifestation of housing abandonment. However, it is possible that by failing to explore the impact of economic change, demographic change, social trends and aspirations, the wider impacts of public policy on the urban form, and recent trends such as the increase in speculative investment in housing, policy makers have become focused on devising housing-based solutions when many of the drivers are located elsewhere (Audit Commission, 2005). A programme of renewal that is based primarily on housing interventions gives many practitioners a sense of comfort as housing abandonment is not a new phenomenon. Bramley (1998) identified a number of local authorities in the Midlands and North that had had a surplus of social housing for many years. The standard solution to this issue has been a mixture of demolition, refurbishment and improved management through policy instruments such as the Estate Action Programme, Housing Action Trusts and the Priority Estates Projects. The scale of downsizing in the social sector has been significant in some cities, with Birmingham, Glasgow and Liverpool all demolishing more than 20,000 dwellings over the 1985-2005 period. But such changes fail to address the wider factors that influence the attractiveness of dwelling types, neighbourhoods and sub-regions.

This chapter is based on the premise that the interaction between surpluses in both the public and private sector at the neighbourhood level in a number of large urban areas, with the emerging problems associated with low values in private sector and multitenure abandonment, did mark a new phase in the evolution of low-income housing markets during the 1990s. However, the chapter also argues that to understand the drivers of this change the debate needs to be placed in an appropriate historical context. Additionally, the reconstruction of local housing markets, and the urban form more generally, will need to take account of new spatial and economic relationships which have emerged over the last three or four decades in the North and industrial Midlands. This is summarised in the conclusion, but firstly illustrated by reference to developments in the inner core of Manchester and Salford in the next section of this chapter.

The structure of inner-city housing markets in central Manchester and Salford

In Manchester and Salford, the housing market renewal intervention area was designed by local authority officials in collaboration with the civil servants who were responsible for delivering the market renewal programme, drawing heavily on the work of Lee and Nevin (2002) referred to above. The final extent of the area was refined with local knowledge and evidence to produce a contiguous intervention area that covered 116,000 dwellings. The characteristics of the housing market at the core of the conurbation are listed in Table 5.1. This shows that the market is predominantly low value, with 74% of properties either being flatted or terraced. Vacancies are high, at 12%, and the rate of owner-occupation at 36% is nearly half the national average (68%).

The *Manchester-Salford housing market renewal pathfinder prospectus* (Manchester City Council and Salford City Council, 2003) highlighted a number of factors that were creating increasing instability within the market renewal area. These included: a concentration of deprivation with 23 of the 27 electoral wards falling within the worst 10% nationally, and eight of these within the worst 1%; an expanding low-value private

Table 5.1: Manchester/Salford housing market renewal area: basic characteristics

Basic statistics	Area (ha)	6,379
	Population (change since 1991)	24,000 (down 8%)
	Number of households	
	(change since 1991)	102,000 (down 7%)
	Number of dwellings	116,000 (down 7%)
	Vacancy rate	12%
Form	Detached	3%
	Semi-detached	23%
	Terraced	47%
	Flats	27%
Tenure	Owner-occupied	36%
	Private rented	21%
	Social rented	43%
Economic	Median sale price 2004	£99,000
	Lower quartile sale price 2004	£55,000
	Annual rate of return since 1986	
	(UK average 14%)	6%

Source: Leather and Roberts (2004); Leather et al (2004); Audit Commission (2005)

rented sector, in an area with a surplus of rented property already; high levels of crime; and a lack of developer confidence restricting new supply. These weaknesses would, however, not have attracted substantial government financial support without significant evidence of abandonment and other problems such as crime and antisocial behaviour. At the beginning of this century that evidence was relatively easy to find, with large-scale abandonment in areas of older terraced housing in Seedley/Langworthy and Higher Broughton in Salford, Lightbowne in north Manchester and lower east Manchester (Beswick and Openshaw).

The decline in these areas in the late 1990s was both severe and rapid. For example, in the Seedley/Langworthy area average prices for a terraced house fell from £30,000 in 1990 to £4,000 in 1998 (Salford City Council, 1998). Similarly, in lower east Manchester a terraced property that was sold in 1992 for £32,000 was selling for £5,000 in 1998. In both of these locations the vacancy rate increased rapidly from the middle of the decade. A study commissioned by Manchester City Council to explain the precipitous decline in the Lightbowne area of north Manchester noted:

> Even if people want to stay in the area and move up the housing ladder they cannot do so. This structural market weakness has meant that economic conditions in the housing catchment area – and better housing choices elsewhere – have resulted in a declining demand for owner occupation. The low level of demand has driven down house prices and resulted in an influx of private landlords, with associated social problems, which in turn has driven down prices in a vicious circle of market decline. (GVA Grimley and Centre for Urban and Regional Studies, 2000, para vii)

The consultants concluded that only radical intervention could ensure that this area of north Manchester would be sustainable in future.

The multitenure areas in Manchester and Salford which have experienced the type of decline described in this chapter have a number of characteristics in common:

- they have benefited from past regeneration expenditure, usually as general improvement areas or housing action areas in the 1970s and 1980s, or as the focus for programmes of acquisition and improvement by RSLs;

- the areas are substantial in size, ranging from between 1,500 to 5,000 dwellings;
- they are characterised by back-of-pavement two-up two-down terraced houses; and
- these clusters of poor-quality terraced houses escaped clearance because of a change of government policy in the mid-1970s. They in effect became a buffer that insulated the more affluent hinterland from the instability inherent to the large public sector housing estates that surround the central business district in Manchester and Salford.

The focus of these low-demand problems in the core of the conurbation lies within an east–west corridor that bisects central Salford and Manchester. It is substantially made up of large social housing estates at the centre, with multitenure terraced areas on the periphery. Other inner-city, low-value owner-occupied areas within the market renewal area, primarily to the south of Manchester city centre, have also been categorised as 'at risk'. However, they are mostly high turnover residential areas that cater for international migration, students, the growing black and minority ethnic community and young professionals. Accordingly they have a function consistent with Manchester's standing as a significant European city. The next section of this chapter examines the drivers of change which have created the imbalance within this inner-city market.

The drivers of change in the inner core of Manchester and Salford

Understanding what drives a complex sub-regional housing market is not an exact science, although the rhetoric of government and the Audit Commission sometimes seems to suggest that it is. It is often easy to confuse cause and effect and to look backwards and identify historic drivers, just as a whole series of new influences are shaping the urban environment. For example, the very phrase 'low demand' has been undermined by house price rises over the 2002-04 period, influenced by speculative demand from potential private landlords, even though price differentials between neighbourhoods in pathfinders and those outside have, if anything, increased.

Of equal importance, it is essential that policy makers and practitioners are able to differentiate between structural causes such as economic change, and fundamental shifts in the urban structure of cities, from those which are generated by a severe dysfunctional relationship between some groups of residents and the neighbourhoods in which they live (as exhibited, for example, by crime and cultural attributes towards education). Clearly British cities operate and trade within radically different sub-regional environments. In the North West, the cores of the two principal conurbations have been affected over the last three decades by a fairly elastic supply of new property outside the inner city (initially planned social rented provision but subsequently dominated by private sector provision). These have combined with a history of severe population decline and significant banks of empty or underused land within their boundaries. The dynamics of urban change will play out very differently in places that have experienced severe and prolonged structural change from those which have relatively tight housing markets.

In the inner core of Manchester and Salford, levels of deprivation are both chronic and widespread. However, given the fact that multitenure housing abandonment is focused on a number of discrete locations it would appear that deprivation, like monolithic provision and tenure skew, is a necessary but not sufficient condition to provoke a collapse in the local housing market. Clearly there are other factors at play that stimulate decline in neighbourhoods that have a certain type of structure. Examples of where simple causality is difficult to demonstrate can be found in the Technical Appendix of the first *Manchester-Salford housing market renewal pathfinder prospectus* (2003). For example, when comparing population change with the concentration of property in Council Tax band A and B, there is no direct correlation between the concentration of low-value property and population loss. Of the 10 wards with the highest concentrations of low-value properties, three experienced population increases between 1991 and 2001, three had major population loss and four moderate population loss (Manchester City Council and Salford City Council, 2003). It is necessary, therefore, to conduct a more detailed analysis of the drivers of change and the interrelationships between them over time, to explain in detail the performance of the housing market in the housing market renewal area.

Historical influences

Some of the most powerful drivers of change in central Manchester and Salford have developed over four or five decades. The process of urban change and renewal is therefore entrenched, and the scale of the issues is quantifiable. This is not the case in other pathfinders such as North Staffordshire and East Lancashire, which are only now beginning to show the type of urban collapse and social stresses that were evident in Manchester and Salford in the mid-1970s. The major long-standing factors that can be identified from the literature are set out below.

Decentralisation

There have been several phases of decentralisation over the past 40 years that have resulted in the loss of nearly 400,000 people in the Manchester/Salford local authority areas. The first wave of change was stimulated by public sector activity in the 1960s and was based on erroneous population projections and a failure to respond to changing tenure preferences (Nevin et al, 2001). This aggressive public sector (over)decentralisation was then followed by a market driven process in the 1970s and 1980s, that was facilitated by a change in planning philosophy towards a pro-development stance. This is no longer such a dominant factor in explaining current change, however, its influence reverberates in several ways:

• past population loss has created intense concentrations of deprivation which are self-reinforcing and very hard to mitigate;
• there is still evidence of net population loss. Even where cities have, like Manchester, succeeded in attracting young people, they struggle to retain them as they age;
• there is a continued danger of planning-led decentralisation, brought about by simplistic 'predict and provide' models influencing land release; and
• there has been a significant and continuing impact on urban densities (see below), which has undermined levels and quality of service provision across the board.

Nature and type of urban redevelopment

Just as Manchester and Salford were planning to (over)decentralise their populations, a significant programme of comprehensive redevelopment was implemented in an east–west corridor which bisected the city centre. The nature and impact of this redevelopment is dramatically revealed by comparisons of before and after maps. The standard of redevelopment within this corridor was among the worst in the UK, replacing around 80,000 terraced dwellings with public sector properties built in large estates using experimental design and construction techniques. Many of these estates have been demolished already (for example, Hulme), while others have been constantly subject to firefighting measures to stabilise them (see, for example, the Ordsall area in Salford). Examples from east to west include:

- Central Salford high rise – 'The precinct' (partial redevelopment)
- Ordsall – Radburn layout (partial redevelopment)
- Hulme – deck access (demolished)
- 'Fort' Ardwick – deck access (demolished)
- Harpurhey – Radburn layout (selective clearance)
- Miles Platting/Colley Hurst – high rise/deck access (significant clearance and estate remodelling)
- Longsight – Radburn layout
- 'Fort' Beswick – deck access (demolished)
- Turkey Lane – deck access (demolished)

Obviously many cities experienced poor-quality redevelopment in the 1960s and 1970s. However, what distinguishes the Manchester/ Salford area from any other English inner city, with the exception of Liverpool, is the scale of the redevelopment, the experimental techniques used to construct the deck access estates, the speed with which these estates failed socially and technically, and the extent to which, when houses rather than flats were constructed, they were developed using Radburn principles – the most unpopular mass housing design in the national local authority portfolio.

Economic change and the collapse of the Victorian mixed-use environment

The Greater Manchester conurbation entered the 20th century with a linear pattern of wealth creation that stretched from Trafford Park and Salford Docks in the west through the city centre to east Manchester. The decline of this wealth creation corridor arguably started in the 1930s, but, without doubt, accelerated throughout the 1950s, 1960s and 1970s, with the remnants of industrial production lost in the 1980s and 1990s. Progressive economic decline resulted in dereliction and a large-scale supply of redundant land being released onto the marketplace, at a time of comprehensive housing redevelopment and the subsequent failure of some large new neighbourhoods. Ultimately this produced an environment of negative change over a six-mile corridor within which few people with income, aspiration or choice would have chosen to stay during four decades of transition. It is in this corridor that the most severe demand problems are concentrated.

Urban population densities

Population density is an important measurement of the health of a modern city. Clearly public policy has historically had the objective of reducing densities where these were injurious to health. However, in a modern city there are minimum levels of population density required to support an efficient public transport system, local shops, medical care services, schools and other facilities. In parts of the housing market renewal area a combination of decentralisation, leading to fewer people using the facilities in a given area, demolition of unpopular estates, and an increase in single people and couples occupying property built for families, have resulted in a collapse of local facilities (see Llewellyn Davies, 2004). This process was well entrenched by the 1970s when the core areas of inner-city Salford and Manchester lost over a quarter of their residents compared to a loss of 1.8% in the rest of Greater Manchester. Between 1951 and 1981 population densities had halved in the inner core (Bristow, 1987). Research by Dorling and Atkins (1995), highlighted in Table 5.2, shows that Manchester and Salford registered greater falls in population density than any other comparable English city in the period 1971-91. Work conducted for Manchester City Council to support their review of the *Housing market renewal pathfinder prospectus* has confirmed this trend. Recent unpublished research carried out as part of preparations for a revised *Housing market renewal pathfinder prospectus* confirms that population densities in the central east–west corridor in Manchester and Salford have moved from a range of 40-87 persons per acre in 1951, to ranges from 0-10 and 10-20 by 2001. Population densities in the core of the conurbation have thus moved from the highest to the lowest in the two cities. Conversely, inner south Manchester has retained its population density over five decades, a factor which has supported a degree of vibrancy in the urban environment in this part of the housing market renewal area.

Table 5.2: Population density (% change) (1971-91) (selected local authorities)

Manchester	−24.11
Salford	−26.24
Bolton	−7.88
Wigan	+1.85
Rochdale	−8.46
Stockport	−3.86
Liverpool	−21.13
Sheffield	−19.54
Newcastle upon Tyne	−20.20
Birmingham	−13.07
Sandwell	−11.93
Inner London	−14.79
Outer London	−5.55

Source: Dorling and Atkins (1995)

Monolithic provision, property type and tenure

The structure of the Manchester/Salford housing market is the product of decisions by public and private sector agencies and individuals taken between 50 and 120 years ago. Other areas, such as Warrington and Macclesfield, have been able to develop their housing markets incrementally to reflect changing aspirations and tastes. The inner Manchester/Salford market, because it has been declining, reflects the provision for a relatively poor community through social rented housing, grafted onto the residue of provision for the respectable working class of the late 19th century. The area has therefore become progressively uncompetitive during the second half of the 20th century (Bristow, 1987).

The housing market function of the housing market renewal area

While the structure of the housing 'offer' in the core of the two cities has failed to compete with peripheral developments, the central areas of Manchester and Salford form the centre of a sub-region of 2.5 million people, where relationships as expressed by economic linkages, travel-to-work patterns and migration have experienced considerable change since the 1970s. Papers produced by Manchester City Council in the early part of the 1990s (see, for example, Manchester City Council, 1996) examined change between the two Census periods 1981 and 1991, migration statistics and inter-local authority moves tracked by the Small Area Statistics in 1991. This data showed the following:

- an outflow of affluent groups, counterbalanced by a significant inflow of poor residents;
- a number of wards where there was little inward movement;
- the increasing use of the older core by young economic migrants, black and minority ethnic groups and students;
- strong linkages with Tameside, Stockport, Trafford and Salford; and
- relatively weak linkages with Oldham, Rochdale, Bolton and Wigan.

The spatial relationships outlined in the last two points above are confirmed by work undertaken by the authors in preparation for the update of the *Manchester-Salford housing market renewal pathfinder prospectus*. An 'area of influence' for Manchester was outlined using ward-level travel-to-work and migration data from the 2001 Census (Figure 5.1). Most journeys to work are of comparatively short distance and only 40% of people in England travelled to work across a local authority boundary. Looking at areas which export at least 10% of their workforce to Manchester reveals a strongly 'south-facing' area of influence for the city, extending across Salford, Trafford, Tameside and Stockport and out into Macclesfield and High Peak, but covering only

Figure 5.1: Manchester – area of influence based on travel-to-work (2001)

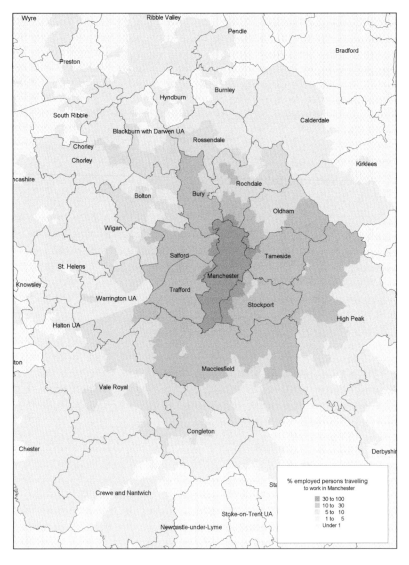

Source: ONS, 2001 Census, Origin/Destination Statistics

parts of Oldham and Rochdale, and having only limited impact on Bolton and Wigan. In contrast, the areas of influence of the other Greater Manchester authorities are much more limited in extent (Figure 5.2) with a strong degree of overlap between neighbouring authorities.

But these linkages are with the city centre and other major employment centres such as the airport and Trafford Park rather than

Figure 5.2: Areas of influence based on travel-to-work for all Greater Manchester authorities (2001)

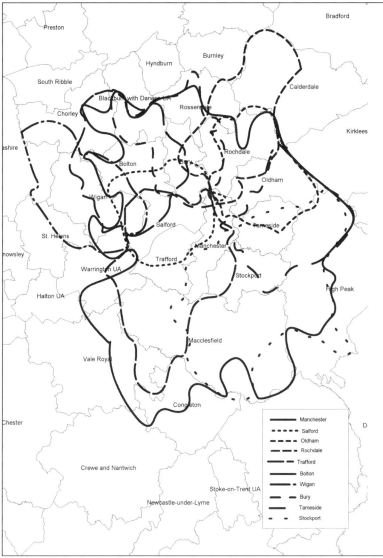

Source: ONS, 2001 Census, Origin/Destination Statistics

with the pathfinder area. Figure 5.3 shows the catchment of Manchester city centre using a finer grained output area analysis. This confirms the widespread area of influence of the city centre in terms of travel-to-work. Figure 5.4 shows the same data for the north Manchester sub-area of the pathfinder. There is little travel into the areas from south of the city centre, and the area of influence extends mainly north but only to the city boundary, with limited crossover from

Figure 5.3: Travel-to-work in Manchester city centre (2001)

Travel to work in Manchester City Centre
% of all travelling to work from origin

30 to 100   (117)
10 to 30   (2485)
 5 to 10   (2830)
 1 to   5   (6169)

Source: ONS, 2001 Census, Origin/Destination Statistics

Figure 5.4: Travel-to-work in north Manchester Area Development Framework (2001)

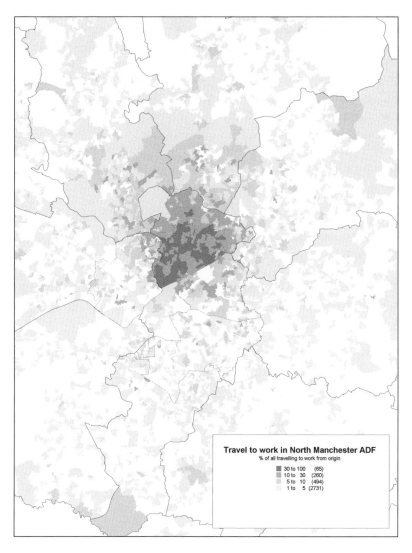

Source: ONS, 2001 Census, Origin/Destination Statistics

Rochdale/Bury. The picture for the east Manchester sub-area is similarly limited, suggesting that both these areas are relatively isolated from links with the city centre and wider areas around them. In contrast, the south Manchester sub-area (Figure 5.5) shows more widespread links, although mainly to the south of the pathfinder area. This reflects the stronger level of integration of this part of the pathfinder into the wider sub-regional economy.

The current functions of the housing market renewal area involve providing low-income housing and areas of transition which allow a dynamic entry point for people coming to or setting up a home in what is demonstrably a southward facing conurbation[4]. The suburbs

Figure 5.5: Travel-to-work in south Manchester Area Development Framework (2001)

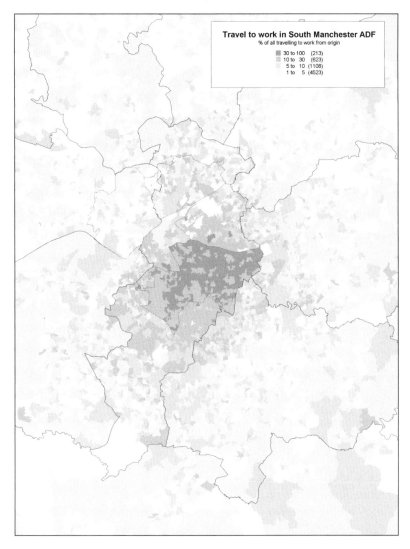

Source: ONS, 2001 Census, Origin/Destination Statistics

for this centre of wealth creation (the Gross Value Added (GVA) per head in south Greater Manchester is more than 40% higher than north Greater Manchester) are mainly outside or on the periphery of the housing market renewal area.

A review of the historical drivers of housing market change potentially shows an interesting temporal variation. Long-standing economic and demographic drivers, combined with planned redevelopment and the provision of social rented housing, have created the conditions whereby a series of predominantly low-income housing markets (including both private and social rented housing) have coexisted with areas undergoing progressive market collapse. A second category of drivers that emerged in the 1990s compounded these processes. These included the declining attractiveness of council housing and its emergence as a mainly residual, short-term tenure, a greater availability of cheap mortgage finance to assist more people on low incomes to become homeowners, and falling male unemployment which facilitated the tenure shift. These factors were less specific to Manchester/Salford and to some extent applied across the whole of the North of England.

These changes, which were well documented by academics in the late 1990s, were more likely in the first instance to impact on specific tenures (council housing) or property types (back of pavement terraces) than neighbourhoods. However, given the unfavourable characteristics of the Manchester/Salford housing market renewal area and the sub-regional housing market relationship that had been developing between the core and its southern neighbours, these societal changes had the effect of seriously aggravating area-based difficulties.

New market drivers and the impact of public policy

More recently, the housing market in the inner core of Manchester and Salford has entered a new and dynamic phase. This has been accompanied by significant house price rises, even in areas such as east Manchester which have experienced sharp falls and high proportions of very low value sales (Leather and Roberts, 2004). The growth of the city centre residential market now accounts for more than half the annual housing completions in the two cities. Manchester absorbs around 25% of the region's international migration, and black and minority ethnic communities now account for more than 20% of the inner-city population with a large potential for growth in the future. As a result of these changes and recent strong economic growth, the population of Manchester has started to rise for the first time in

20 years. A key question for local policy makers is whether the housing market renewal programme can restructure local provision in a way that changes its regional and sub-regional function and thereby retains these groups as their aspirations change or increase.

Given that new markets are emerging in Manchester/Salford, and that the area has seen increases in house prices, some are already questioning the need for a Housing Market Renewal Fund. Figures 5.6 to 5.9 show annual rates of price increase by postcode sector for the Greater Manchester and Cheshire area, every two years from 1996 to 2003. In the mid-1990s there was a clear band of low-value housing at the core of the conurbation, but from about 2000 even the neighbourhoods with the most intractable problems registered robust price increases.

Figures 5.10 to 5.12 show recent trends in house prices in the Manchester/Salford pathfinder relative to the rest of the North West over the 1996-2004 period. Despite absolute price growth in the pathfinder, the gap between the housing market renewal area and the rest of the region remains wide and has only narrowed slightly since 2002 (Figure 5.10). Figure 5.11 shows the difference in the profile of prices between the pathfinder and the rest of the region in 2004. The peak price in the pathfinder was still only in the £30,000-£40,000 band, and the proportion of sales in the pathfinder greatly exceeds that for the rest of the region in all bands up to £80,000, after which it falls well short. Figure 5.12 shows the proportion of sales in the pathfinder that fell below the regional lower quartile threshold. This remained at between 60% and 80% (around three times the expected level if prices were similar in distribution to those for the rest of the region), falling only slightly in 2004. Additionally, the Audit Commission has estimated that the annual rate of return for owner-occupied property in Manchester/Salford has been 6% compared to a national average of 14% (see Table 5.1). Housing in the pathfinder area thus continues to be a very poor investment.

Despite the continuing underperformance, recent price rises still require some explanation given the higher turnover, vacancies and general level of decay which exists in many of these neighbourhoods. At least part of the answer may be found in the effects of public sector intervention in the market. Over the 2000-2005 period the two cities have averaged 1,500 demolitions per annum, and a clearance programme is likely to be maintained over the short-term lifetime of the housing market renewal programme. The crude surplus of accommodation that contributed to the problem of low demand is therefore disappearing quite quickly. The supply of units of affordable

Figure 5.6: House price changes in Greater Manchester (1996-97)

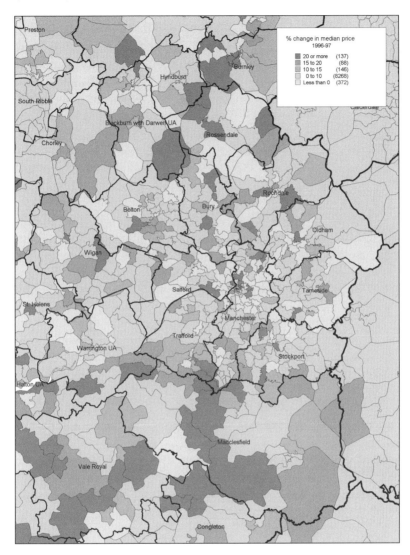

Source: ODPM, HM Land Registry

housing and social housing relets are being reduced while the demand for low-income housing is being increased by the decanting process. In the absence of a new affordable housing supply local shortages will be inevitable for the duration of the clearance programme. An increase in speculative purchase also lies behind price rises in some areas, particularly those with the lowest values (Leather and Roberts, 2004).

Figure 5.7: House price changes in Greater Manchester (1998-99)

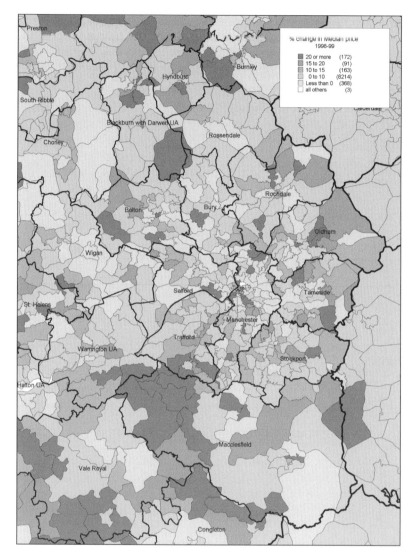

Source: ODPM, HM Land Registry

The housing market renewal area is undergoing a period of rapid change, with market forces predominating in the new city centre and the public sector leading in the areas where the private sector has largely been absent for a century. The extent to which the inner core of Manchester will be able to retain the new sources of demand is dependent on the ability to introduce a new mix of properties and to

Figure 5.8: House price changes in Greater Manchester (2000-01)

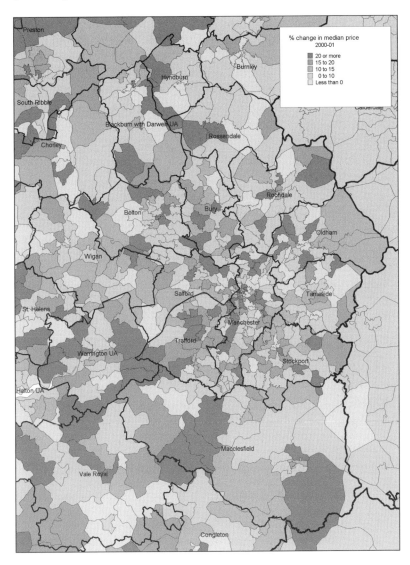

Source: ODPM, HM Land Registry

increase densities in the shattered urban form that characterised much of the inner city. This will be critically dependent on engineering a tenure shift in areas of north and east Manchester and central Salford that are still predominantly populated by social housing in neighbourhoods which experience comparatively low inflows of population.

Figure 5.9: House price changes in Greater Manchester (2002-03)

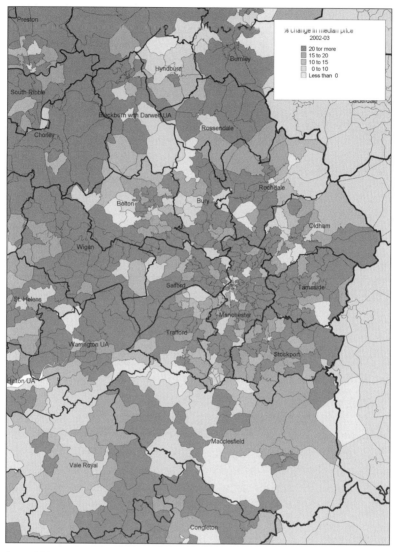

Source: ODPM, HM Land Registry

Figure 5.10: Ratio of pathfinder median prices to median price for North West region outside pathfinders

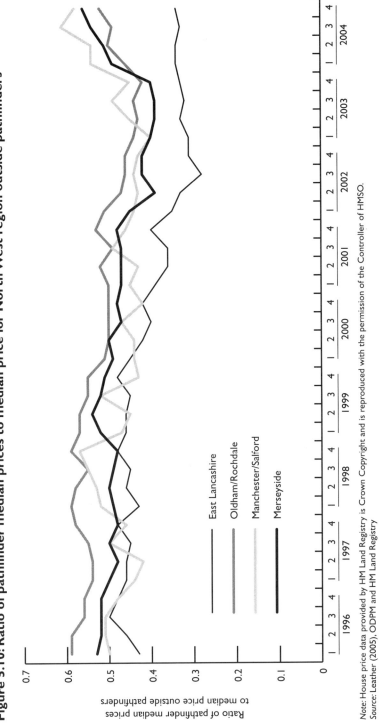

Note: House price data provided by HM Land Registry is Crown Copyright and is reproduced with the permission of the Controller of HMSO.
Source: Leather (2005), ODPM and HM Land Registry

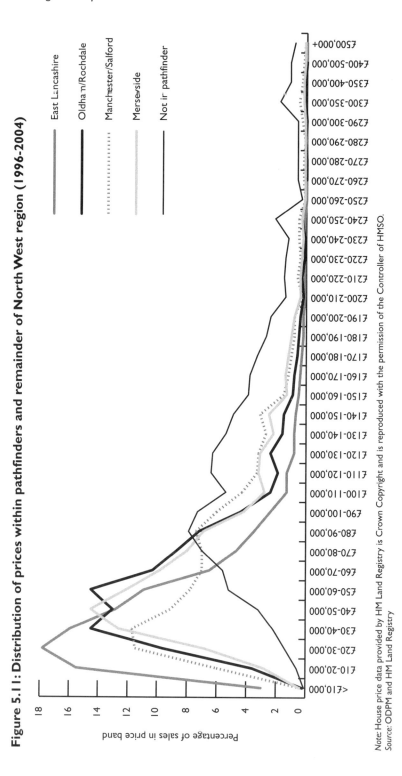

Figure 5.11: Distribution of prices within pathfinders and remainder of North West region (1996-2004)

Legend:
- East Lancashire
- Oldham/Rochdale
- Manchester/Salford
- Merseyside
- Not in pathfinder

Note: House price data provided by HM Land Registry is Crown Copyright and is reproduced with the permission of the Controller of HMSO.
Source: ODPM and HM Land Registry

Figure 5.12: Percentage of sales below regional 25th percentile threshold, North West pathfinders (1996-2004)

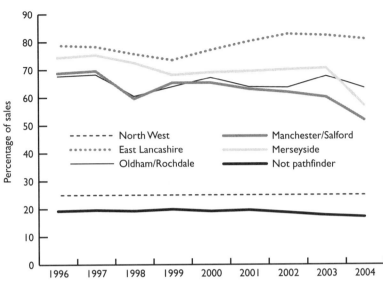

Note: House price data provided by HM Land Registry is Crown Copyright and is reproduced with the permission of the Controller of HMSO.
Source: ODPM and HM Land Registry

Conclusion

This chapter has emphasised the importance of understanding the historical drivers of change that have shaped our older industrial cities. Their function and form have been determined by past and current market forces and a legacy of public sector intervention that has on occasion been misguided. It is therefore essential that initiatives such as the housing market renewal programme are based on a robust forward strategy which takes into account societal change and the reality of economic restructuring which often has a strong spatial dimension.

The emerging evidence base being produced by the nine housing market renewal pathfinders is emphasising the power of the social and economic forces which are reshaping cities and regions. In the context of economic restructuring in the North of England and the industrial Midlands, the poor quality of inner-city housing markets has reinforced social exclusion and filtered the poorest people into neighbourhoods with intense concentrations of deprivation. In Manchester and Salford the process of neighbourhood disintegration has been an ongoing process for more than four decades, during which time the pattern of land and employment use also collapsed in the inner core. In retrospect, it should have come as no surprise that the most marginal areas of owner-occupation on the fringes of comprehensive redevelopment areas that have been unstable for nearly half a century eventually collapsed. This should be a potent warning for the future.

A series of urban policy initiatives since 1977 have not proved capable of addressing the profound loss of competitiveness of the urban environment in the older industrial towns and cities. For the housing market renewal programme to be successful in the long term, a coordinated response from the government will be necessary which integrates transportation, economic development, planning, skills and training and housing strategies at regional, sub-regional and district levels. Clear priorities will need to be developed and a volume of public sector investment commensurate to the task will need to be committed. Without this level of commitment it is possible that the Housing Market Renewal Fund will merely address the effects of change, and not alter the long-term trajectories of the older urban areas.

Notes

This note applies to all figures reproduced in this chapter: Census data is Crown Copyright and is reproduced with the permission of the Controller of HMSO. Map boundaries are based on data provided through EDINA UKBORDERS with the support of the Economic and Social Research Council and Joint Information Systems Committee and use boundary material that is copyright of the Crown.

[1] The nine pathfinder areas are: Newcastle and Gateshead; Hull and East Riding of Yorkshire; South Yorkshire (Sheffield, Barnsley, Rotherham and Doncaster); Birmingham and Sandwell; North Staffordshire (Stoke on Trent, Newcastle under Lyme and Staffordshire Moorlands); Manchester and Salford; Merseyside (Liverpool, Sefton and Wirral); Oldham and Rochdale; and East Lancashire (Blackburn with Darwen, Hyndburn, Burnley, Pendle and Rossendale).

[2] Except Hull and East Riding. Here the intervention area corresponds with Hull City Council's boundary but the partnership to implement the programme also includes East Riding Council.

[3] At the end of 2004. The Hull pathfinder submitted its proposals early in 2005.

[4] The central business district of Manchester has a fairly even impact on travel-to-work areas across the Manchester reference area. However, the economy is southward facing in terms of GVA and flows of commuters because of the location of the universities, the airport and a number of high-technology clusters.

References

Audit Commission (2005) *Housing market renewal: Best practice handbook*, London: Audit Commission.

Bramley, G. (1998) 'Housing surpluses and housing need', in S. Lowe, S. Spencer and P. Keenan (eds) *Housing abandonment in Britain: Studies in the causes and effects of low demand housing*, York: Centre for Housing Policy.

Bristow, M. (1987) 'The North West', in P. Damesick and P.V. Wood (eds) *Regional problems, problem regions and public policy in the United Kingdom*, Oxford: Clarendon Press.

Cole, I. and Nevin, B. (2004) *The road to renewal*, York: York Publishing Services.

Cole, I., Hickman, P. and Reeve, K. (2003) *The Leeds housing market: Perceptions of change*, Sheffield: Sheffield Hallam University.

DETR (Department of the Environment, Transport and the Regions) (2000) *National strategy for neighbourhood renewal. Report of Policy Action Team 7: Unpopular housing*, London: The Stationery Office.

Dorling, D. and Atkins, D. (1995) *Population density change and concentration in Great Britain 1971, 1981 and 1991*, Studies on Medical and Population Subjects, No 58, London: HMSO.

GVA Grimley and Centre for Urban and Regional Studies (2000) *Moston, Harpurhey and Lightbourne: Housing market study*, Report for Manchester City Council and North Manchester SRB Partnership, Manchester: GVA Grimley.

Leather, P. (2005) *Housing market trends in the North West of England: 2004 update*, Manchester: Government Office for the North West.

Leather, P. and Roberts, J. (2004) *Housing market trends in the North West of England*, Manchester: Government Office for the North West.

Leather, P., Murie, A. and Roberts, J. (2004) *Home ownership solutions for low demand areas*, London: ODPM/Council of Mortgage Lenders.

Lee, P. and Nevin, B. (2002) 'Using GIS to research low and changing demand for housing', in D. Kidner, G. Higgs and S. White (eds) *Socio-economic applications of geographic information science*, London: Taylor & Francis.

Lee, P. and Nevin, B. (2003) 'Changing demand for housing: restructuring markets and the public policy framework', *Housing Studies*, vol 18, no 1, pp 65–86.

Llewellyn Davies (2004) *Manchester-Salford housing market renewal. What does it take to make a neighbourhood?*, London: Llewellyn Davies.

Manchester City Council (1996) *Migration in Manchester – An analysis of the small area migration statistics 1991 Census*, Planning Studies Group April, Manchester: Manchester City Council.

Manchester City Council and Salford City Council (2003) *Manchester-Salford housing market renewal pathfinder prospectus*, Manchester: Manchester City Council.

Murie, A., Nevin, B. and Leather, P. (1998) *Changing demand and unpopular housing*, Working Paper No 4, London: The Housing Corporation.

Nevin, B. (2002) *Housing market renewal: Submission to the Comprehensive Spending Review*, Birmingham: Centre for Urban and Regional Studies.

Nevin, B., Lee, P., Goodson, L., Murie, A. and Philimore, J. (2001) *Changing housing markets and urban regeneration in the M62 corridor*, Birmingham: Centre for Urban and Regional Studies.

Pawson, H. and Bramley, G. (2000) 'Understanding recent trends in residential mobility in council housing in England', *Urban Studies*, vol 37, no 8, pp 1231–59, July.

Salford City Council (1998) *A sustainable community in Seedley and Langworthy, Salford. An action plan*, Salford: Salford City Council.

Weaver, M. (1999) 'Mayer defends approval of demolished estate', *Housing Today*, 5 August, p 7.

Webster, D. (1998) 'Employment change, housing abandonment and sustainable development: structural processes and structural issues', in S. Lowe, S. Spencer and P. Keenan (eds) *Housing abandonment in Britain*, York: Centre for Housing Policy.

SIX

Affordability comes of age

Glen Bramley

Introduction

In 1980 the term 'affordability' was not widely used in relation to UK housing policy. Now, however, we have a freer housing market than at any time since 1915, and a social rented sector that has been in numerical and proportionate decline for 25 years; for 80% of households in the UK housing consumption is essentially based on ability to pay what the market will bear, and we have embarked on an era in which affordability has become a key concept. We have moved, as Whitehead (1991) predicted, from a needs-based to an affordability-based housing policy. While it can be argued that affordability has always been one of the pillars of the central goals of housing policy ('a decent home for all families at a price within their means'; see Stephens et al, 2005), for the foreseeable future it appears certain to occupy an even more central place in policy debate. There have been earlier 'affordability crises' associated with cyclical peaks in the housing market, particularly during 1988-90. Bramley (1994) discussed the wave-like character of this policy concern, but suggested that there were structural and secular elements to the new emphasis on affordability, and that this wave would leave certain policy legacies. An example of the latter would be planning policies for affordable housing (Monk and Whitehead, 2000; Crook et al, 2002). Others have linked the issue to structural changes in the labour market (Ford and Wilcox, 1994; Ford et al, 2001). The central role of Housing Benefit in public spending on housing and in debates about reform is further testament to the centrality of affordability.

In view of the new significance of affordability, this chapter reviews the issue, asking some broad questions: Where have we got to? What do we know? Where next? It starts by addressing the concept of affordability, focusing on some issues that have continued to be problematic. It then presents some evidence on the incidence of affordability problems in England, contrasting normative and behavioural approaches and drawing out some implications of this evidence for criteria that might guide policy. Increasing attention has as noted been given to one aspect, the ability of households to access owner-occupation, and more detailed evidence is presented on this, looking both backwards and forwards as well as at the very striking cross-sectional picture of regional differences. This analysis draws particular attention to certain critical assumptions to which the results are sensitive.

The chapter then looks at a range of policy responses to the need for affordable housing which this analysis demonstrates, including innovations in forms of 'intermediate sector' provision and in the planning and supply systems. Again the emphasis is on England. The concluding discussion ranges informally over a number of policy ideas relating to affordability whose time seems to have come.

Moving the concept forward

This section addresses four issues in the conceptualisation of affordability that have created and continue to create considerable difficulty. These are:

- the issue of affordability ratios versus residual income approaches to measuring affordability;
- the notion of different levels of affordability problem;
- what is meant by 'affordable housing' and the utility of this concept; and
- the geographical basis for affordability analysis.

Ratios versus residual income

The choice between affordability ratios and residual incomes has been well rehearsed (see Grigsby and Rosenburg, 1975; Hancock, 1993; Bramley, 1994; Hulchanski, 1995; Stone, 1995; Chaplin and Freeman, 1999; Yip and Lau, 2002). Figure 6.1 presents the issue in a standard economic framework, plotting households' consumption of housing and non-housing relative to two normative standards, one for minimum acceptable housing ($H^\star$) and the other for minimum acceptable residual income ($N^\star$). Households with an 'affordability problem' may be defined in various ways. Those in quadrant A have an unambiguous problem, while those in quadrants B and C fall below at least one standard and could not move to an acceptable situation given prevailing housing price (given by the slope of the budget line from point Y

Figure 6.1: Housing and non-housing consumption identifying categories of affordability relative to income and housing standards, England (1998-2001) (% of all households in each category)

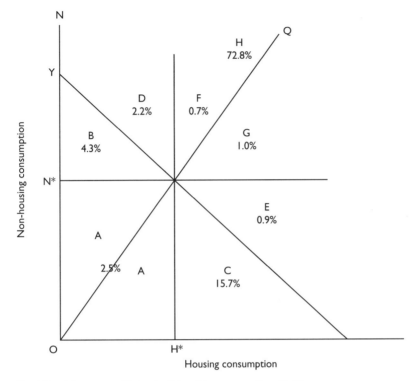

Note: H* = minimum acceptable housing; N* = minimum acceptable residual income

through the intersection of H* and N*). Households in quadrants G and E appear to have a problem in terms of high affordability ratios (housing cost relative to income) but how far this is a policy problem depends on whether they are constrained in adjusting their consumption. This presentation underlines the substantial difference between the affordability ratio criterion and the residual income criterion.

In summary, *affordability ratios* are appealing to common sense, can be rationalised from behavioural evidence and tie in with notions of comparability (horizontal equity). They have actually been widely used in practice in rent setting and housing allowance schemes in different countries. However, the *residual income approach* seems to represent a more rigorous application of the concept that is fully consistent with the mainstream analysis of poverty. The residual income approach still faces certain problems. In particular, the poverty line either uses the Housing Benefit/Allowance system scales, implying that affordability problems have been solved, or uses a different set of scales, leading to a debate about the most appropriate scales to use. This would appear to lead to the conclusion that housing affordability is a non-issue (even though income inadequacy may be an issue), but in practice there remain a range of issues relating to housing costs, including the situation of households not eligible for (full) Housing Benefit/Allowance, and the situation of people with incomes above the scale who face sharp increases in housing costs and high marginal 'tax' rates. The residual income approach does not connect well with housing practitioner concerns about housing supply and pricing, and does not deal with the points about behaviour and horizontal equity mentioned above.

Both criteria are relevant and should ideally be combined. In simple terms, a household's situation is clearly 'unaffordable' if it faces *both* a ratio of housing cost to income above certain norms *and* a ratio of residual income to household requirements that is below certain other norms (a wider definition could substitute *either … or* for *both … and*). Several analysts have suggested that a problem should be defined as being one of affordability, rather than inadequate income, where the problem arises only because housing costs are above some norm, for example because of tight regional housing markets (Yip and Lau, 2002). This literature also looks at the issue of whether high housing costs result from 'voluntary' decisions by households to occupy housing of above minimum standard, when they could have accessed more basic housing at a lower cost. Another compromise between the approaches is to say that the housing cost to income ratio does not matter above a certain income level (Grigsby and Rosenburg, 1975).

Is it possible to get away from normative 'third party' judgements (Maclennan and Williams, 1990), or rather to bolster particular judgements, by appealing to *empirical evidence* of some kind? There are two kinds of evidence that may be relevant. Firstly, evidence of behaviour in general, which tends to indicate that most households, given a degree of choice, tend to spend certain proportions of their income on housing. This provides a general underpinning to the 'affordability ratios' approach, and can also be invoked as an argument of horizontal equity when households with limited choices are having housing solutions determined by the government. Secondly, there is evidence about the incidence of problems people actually experience in paying their housing costs, whether subjective self-reported problems/hardships or more objective indicators like arrears and possession actions. It is possible to investigate these relationships using micro-data to identify potential threshold indicator values that seem to be associated with heightened risk. Although Bramley (1990) suggested such an approach, there has been surprisingly little published work that attempts to pin things down in this way.

Levels of affordability

Is housing (un)affordability a form of deprivation? It is, partly because of the interdependence of affordability with housing availability and decency, and partly because housing is regarded as one of the most basic or essential human needs (Gordon and Pantazis, 1997; Gordon et al, 2000). However, it is important to note that there are different *levels* of housing (un)affordability which affect different strata of the population. The household that is in primary poverty because of the burden of its mortgage payments, not covered by benefits, or the household which is homeless because of an inability to afford available private market rents, are examples of households experiencing the more basic level of affordability problem. Potential new households facing house prices in their locality which are beyond the level that they are likely to be able to afford unassisted exemplify a different level of affordability problem. Theirs is a less direct and intense problem, because (a) these people have not yet formed a separate household, and (b) they face a range of alternatives, such as moving to a cheaper area, living with relatives, or sharing, which although 'second best' do not in themselves constitute primary poverty. On the other hand, this second group is probably larger in numerical size and quite clearly relevant to significant policy interventions (for example, provision of new affordable housing and use of the planning system).

This idea of different levels of affordability problem finds some support in past literature on affordability. For example, Linneman and Megbolugbe (1992) and Bramley (1994) both distinguish the problems facing low-income renters (which in Britain are closely bound up with Housing Benefit) from problems facing middle-income aspiring homeowners. As a development from this work it is possible to identify three groups:

1. households directly experiencing basic problems of housing affordability;
2. households at significant risk of experiencing such problems in their current housing situation; and
3. existing or potential households facing a problem accessing mainstream market housing at affordable levels.

Type 1 problems focus primarily on households with very low incomes and limited housing options, who are likely to be dependent on the basic safety nets of Income Support and social housing. Type 3, by contrast, extends the range of concern up the income scale, and recognises that in certain market conditions a wider range of households (including many working households) may experience problems of access or risk of unaffordability (type 2). It is this wider arena, contingent on house price–income relationships, which constitutes what has come to be termed recently 'the intermediate market'.

This chapter is concerned with the measurement of problems at all of these levels. It illustrates the measurement of type 1 or type 2 problems of affordability, based on micro-data. Problems of type 1 may be argued to be more pressing and higher priority from a social policy point of view. However, a focus on type 3 is still justifiable, for several reasons. First, type 3 problems are broader in scope and can be said to encompass the narrower and more extreme problems within the broader population identified. Second, it is logical to expect that the key drivers of type 3 problems, house prices and incomes, are also drivers to problems of types 1 and 2. Third, this logic is bolstered by evidence from the analysis of micro-data on the incidence of these narrower problems, which confirms that prices and incomes are among the strongest predictors of the incidence of such problems. Finally, type 3 problems are (as shown below) the focus of policy concerns in the housing and planning field, concerns which go wider than simply responding to particular aspects of poverty and deprivation and embrace the broader functioning of regional economies and housing markets.

Affordable housing

Much of the policy response to the apparent crisis of housing affordability is concerned with the provision of new or additional housing opportunities, and increasingly this supply policy has operated under the banner of 'affordable housing'. This seems, however, to be rather a loose, portmanteau term, which raises a number of concerns among analysts and practitioners alike.

Some are concerned that this term is too vague and distracts attention from the key attributes of tenure. They would argue that the central concern should be with rented housing, particularly rented housing of a regulated adequate standard allocated on a basis of need with security of tenure (that is, social housing). This group also tend to argue that those whose needs can only, or should properly, be met through social rented housing provision are the highest priority group for policy attention – the homeless and others on very low incomes, many of whom have other support needs. This group broadly constitute type 1 in the levels typology sketched above.

Others are concerned that the term 'affordable housing' is too easy a let-out clause for developers or public agencies. Housing may be portrayed as 'affordable' because it is either small and of poor standard or because it is discounted in some way below the price of new build market housing, without actually being cheaper than what may be available elsewhere in the market. This issue has been a major source of dispute and delay in the negotiation of planning agreements for affordable housing.

A third group are concerned that attaching the 'affordable' label to specific housing units is not logically the right solution to the problems of affordability experienced by individual households. This would include those who favour general solutions in the form of individual housing allowances geared to the particular incomes and needs of particular households, rather than 'bricks and mortar' subsidies to supply. Those like Ford et al (2001) and Burrows and Wilcox (2001), who have examined the situation of owner-occupiers experiencing financial difficulty, point out that typically such households were not poor (and hence not experiencing an 'affordability' problem) when they bought their home, but have experienced a change in circumstances, for example loss of a job, partner or good health. It is difficult to predict and anticipate such problems and to allocate the affected households to particular 'affordable' housing units in advance. Furthermore, the general concern with mixed and balanced communities leads to the view that it is not desirable to concentrate low-income households in particular blocks or estates which are the typical product of supply-side initiatives.

To be set against these views, there are several weighty arguments to consider. First, 'affordable housing' appears to be a very serviceable political concept, which is capable of building a wide coalition in support of useful policy measures at both national and local levels. It appears to have much more positive connotations than social housing, and to appeal to a 'middle Britain' which is clearly of electoral importance.

Second, it can be argued that, for most of the past 25 years, housing policy in Britain has conspicuously neglected the supply side. This is a major conclusion of the Barker (2004) review, which makes a strong economic and social case for a 'step-change' in housing supply. While much of this agenda is concerned with the planning system and general market housing, this is intended to bear down on affordability problems which arise in the general market, and at the same time the need for additional social and intermediate provision is also highlighted.

Third, it can also be argued that the principal housing finance strategy of the past 25 years, that of concentrating subsidy on individual means-tested Housing Benefit, has not been a conspicuous success. Housing Benefit has not solved affordability problems, as is shown below, while it has created considerable incentive problems in relation to both the housing and the labour markets. The kind of reforms now canvassed for Housing Benefit seek to overcome these problems by introducing more market-like mechanisms. But, if these are not to create unacceptable side-effects, there needs to be a functioning supply system which delivers a range of housing at prices or rents which are not wholly unaffordable for households which may receive only partial or limited assistance.

For these reasons I would argue that supply-oriented policies which focus on the provision of 'affordable housing' opportunities do have a substantial role to play.

Geography of affordability

Many of the basic problems of poverty and disadvantage in our society can be seen to operate across the whole country in a similar way, impacting on particular demographic and social groups but without being a strong function of geography. Considerable debate has raged about the significance of 'area effects' in exacerbating poverty, deprivation or social exclusion, but much of the evidence emerging has suggested that place is rather marginal in all this.

However, it is clear that problems of housing affordability have a very pronounced geography. A relatively fixed housing supply confronting widely varying economic demand gives rise to dramatic variations in housing prices across regions and localities. The analyses presented later in this chapter underline the extent of these geographical variations. They also show that resulting needs for affordable housing show even greater variation, because they are compounded by variations in the inherited supply of existing affordable housing opportunities, particularly lettings of social rented housing. Thus, the risks that particular types of household face of experiencing housing affordability problems, and their opportunities to find affordable solutions, vary greatly depending where they live.

It follows that the measures developed for housing affordability should reflect that geographical variation, and that the policy solutions promoted should be geographically targeted if they are to be effective.

However, this leaves open some important questions about the geographical level or scale at which these measures are constructed and at which policy solutions are planned and implemented.

For access to housing the most appropriate geographical unit is the local housing market area (HMA), the normal search area which households originating in (or working in) a particular place are likely to seek accommodation. In practical terms, reflecting data availability, this is currently best proxied by local authority (district) areas. This reflects the relatively limited search areas of lower-income households and the tendency of social housing allocation systems to operate at this level. Nevertheless, it is true that for middle- and higher-income households search areas may be wider than this, particularly in regions like the South East where prices and incomes are higher and longer distance commuting is more common. However, if some needs can reasonably be met in districts other than those where they arise, this calls into question a system of local housing strategies and needs assessments. It is perhaps therefore not a coincidence that, in the context of recent changes in the planning system and regional governance, there has been a pronounced shift of emphasis from the local to the regional or sub-regional level. In principle, one could construct an affordability indicator for neighbourhoods based on the incomes and household characteristics of residents of each neighbourhood and the housing prices and opportunities of the wider HMA within which it is located. However, the current limitations on income data availability lead back to an approach that constructs both sides of the calculation on district areas.

One of the most important recommendations of Barker (2004) was that there should be regional affordability targets and that these should play a key role in the planning system. If followed through, this recommendation could profoundly alter the dynamics of the planning system. There are many detailed questions to be asked about the way these targets are specified – the proposed main emphasis is to be on ratios of lower quartile house prices to lower quartile earnings. However, the biggest issue, and one on which there is much uncertainty from an evidence and even from a theoretical viewpoint, is the question of how much extra housing supply is required to bring about a given, desirable, reduction in price–earnings ratios. The current phase of research on this is only geared to producing an answer at a regional level, whereas what is suggested here is a need for a sub-regional answer.

Incidence of problems

Normative affordability

Although academics have disagreed on the 'best' basis for defining affordability, there has been a degree of commonality in the broader analytical frameworks. In other words, it is fairly clear what the alternative options are and what kinds of data are relevant to measuring these. Some studies, particularly in countries other than the UK, have attempted to quantify the incidence of different types of affordability problem (for example, Yip and Lau, 2002). There has been rather less of this kind of analysis than one might have expected in the UK, although relatively rich micro-datasets are available to tackle the question.

Figure 6.1 provides a classification of affordability-related problems, framed in terms of the classic economic analysis of the consumption of housing and non-housing goods. It is interesting and informative to look at the relative magnitude of the populations experiencing the different kinds (and levels) of affordability problem represented by the different quadrants of this diagram. This can give some pointers to strengths and weaknesses of the current finance system. Analysis by tenure and by region helps to target concern on the particular institutional or geographical parts of the system that exhibit more problems. Table 6.1 and Figures 6.2 and 6.3 provide such an analysis for England in 1998-2001, based on the Survey of English Housing. Ideally one would also look at changes over time in the magnitude of the different groups. Owing to definitional changes in the key data source, it is difficult to do this precisely for this classification.

Our prime candidates for what was termed above type 1 affordability problems are those households in category A, being both poor in terms of having a very low residual income and also being in housing need in terms of suffering one or more shortfalls from reasonable housing standards. This group comprised only 2.5% of households in 1998-2001. By contrast, 72.8% of households had none of the problems considered. On this basis, England appears quite a well-housed nation. It is noteworthy, however, that the incidence of category A is markedly higher in the rental tenures (4-7%) than in owner-occupation (<1%), and markedly higher in London than in other regions (>5% versus approximately 2%). A possible cause for concern, however, is that the highest rate of category A is in the social rented sector. We used to think of social renting as the solution to the problem rather than, as it appears here, the focus for (if not the cause of) the problem.

Table 6.1: Households in different normative affordability categories by tenure and region, England (1998-2001)

	Tenure			Broad region			
	Own	Social	Private rented	London	South	Midlands/North	Total
A In need, poor	0.9	7.3	4.1	5.3	1.6	2.4	2.5
B In need, not poor, can't buy	2.2	6.3	14.9	9.5	4.0	3.0	4.3
C Not in need, poor, can't buy	9.1	36.9	17.6	17.0	14.3	16.3	15.7
D In need, not poor, can buy	1.8	1.7	5.7	2.7	1.9	2.2	2.2
E Not in need, poor, can buy	0.7	1.8	0.8	0.0	0.2	1.8	0.9
F Not in need, not poor, can't buy, high AR	1.0	5.0	2.0	0.8	0.2	0.7	
G Not in need, not poor, can buy, high AR	0.9	0.7	1.7	0.8	1.1	1.0	1.0
H None of these problems	84.4	44.3	50.3	62.7	76.1	73.2	72.8
All households	100.0	100.0	100.0	100.0	100.0	100.0	100.0

Notes:

'In need' includes being below the bedroom standard; being very dissatisfied with state of repair, heating system or landlord; sharing parts of the accommodation including WC or bathroom or circulation space; having repair costs that cannot be afforded; or having major repairs which should be done.

'Poor' means having residual income below 1.1 times the Housing Benefit Applicable Amount.

'Can't buy' is based on a lending multiplier of 3.5 times gross income compared with a threshold price based on the lower quartile of all sales in the Land Registry price data at district level.

AR = affordability ratio.

Source: Author's analysis of the Survey of English Housing 1998-2001

Figure 6.2: Normative affordability categories by tenure, England (1998-2001)

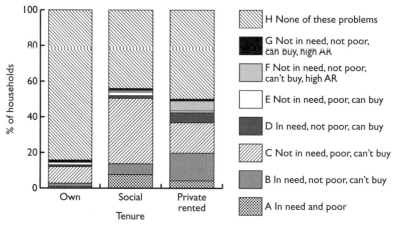

Note: AR = affordability ratio.

Figure 6.3: Normative affordability categories by region, England (1998-2001)

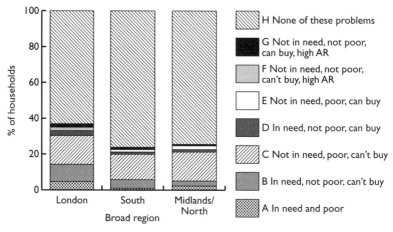

Note: AR = affordability ratio.

The next two categories (B and C) suffer one but not both of the basic problems, poverty and housing need, and in addition would not have enough income to be able to buy locally (without some initial equity). This latter point provides a partial indicator that these households could not necessarily easily trade their way out of their problem, although they might be able to exchange their poverty for housing need or vice versa. The striking feature here is not so much the larger overall number but rather the preponderance of households in one of the two categories – poor but not in need. Unlike some other measures, this group is more evenly distributed across the regions. Furthermore, this group is particularly concentrated in social rented housing, where it comprises 37% of all households. This finding encapsulates a characteristic outcome of British housing policies of the past 25 years: we have solved most traditional housing needs, but trapped a large number of people in relative poverty within our public housing stock.

The remaining groups are smaller in number, comprising households with one or other problem who could buy (perhaps a transitional group, particularly common in private renting), and others with neither needs nor in poverty but who either cannot buy or who face a high 'affordability ratio'. Again, these groups are more common in private renting. The cannot buy/high affordability ratio group is unsurprisingly more common in London.

This kind of analysis is informative in painting a picture of affordability problems in contemporary England. It may also be useful as a step along the way to providing a more comprehensive set of indices of affordability problems at a more localised level, as well as for monitoring change over time. One approach to index construction is to see whether problems revealed in such surveys as this can be predicted fairly well on the basis of plausible and acceptable proxy indicators. Initial tests of this proposition, still using the Survey of English Housing dataset and treating categories A–C as the target group, indicated that this could be feasible, and confirmed that by far the strongest predictor variables were (individual household) income and (local) house price. This provides indirect support for the current Index of Multiple Deprivation (IMD) affordability index, for which income and price variables are the main components.

Behavioural/subjective evidence on ratios issue

The above analysis is set within a normative framework. However, it was suggested earlier that there was scope for more empirical investigation of households' expenditure behaviour and of affordability problems as experienced or perceived by households themselves. Conventional economic analysis of demand functions provides an example of the first approach. The second approach entails using data on households actually experiencing problems, which are generally best obtained from household survey datasets. The problems may be objectively defined, but with the data still self-reported, as with arrears; or they may be subjectively defined, such as when households say they are finding payments fairly difficult to manage. The measures used here, again based on the Survey of English Housing, are based on a composite of both types, in the case of owner-occupiers, but on the former type of measure only in the case of renters.

One way of settling the long-rumbling dispute over affordability ratios versus residual income might be to subject it to an empirical test. Which is the better predictor of problems? Table 6.2 summarises the incidence of any self-reported mortgage payment problems and more serious payment problems, for all owner-occupiers in England (using Survey of English Housing, 1998-2001). Rates are shown for those with a very low residual income after housing costs (less than 110% of the benefit system norm) and for those with a very high ratio of housing costs to net income (above 35%), and for those with both of these characteristics. This table suggests that *both* low residual income *and* high affordability ratios are strongly associated with payment problems. The fact that the top right cell contains a bigger number than the bottom left suggests that affordability ratios appear to have a stronger relationship than residual income. Figures 6.4 and 6.5 show these relationships separately across banded values, again suggesting both are relevant, although emphasising the marked steepening of the relationship with low residual incomes below ratios of around 120% of the poverty line.

The last section on the right of Table 6.2 looks in a similar way at tenants with (recent or current) rent arrears. Here the picture is less clear-cut, with some evidence that low residual income increases problems but no such evidence for high affordability ratios. Figure 6.6 shows the broadly expected but unsteady inverse relationship between rent arrears and residual income. There is no very clear relationship with affordability ratios. This may reflect the confounding role of Housing Benefit.

Logistic regression models controlling for household demographic and other characteristics provide a more refined test, and an example is reported in Table 6.3. These confirm that both indicators (high affordability ratio, low residual income) contribute independently to the explanation of mortgage problem incidence, but that if anything it is the affordability ratio factor which has a bigger impact. In the example illustrated, high affordability ratio has a larger and more significant impact than low residual income, whether or not the other variable is included. These models also confirm the strong overall role of general price and income levels.

Similar models may be fitted to data on rent arrears, but their performance is unsatisfactory, especially in relation to these two

Table 6.2: Incidence of mortgage payment difficulties by whether high affordability ratio and/or low residual income

Any payment problem (%)

Low residual income?	High AR	
	No	Yes
No	6.2	29.9
Yes	12.1	50.4

Serious payment problem (%)

Low residual income?	High AR	
	No	Yes
No	0.6	4.9
Yes	2.1	13.4

All renters: any payment problem (arrears) (%)

Low residual income?	High AR	
	No	Yes
No	9.8	5.6
Yes	16.1	11.4

Notes:

'Any payment problem' includes cases where the mortgage is being paid by the Department of Social Security or a third party, cases where there are any arrears, cases where the household finds payments fairly or very difficult to manage, and cases where they have been in arrears in the past.

'Serious payment problem' includes cases more than six months in arrears, cases where the household finds it very difficult, and cases where payments are currently falling further behind.

For renters, any payment problem includes arrears (>2 weeks) currently or in the last year.

AR = affordability ratio.

Source: Author's analysis of the Survey of English Housing, 1998-2001

Figure 6.4: Mortgage payment difficulties by residual income ratio

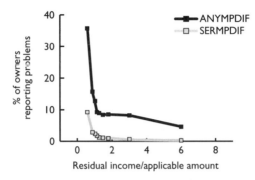

Figure 6.5: Mortgage payment difficulties by affordability ratio

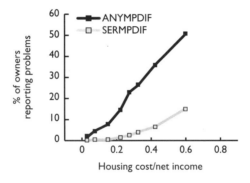

Figure 6.6: Rent arrears by residual income ratio

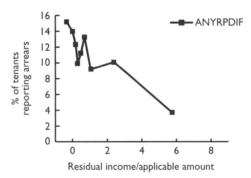

Table 6.3: Logistic regression model for owners with any mortgage payment difficulty

		B	SE	Wald	df	Sig	Exp(B)
Step 1	RELPRICE	0.270	0.044	38.209	1.000	0.000	1.310
	LOGINC	−0.744	0.039	357.193	1.000	0.000	0.475
	RELSAINC	−0.209	0.061	11.636	1.000	0.001	0.811
	AGEU30	0.000	0.062	0.000	1.000	0.998	1.000
	ELD	−0.241	0.079	9.159	1.000	0.002	0.786
	LONPAR	0.449	0.081	30.587	1.000	0.000	1.567
	CFAM	−0.036	0.066	0.293	1.000	0.589	0.965
	NAGE16	0.247	0.029	72.628	1.000	0.000	1.280
	NUMWKR	−0.271	0.035	58.885	1.000	0.000	0.763
	NUNEMPF	0.571	0.090	40.459	1.000	0.000	1.770
	NSTUDF	0.310	0.048	41.248	1.000	0.000	1.363
	DISAB	1.083	0.094	134.079	1.000	0.000	2.953
	OUTRIGHT	−6.840	0.450	230.908	1.000	0.000	0.001
	LOWRIR	0.202	0.063	10.221	1.000	0.001	1.224
	HIGHAR	0.768	0.055	196.948	1.000	0.000	2.156
	Constant	2.635	0.221	142.086	1.000	0.000	13.939

Model summary

	−2 log likelihood	R^2 Cox and Snell	Nagelkerke
Step 1	20683.768	0.153	0.335

Classification table

	Observed		Predicted ANYMPDIF		% correct
			0	1	
Step 1	ANYMPDIF	0	41,650	475	98.872
		1	3,454	796	18.729
	Overall %				91.528

Build up of model

	−2 log likelihood	R^2 Cox and Snell	R^2 Nagelkerke	% correct Positive	All	Rank
Neither	20,946	0.149	0.325	16.52	91.55	4
LOWRIR	20,873	0.150	0.328	18.12	91.55	3
HIGHAR	20,694	0.153	0.335	18.14	91.53	2
BOTH	20,684	0.153	0.335	18.73	91.53	1

Coefficients

		B	SE	Wald	df	Sig	Exp(B)
Separate	LOWRIR	0.509	0.059	73.810	1.000	0.000	1.664
	HIGHAR	0.829	0.051	262.021	1.000	0.000	2.291
Together	LOWRIR	0.202	0.063	10.221	1.000	0.001	1.224
	HIGHAR	0.768	0.055	196.948	1.000	0.000	2.156

Source: Survey of English Housing, 1998-2001

variables. This remains the case even when cases receiving Housing Benefit are removed from the sample. Income and house prices continue to play a significant role. There is also evidence of a significant effect from neighbourhood-level poverty.

To get behind these less clear patterns for rent arrears, it is instructive to review other research evidence looking at arrears from different perspectives. From a recent review of arrears and possessions, a number of features stand out, including a rising level of arrears per case, a focus on families with children, younger single males and vulnerable groups and the significance of fluctuating employment interacting with the

Housing Benefit system (CIPFA, 2004; More et al, 2004; ODPM, 2004). While many argue that the fundamental causes of rent arrears are poverty and residualisation (Audit Commission, 1993; Evans and Smith, 2002), the growing tolerance of high levels of unsecured and multiple debt is a factor affecting different income groups (Kempson et al, 2004). If rent arrears are in part an expression of housing affordability problems, they should also be seen as linked in with an agenda of 'financial inclusion' and indebtedness.

Problem and undischarged debt can lead to exclusion from the formal circuits of consumer finance, including mortgage finance. On the margins of ownership and rental tenures, there may be a significant, possibly increasing, numbers of households who are ineligible for conventional mortgage finance, despite having nominally sufficient income, because of undischarged previous debts. It is difficult to measure this group in a way that enables it to be incorporated in more general measures of access to owner-occupation.

Within the formal mortgage sector, lenders apply rules and norms, including increasingly sophisticated credit-scoring techniques to reflect people's credit history and prospects. But their fundamental lending norms remain related to income, and can be expressed by ratio measures such as lending multipliers. It may be assumed that these norms, although they may seem arbitrary, reflect accumulated experience of what criteria give a reasonable guide to risk, or its avoidance. The continued use of such ratio norms is consistent with our finding from the Survey of English Housing that affordability ratios are good predictors of payment problems for homeowners.

Access to owner-occupation

Modelling access

Over the last 15 years measuring access to owner-occupation has come to occupy a central place in assessments of the need for social housing and other forms of affordable housing, particularly at local and regional scales. Housing needs assessment itself has assumed a greater significance, as a key part of local housing strategies and as a basis for the 'enabling' role of local authorities, and particularly as a basis for local planning policies and 'Section 106' planning agreements. Official guidance on local needs assessments (DETR, 2000a) gives a central role to estimating the ability of various groups of households to access home ownership, based on affordability. Many local assessments utilise local household surveys to provide the main evidence base for such assessments, but it is also possible to construct such estimates from secondary data sources. I have developed a model to perform the latter task, which can be applied to data at local authority level across the whole country, as well as for smaller sub-areas in some local studies. This model has proved quite serviceable, placing local assessments in a wider regional and national context by applying common measures and criteria and overcoming continuing limitations with official data on incomes. The latter point is important because affordability is essentially about the intersection between two distributions, the distribution of house prices and the distribution of incomes. Output from the model has been used in a number of government-sponsored studies, including the work of the Home Ownership Task Force (Housing Corporation, 2003), the Barker (2004) review and the Scottish Executive's 2004 affordable housing review (Bramley, 2004).

It is not necessary to dwell on the model's assumptions and mechanics and their underlying justification (for a fuller discussion see Bramley and Karley, 2005). The main features and assumptions include the following:

- local income distributions are modelled from Census and other data, calibrated against Family Resources Survey income data pooled over several years;
- the key target group are households aged under 35, taken as representative of the cohort of newly forming households who are the key group seeking to access the market;
- threshold house prices are based on lower quartile prices by size, using data from the Survey of Mortgage Lending, backed up (where sample sizes are inadequate) by data from the Land Registry;
- the primary test of affordability is based on a lending multiplier of 3.5 times gross income for a single earner (or 0.85 times this for two-earner households). A secondary test based on residual income after housing costs being above 1.2 times the Housing Benefit applicable amount (a form of poverty line taking account of household composition) is also applied. Thus, the model encapsulates both approaches to affordability discussed above;
- the net need for additional affordable housing is derived from this by applying the affordability rate for under-35s to a demographic estimate of the flow of new household formation, and deducting the supply of net relets of existing social housing. Further allowances are made (in some versions) for existing owners moving into social renting, for migrants and for backlogs of existing need based on waiting lists.

Some representative results from this model are shown for the English regions in 2004 in Tables 6.4 and 6.5. The first column of Table 6.4 shows the proportion of households aged under 35 able to buy in the market in that year, based on their incomes and threshold house prices. It was a particularly bad year for affordability in 2004, with only a third of such households able to buy in England. The rates ranged from 15.5% in London and rather over a quarter in three southern regions to just over 45% in three northern regions.

The second column shows ability to buy after an adjustment is made to reflect access to family wealth to enable some additional marginal households to buy. This is discussed further below under the heading of 'some critical assumptions'. The third column shows affordability for working households separately, based again just on income. These figures are significantly higher, ranging from 21.7% in London to nearly 60% in the northern regions. It should be noted that these estimates are lower in the northern regions than those produced by Wilcox (2003) in recent Joseph Rowntree Foundation studies. The main reason for this difference is that our model applies the secondary residual income test, which means that significant numbers of lower-income working households would be close to the poverty line if they bought in these lower-priced areas.

The last two columns look at the incremental affordability offered by two main forms of low-cost home ownership (LCHO) provision. The role of LCHO and the 'intermediate sector' is discussed further later. However, it should be noted that the column headed 'Homebuy

Table 6.4: Affordability rates by region (2004) (% of households aged under 35 able to buy)

Region	Able to buy (income)	Able to buy (wealth adjusted)	Able to buy (working)	Shared ownership increment	Homebuy increment
North East	45.7	50.2	59.9	10.4	9.9
Yorkshire and Humberside	45.5	50.5	57.4	12.1	11.2
North West	45.5	50.4	58.8	11.3	10.6
East Midlands	40.7	46.7	50.6	14.0	14.1
West Midlands	38.9	43.8	49.8	13.9	13.5
South West	28.5	34.6	35.5	16.9	15.8
East	29.4	35.3	37.2	20.7	16.1
South East	26.2	31.8	33.7	21.5	16.2
London	15.5	20.4	21.7	23.4	12.2
England	33.4	38.7	42.9	16.8	13.5

increment' provides a measure of the sensitivity of affordability to a given (25%) reduction in price thresholds. This can be useful as a sort of 'ready reckoner' in judging the impact of price changes on affordability. This sensitivity is generally greater in the southern regions.

Table 6.5 shows some estimates of need derived from this affordability analysis for the same date. As an annual flow, the net need for England appears to be about 65,000 household units per year. But this nets off substantial surpluses of lettings over new need concentrated mainly in the northern regions. If we simply add up the positive needs at district level we get a total of around 127,000. Meanwhile, the surplus lettings add up to nearly 63,000. This feature of the model has been valuable in highlighting the problem of low demand for social rented housing in wide areas of the country since the mid-1990s (for example, Bramley et al, 2000). It is noteworthy that this evidence of low demand persists in 2004, despite the general rise in house prices in all regions. The key factor driving this finding is the continuing high level of relets, particularly in the northern regions.

Two critical assumptions

Deposits and wealth

It is assumed that income is the main constraint on house purchase, because 100% or high loan-to value (LTV) ratio lending is widely available. The argument for making this assumption is partly one of

Table 6.5: Affordability-based needs by region (2004) (number of units per year)

Region	Gross household formation	Net relets	Net need	Positive need	Surplus lettings
North East	24,099	28,275	−14,401	353	14,754
Yorkshire and Humberside	48,503	41,098	−12,713	2,580	15,293
North West	64,811	51,923	−14,260	3,691	17,951
East Midlands	40,399	26,628	−910	5,598	6,508
West Midlands	50,815	35,094	−1,861	5,336	7,198
South West	45,943	16,779	19,482	19,482	0
East	51,232	23,508	15,501	16,474	972
South East	77,216	27,128	34,694	34,786	92
London	81,428	32,204	39,014	39,014	0
England	484,445	282,636	64,547	127,314	62,768

Note: Positive need sums positive net needs at district level, ignoring surpluses. Surpluses sum negative net needs at district level.

simplicity, and partly that the model focuses on limits or boundaries of affordability. Also, where households fund deposits from savings, this incurs an opportunity cost in loss of income from savings, and we are (partly for consistency) using a comprehensive definition of income including income from savings and investments.

Recent lending data suggest that use of wealth, probably from family sources, is becoming relatively more important among the diminishing number of first-time buyers who are still able to get into the market (Bramley and Karley, 2005; Joseph Rowntree Foundation, 2004). Modelling the availability of such wealth is difficult, given data limitations and the complexity of the intra- and inter-household transfers involved. Nevertheless, this issue of wealth is now so important that it cannot be ignored, and one can make an allowance for it, based on plausible assumptions and some evidence, within the needs estimates presented.

Table 6.6 shows the proportion of first-time buyers in each region in 2001 who made a deposit of more than 20%, and who at the same time appear not to have had enough income to buy (without the extra capital). This proportion averages 13.2% for England as a whole but ranges from just over 5% in the North to around 20% in London. Rates are also relatively high in the South West (19%) and South East (16.7%). Given the levels of income-based affordability at that time (averaging around 40% of new younger households), this implies that about 6% of the whole cohort were being enabled to buy thanks to access to family wealth in 2001. A proxy-based formula is used to predict local variations in this proportion as an adjustment to the income-based affordability calculations used to generate need estimates in this study. In brief, this is based on:

- sub-regional values from the Survey of English Housing for the proportion of first-time buyers whose primary source of deposit was 'gifts, inheritance, informal loans, etc';
- an indicator based on evidence from the Family Resources Survey of the proportion of mature families

Table 6.6: Percentage of first-time buyers making 20%+ deposit without enough income to buy, by region (2001)

Standard region	%
North	5.3
Yorkshire and Humberside	6.9
North West	7.1
East Midlands	9.1
West Midlands	11.5
South West	19.0
East Anglia	12.3
South East	16.7
London	20.1
England	13.2

Source: Author's analysis of Survey of Mortgage Lending linked to local authority level house prices (couple families or large adult households aged over 40) with enough savings to finance a substantial deposit, predicted using a proxy formula based on income, house prices, working households, social renting and high social class; and

• the marginal affordability increment identified above under the heading 'Homebuy'.

Table 6.4 (column 2) shows the impact of this wealth adjustment on the affordability calculations. Overall, 5.4% more households would be enabled to buy. There is slight variation between the regions, with a slightly larger increment in the more rural regions (South West, East, East Midlands). Table 6.7 shows the same calculation for an earlier year, but also shows the impact on net need numbers. This one adjustment to the affordability calculation has the effect of reducing net needs by 15,000 (13%). Although the basis of calculation is approximate, this adjustment is arguably a step towards greater realism. We may also anticipate that access to wealth will be an increasingly important feature in the housing market of the future, and there will be a need to develop further methods of modelling it.

Table 6.7: Sensitivity of affordability and need estimates to wealth adjustment and access to lower-priced adjacent districts, by region (2002)

	Affordability rates (% can buy)			Net positive need		
	Baseline	Wealth adjusted	Lowest adjacent	Baseline	Wealth adjusted	Lowest adjacent
North	54.5	57.9	63.3	94	14	0
Yorkshire and Humberside	54.6	58.5	66.7	1,737	1,236	224
North West	54.0	57.9	65.1	2,257	1,691	376
East Midlands	51.1	55.7	64.3	3,813	2,957	924
West Midlands	46.5	50.6	59.0	3,785	3,020	1,031
South West	35.2	40.7	48.2	17,961	15,373	11,906
East	38.1	43.4	55.5	13,992	11,936	6,801
South East	31.7	36.9	48.7	33,537	29,589	21,118
London	20.0	24.7	34.5	38,024	34,362	25,709
England	40.8	45.4	54.6	115,200	100,179	68,089

Note: Columns 3 and 6 show combined effect of wealth adjustment and access to lowest-priced adjacent district.

Net need is new need excluding backlog.

Geographical scale

The analysis reported so far has relied on the assumption that effective HMAs equate with local authority districts, at least as far as marginally affordable households and potential social renters are concerned. This does reflect the traditional pattern of local housing strategies and resource allocation based on local authorities. However, there is, as noted earlier, a strong argument for looking at affordability, needs and supply at a sub-regional scale. A simple way of modelling the effect of such a shift is illustrated also in Table 6.7. For each local authority we look at its six nearest (usually contiguous) neighbour districts and select the one with the lowest house prices. The model then tests the impact of substituting that price level as the threshold, rather than the within-district value. This then effectively assumes that marginal new buyers can and will move to cheaper areas within their same sub-region.

Table 6.7 shows that this alternative assumption makes a dramatic difference to the results. Affordability jumps by a further 9 percentage points (a fifth), with a proportionately greater increase (two fifths) in London and the South East. Net need drops by 32,000 (32%), with the main impact inevitably in London and the South East. One could describe this reduction as being from an unattainable to a potentially attainable level of provision. These very big impacts from this assumption confirm the importance of geographical scale. They also remind us that, in practice, this is one of the main ways in which people and the market respond to shortage and pressure – by moving to less preferred locations, and possibly by having to commute further to work. Bramley (2004a) showed a similar impact, on a smaller scale, when analysing affordability-based needs in Scotland on the basis of HMAs rather than local authority areas.

Responding to the need for affordable housing

A wider menu

The kind of analysis just presented, although it is clearly subject to margins of uncertainty and debate, does underline that there is a large-scale problem that seems to call for some substantial policy responses. But, to pick up the theme from our earlier discussion of 'affordable housing', what sort of provision should the government be promoting? Some would argue that, as always, social rented housing targeted at the poorest groups should be the highest priority. However, such a view is somewhat tainted by producer interests – social landlords like to promote their core product – and may not be the smart way to respond in terms of the nature of the problem, the cost-effectiveness of solutions, or popular preferences. An alternative view, which seems to be increasingly reflected in government policy, places greater emphasis on the intermediate market and LCHO-type solutions. In the run-up to the General Election in 2005, the government's housing strategy headlined 'a million new homeowners' over five years.

There is a strong logic for greater emphasis on LCHO within the new provision programme. As shown in Bramley et al (2002), both shared ownership and Homebuy (equity loan) are excellent value for money for the public/social housing sector in the longer term (because of shallower subsidy and staircasing receipts). Recent initiatives and announcements by the Council of Mortgage Lenders indicate that a joint programme between the government and lenders involving 'lender-financed equity loans' is now likely to happen. This approach, discussed in Bramley (2004b), is potentially as significant in the longer term as private finance for housing associations was in 1989. It means that equity loans can be offered in large numbers without being a call on scarce public capital subsidy resources. The affordability-based analysis of needs exemplified in this chapter shows that it is in the marginal 'intermediate' sector of demand that the problem lies; that is, households who only need a moderate amount of help to attain owner-occupation. The potential portability of Homebuy also fits easily with a sub-regional scale of analysis and solution, and Homebuy has certainly proved popular with key workers. On the supply side, Bramley et al (2002) showed that LCHO fits well with efforts to use the planning system to deliver affordable housing through Section 106 planning agreements on general housing sites. It is preferred by developers and can be delivered often without public subsidy.

Private renting, or new intermediate renting models, are another area for response to need in this intermediate affordability sector. There is more work to be done on this, but it is clear that in some circumstances private renting can look more affordable than owner-occupation, a reversal of the normal (and long-run) tendency for private renting to cost more. Mid-market rent could certainly be provided by RSLs or others for relatively shallow subsidy. The proposed introduction of Real Estate Investment Trusts could underpin the development of a larger sector here.

Feasible scale of provision

If LCHO is better value for money than social renting, this suggests programmes should be shifted in this direction. But how much LCHO is warranted, given that only some households in need can afford these options? Table 6.8 shows the incremental affordability offered by two LCHO options, shared ownership of a new RSL dwelling buying a minimum tranche of 25%, and Homebuy equity loan enabling purchase of a 75% share of a second-hand home at threshold price levels (lower quartile). Shared ownership on this basis is only affordable by slightly more households than Homebuy, particularly in the northern regions. This is because new housing typically has a higher market value than second-hand housing. These options are illustrative of current products, but may be modified. For example, Homebuy could be available in lower tranches, possibly with a deferred real interest charge on part of the equity loan (Bramley, 2004b), and could in principle be applied to new build housing.

Table 6.8 also shows the number of new households in need of affordable housing who could be helped by these schemes. In these calculations, need is discounted where there is a surplus or near-balance in supply of relets relative to new need, giving rise to rather small numbers in the northern regions. Nevertheless Table 6.8 suggests that between 27,500 and 37,500 households could be helped by these

Table 6.8: Low-cost home ownership potential by region (2002) (extra % able to buy; number of new households per year; number of existing renters per year)

Region	Shared own % extra	Homebuy % extra	Shared own need	Homebuy need	Social renters LCHO	Private renters LCHO
North East	10.4	9.9	95	82	1,079	1,204
Yorkshire and Humberside	12.1	11.2	836	656	2,060	4,453
North West	11.3	10.6	1,169	939	3,243	5,788
East Midlands	14.0	14.1	1,856	1,745	2,027	4,167
West Midlands	13.9	13.5	1,389	1,342	2,690	4,435
South West	16.9	15.8	4,981	4,654	3,716	13,963
East	20.7	16.1	5,071	3,975	4,805	11,682
South East	21.5	16.2	10,883	8,129	6,260	20,660
London	23.4	12.2	11,332	5,916	6,655	24,906
England	16.8	13.5	37,613	27,438	32,536	91,258

mechanisms. This represents a very substantial share of the overall need described above.

Furthermore, Table 6.8 also illustrates that there is further potential scope for using LCHO to meet need, indirectly, by freeing up existing social rented housing which could then be used to house homeless or other low-income households. It is estimated that around 32,500 existing social renters per year might take up LCHO opportunities to move and buy (based on analysis for the Home Ownership Task Force [Housing Corporation, 2003]). Existing LCHO mechanisms have been partly targeted towards this group, and current government proposals envisage an expansion of such options.

Affordability is only part of the story as far as feasibility is concerned. It is also necessary to consider the supply side. Both the *Sustainable Communities Plan* (ODPM, 2003) and the Barker (2004) report envisage a substantial increase in supply of both affordable and general market housing. However, current thinking on good practice in new housing provision, reflected in government planning guidance, emphasises a 'mixed and balanced' provision in terms of tenure, price and type of housing. In future, most new affordable housing will be delivered on mixed development sites. Most local authorities are now using planning powers to negotiate such mixed schemes on the basis of local targets based on evidence of need. The highest targets achieved to date, and likely to be achieved in the future, are for 50% of units to be affordable (in parts of London and a few other localities). In most areas the targets are less than 50%, partly because of needs evidence and partly because of considerations of financial viability. There is therefore a supply-side constraint on the total level of new affordable provision, based on the overall level of planned development and the affordable housing targets to be applied to this. This is reinforced by the inevitable constraint on public sector financial resources to provide the subsidies for such development, only a part of which can be funded by so-called planning gain (Crook et al, 2002).

Use of Homebuy and similar mechanisms that give a portable subsidy to potential buyers to go out and buy existing second-hand housing provide a partial way around this supply constraint. Some needs can be met in this way without being a claim on the affordable share of new housing development. If this can be largely funded by lenders, with a more limited (possibly revenue-based, time-limited) public subsidy, then this mechanism is attractive to a government seeking to meet affordable needs (for example, for key workers) and to promote home ownership further. However, the use of this mechanism is ultimately limited by the proportion of those in need who can afford such options, as described above. There are also additional policy considerations to be weighed here. Subsidising people to buy in the existing market adds to demand without adding to supply, and carries some danger of pushing up already high price levels. The size of this impact has not been quantified and is rather difficult to estimate, in the same way that the supply requirements of the Barker agenda are difficult to quantify. There are also arguments against too heavy an emphasis on encouraging existing social renters to move and buy, rather than, for example, buying in situ, because this exacerbates an already serious problem of residualisation of social housing estates.

The affordability model can be used to explore the possible scale and distribution of a feasible programme 'optimised' through the maximal use of LCHO and planning agreements. Lack of space prevents a full analysis of this kind here, but in short it does indicate that most, if not all, of the indicated needs could be met in theory. Practical limitations include, obviously, public spending resources, not just directly to fund the social rented housing (in particular) but also the infrastructure needed to support the higher overall level of new housing provision which Barker (2004) envisages but which regional planning bodies may be reluctant to provide for.

Affordability and the future agenda

The final section of this chapter draws together some ideas for the future policy agenda, focused on affordability.

Affordability standards

A number of commentators have pointed out that successive governments have been reluctant to lay down official standards of affordability, despite this concept coming to play a more central role in housing policy. It is understandable that, in the past, governments were reluctant to commit themselves in this area, knowing that their policies and programmes would be unlikely to enable reasonable standards to be met. However, the policy context has changed somewhat, with a greater commitment from the present government to recognise and respond to affordable housing needs and a general emphasis on policy frameworks that define standards and set outcome targets relating to these. 'Decent homes' is a major example in the housing field.

Some of the preceding discussion has indicated that the choice and definition of any affordability standard is not completely straightforward.

Should the emphasis be on ratios or residual income? How are the different levels of problem to be reflected? What types and tenures of housing are approved as 'affordable'? Is the standard an aspiration to be achieved on average, or something that all households should achieve? For example, there may be trade-offs or compromises with other principles relating to choice and efficiency.

There are four areas of policy where some sort of standard seems to be inevitable or emerging, and these are discussed further in turn. First, the Barker (2004) proposal for regional affordability targets seems to imply a normative notion of a desirable standard of 'type 3' affordability, albeit on a fairly aggregated basis. Second, local and (sub-)regional housing strategies are expected to be underpinned by housing needs assessments that follow an approved methodology which takes account of affordability (again at the type 3 level). Third, social sector housing rents are based on a restructuring formula that is based in part on an affordability criterion. As in the past, Social Housing Grant formulae need to be geared to deliver new housing at this rent level. In future, Housing Benefit is likely to be increasingly based on these target rents rather than on actual rents. This leads on to the final area, which is the design of Housing Benefit itself. Currently, Housing Benefit is the main determinant of 'type 1' affordability; in future this role may be shared more with other mechanisms including rent setting and tax credits.

Affordability indicators

Affordability indicators would naturally be associated with any affordability standards, but indicators may be used whether or not formal standards are adopted. An important Barker (2004) recommendation, accepted in principle by the government, is that there should be regional affordability targets, expressed in terms of the ratio of lower quartile house prices to earnings. These targets would not initially be all at the same level, but there is some implicit expectation of regional convergence. Supplementary indicators may also be used for monitoring regional affordability. This initiative is a serious attempt to tackle regional imbalance and change the ground rules of land use planning. However, there are naturally detailed concerns about the operation of this system, particularly if local authorities distort decisions simply to get a favourable indicator score.

There are various other 'type 3' (that is, home ownership access/affordability) indicators around in the system anyway. For example, there is a Public Service Agreement (PSA 5) for reducing regional housing market imbalance, which refers to an affordability indicator. There is also an indicator of access to owner-occupation produced by the present author contained within the Indices of Multiple Deprivation (IMD) 2004. Wilcox (2003) has produced a series of indicators in publications for the Joseph Rowntree Foundation and in *Roof* magazine.

What about more basic 'type 1' affordability indicators? The routine monitoring of rents versus incomes of new social housing lettings through the Continuous Recording (CORE) system would be one example (soon to be extended to the local authority sector). Problems/pressures in the private rented sector can be monitored in part through Housing Benefit statistics, including the related Rent Officer referred and determined rents, although there are significant issues of non-eligibility (for example, students) and non-take-up. The kind of classification exemplified by Table 6.1 and Figures 6.2-6.3 in this chapter, based on the Survey of English Housing, could be replicated on an annual basis. The advantage of this kind of approach is that it looks jointly at affordability and housing need shortfalls, although there are problems with some of the need measures not being repeated every year. It is also important to pay attention to the mainstream monitoring of poverty (including child poverty) in Britain, which makes use of the Family Resources Survey and applies certain explicit poverty lines based on percentages of median equivalised income. Particular attention would focus here on the difference between before and after housing costs measures of poverty.

Planning targets

Since 1991, planning policies and planning agreements have played an increasingly important part in the delivery of affordable housing. Within this approach a key element is a local, needs-based target share of affordable housing to be included within new housing developments. Despite continuing doubts about its legality and efficacy, this policy has a strong logic and momentum behind it, as a way of stretching public programmes by capturing windfall development gains and as a way of promoting mixed communities. The Barker (2004) review, while highlighting the need for additional affordable housing, has raised a question mark about the continuance of this mechanism, by proposing a more generalised 'planning gain supplement'. If Barker's general supply-increasing measures were successful in reducing prices, the need for such mechanisms might reduce in time, and it is also likely that more of the planning gain capture will be needed to fund infrastructure. However, there remain doubts about the political/policy feasibility of the requisite supply increases, whatever these may be, and there is strong local support for Section 106 type policies. These are likely to remain part of the menu in some form.

Sub-regional affordability-based needs assessments

Since the 1990s there have been waves of local housing needs assessments, often driven by planning policy. There have also been repeated attempts to tighten up the methodology of these assessments, but affordability continues to occupy a central role within them. The current phase appears to involve a shift towards (sub-)regional assessments rather than local assessments, with a stronger emphasis on market analysis rather than traditional needs assessment, and this may help to increase the rigour and realism of the process. The sub-regional perspective draws attention to the phenomenon of potential mobility, which was shown earlier to be a critical assumption in affordability-based assessments. This in turn gives a greater role to provision mechanisms that allow mobility, such as Homebuy. It also provides a more appropriate scale at which to bring the planning of housing into a closer relationship with planning for economic development. Some current research is directed towards refining the tools that may be used in such assessments and forward planning, particularly in relation to the usability and predictability of housing market information.

Affordability and financial inclusion

In reviewing the incidence of basic affordability problems among renters earlier in this chapter, it became clear that traditional ratio measures were inadequate. Part of what underlies this are the continuing problems with the Housing Benefit system, but part of it is to do with interactions between housing affordability and wider problems of personal debt and personal financial management. There is a need to connect the traditional housing concerns with affordability and rent collection with the emerging policy focus on financial inclusion and financial literacy. Although this focus is frequently allied with a concern about poverty and the poorest, it is clear that these problems extend up the income scale. Furthermore, as home ownership continues to expand, strongly encouraged by government, these problems overlap with those of sustainable home ownership. Thus, housing policy and practice need to move beyond their traditional focus on development and management to embrace information, advice and regulation relating to financial products and mechanisms.

Equity loans

The analysis in this chapter draws attention to the potentially significant role of the intermediate market. Of all the mechanisms tested in this arena, the one that seems to have the most generic potential is that of the equity loan, currently mainly represented in England and Wales by the Homebuy scheme. It is clear that this mechanism is highly attractive to both buyers and lenders, and that with additional flexibility it could find much wider application. The Home Ownership Task Force foreshadowed this by speculating on the attractions of this model as a future basis for Right to Buy which would be fairer to all parties, and this is reflected in recent government proposals for a Social Homebuy scheme for RSL tenants. The Council of Mortgage Lenders has taken up the cause and is now promoting a large-scale addition to equity loan provision primarily funded by lenders themselves, with relatively limited subsidy requirements on the public sector. Equity loans also have a role to play with older owners in funding equity release and repair/improvement investment. We have moved from an era of general, untargeted tax relief subsidy to home ownership to one where there is no general subsidy, but many are excluded from the market. The equity loan is the right instrument to bridge this gap with flexible, shallow and time-limited subsidies that enable many more households to afford home ownership and participate in the asset economy.

Housing Benefit reform

Last, but by no means least, we have the great unfinished business of Housing Benefit reform. The present system is costly, only partially successful in ensuring affordability, difficult to administer and characterised by damaging disincentive effects – disincentives to work, disincentives to exercise housing choice and disincentives to hold landlords to account for their services. The traditional arguments for separate housing payments based on actual rents are losing their force, as social rents are restructured and private rents become market based. More adequate benefit, pension and tax credit incomes can float more households off the need for dependency on Housing Benefit. Pilot projects are showing the way towards a benefit scheme based on flat rate entitlements. Reform is risky, in the sense that some households could be worse off and some social landlords could face a more uncertain income. This is the price to be paid for a system which would be more in tune with the times, promoting efficiency, choice and accountability.

References

Audit Commission (1993) *Remote control: The national administration of Housing Benefit*, London: Audit Commission.

Barker, K. (2004) *Review of housing supply: Delivering stability: Securing our future housing needs, Final report: Recommendations*, London: HM Treasury/ODPM.

Bramley, G. (1989) *Meeting housing needs*, London: Association of District Councils.

Bramley, G. (1990) 'Access, affordability and housing need', Paper presented at ESRC Housing Studies Conference, University of Surrey, September, mimeo, SAUS, University of Bristol.

Bramley, G. (1994) 'An affordability crisis in British housing: dimensions, causes and policy impact', *Housing Studies*, vol 9, no 1, pp 103-24.

Bramley, G. (2004a) *Local housing need and affordability model for Scotland – update*, Report 34. Edinburgh: Communities Scotland.

Bramley, G. (2004b) *The potential scope for lender financed equity loans*, London: Council of Mortgage Lenders.

Bramley, G. and Karley, N.K. (2005) 'How much extra affordable housing is needed in England?', *Housing Studies*, vol 20, no 5, p 685.

Bramley, G., Lancaster, S. and Gordon, D. (2000) 'Benefit take-up and the geography of poverty in Scotland', *Regional Studies*, vol 34.

Bramley, G., Cousins, L., Dunmore, K. and Morgan, J. (2002) *Evaluation of the low cost home ownership programme*, ODPM Housing Research Report, London: ODPM.

Burrows, R. and Wilcox, S. (2001) *Half the poor: Homeowners with low incomes*, London: Council of Mortgage Lenders.

Chaplin, R. and Freeman, A. (1999) 'Towards an accurate description of affordability', *Urban Studies*, vol 11, pp 1949-57.

CIPFA (Chartered Institute of Public Finance and Accountancy) (2004) *Housing rent arrears and benefits statistics 2003*, London: CIPFA.

Crook, A., Curry, J., Jackson, A., Monk, S., Rowley, S., Smith, K. and Whitehead, C.M.E. (2002) *Planning gain and affordable housing: Making it count*, York: Joseph Rowntree Foundation.

DETR (Department of the Environment, Transport and the Regions) (2000a) *Local housing needs assessment: A guide to good practice*, London: DETR/ODPM.

Evans, A. and Smith, R. (2002) *Closing the gap: Working together to reduce rent arrears*, Cardiff: Audit Commission Wales.

Ford, J. and Wilcox, S. (1994) *Affordable housing, low incomes and the flexible labour market*, Research Report 22, London: NFHA.

Ford, J., Burrows, R. and Nettleton, S. (2001) *Homeownership in a risk society*, Bristol: The Policy Press.

Gordon, D. and Pantazis, C. (1997) *Breadline Britain in the 1990s*, Aldershot: Ashgate.

Gordon, D., Adelman, A., Ashworth, K., Bradshaw, J., Levitas, R., Middleton, S., Pantazis, C., Patsios, D., Payne, S., Townsend, P. and Williams, J. (2000) *Poverty and Social Exclusion Survey of Britain*, York: Joseph Rowntree Foundation.

Grigsby, W. and Rosenburg, L. (1975) *Urban housing policy*, New York, NY: APS Publications.

Hancock, K.E. (1993) '"Can pay? Won't pay?" or economic principles of "affordability"', *Urban Studies*, vol 30, no 1, pp 127-45.

Housing Corporation (2003) *A home of my own*, Report of the Low Cost Home Ownership Task Force. London: Housing Corporation.

Hulchanski, J.D. (1995) 'The concept of housing affordability: six contemporary uses of the housing expenditure-to-income ratio', *Housing Studies*, vol 10, no 4, pp 471-91.

Joseph Rowntree Foundation (2004) 'Survey reveals the price parents will pay to put children on the home ownership ladder', Press release, 17 June (www.jrf.org.uk/pressroom/releases/170604.asp).

Kempson, E., McKay, S. and Willitts, M. (2004) 'Characteristics of families in debt and the nature of indebtedness', DWP Research Summary (www.dwp.gov.uk/asd/asd5/summ2003-2004/211summ.pdf).

Linneman, P. and Megbolugbe, I. (1992) 'Housing affordability: myth or reality?', *Urban Studies*, vol 29, nos 3/4, pp 369-92.

Maclennan, D. and Williams, R. (eds) (1990) *Affordable housing in Britain and the United States*, York: Joseph Rowntree Foundation.

Monk, S. and Whitehead, C. (2000) *Restructuring housing systems: From social to affordable housing?*, York: York Publishing Services for the Joseph Rowntree Foundation.

More, A., Pawson, H. and Scott, S. (2004) *Evaluation of English housing policy since 1975: Theme 5 – Management effectiveness*, London: ODPM (www.odpm.gov.uk).

ODPM (Office of the Deputy Prime Minister) (2003) *Sustainable communities: Building for the future*, London: ODPM.

ODPM (2004) *Survey of English Housing 2002/03*, London: ODPM.

Stephens, M., Munro, M. and Whitehead, C.M.E. (2005) *Lessons from the past, challenges for the future*, ODPM Housing Research Summary 214 (www.odpm.gov.uk/index.asp?id=1155461).

Whitehead, C.M.E. (1991) 'From need to affordability: an analysis of UK housing objectives', *Urban Studies*, vol 28, no 6, pp 871-87.

Wilcox, S. (2003) *Can work – can't buy: Local measures of the ability of working households to become home owners*, York: Joseph Rowntree Foundation.

Yip, N.M. and Lau, K.Y. (2002) 'Setting rent with reference to tenants' affordability: public housing rent policy in Hong Kong', *Journal of Housing and the Built Environment*, vol 17, no 4, pp 409-18.

SEVEN

Mob mentality: the threat to community sustainability from the search for safety

Rowland Atkinson

Introduction

It is difficult to separate public policy interventions, even those as central as the provision of public housing, from utopianism and desires to affect both the housing and social futures of citizens (Ravetz, 2001). Government action and academic research is full of assessments of the likely future impacts of extrapolated trends, such as housing expenditure, economic growth and change, social need, household mobility and likely regional and labour market changes which will affect the type and scale of need for social and private housing. Among these anticipated changes, any attempt to prophesy the future is deeply linked to how we measure our progress to a future and better place (Kumar, 1978). Of course, this is to say nothing of the complexities and dangers of applying such visions. This chapter builds on recent empirical work and policy to consider aspects of current social and urban change that appear likely to lead to increasingly inequitable outcomes in the future.

In documenting the extreme poverty of 'The bend' in 19th-century New York, Jacob Riis's essays and photographs, entitled *How the other half lives*, threw light on the relative seclusion of poverty from the gaze of the middle classes who did not know because they did not care (Riis, 1971). Rather than referring, as has become common, to the affluent, Riis was concerned with a voiceless and growing urban poverty with few champions. While retaining a clear focus on continuing issues of poverty it is also necessary to consider the impacts of choices and patterns of mobility by higher-income groups to develop a fuller impression of the future connections between poverty, affluence and segregation in British housing. While social policy, housing and urban analysts have long cast their gaze over those less fortunate, the task of thinking about the future also hinges on recapturing and reconnecting the affluent and households with choice in order to promote the kinds of diverse communities that appear to hold out the prospect of greater sustainability and social equity. In this chapter it is argued that in future private residential choices may have increasingly pronounced public consequences, the beginning of which can already be seen in our towns and cities.

In both the residential choices and daily negotiated patterns of association and social interaction of high-income households the need for safety is playing an increasingly significant role. Gated communities, enclave-style executive homes and tower-block lofts with secure entry systems bear testament to the growth of secluded and exclusive lifestyles, which also provide aspirational models of living for many others. Social affinity, grouping together with people like ourselves, also forms a powerful imperative and one which is leading to socially 'tectonic' relationships (Butler with Robson, 2003) in which the middle classes live disengaged from those different from themselves, even those living in the same neighbourhood. If housing studies in general, and the study of citizenship in particular, have been concerned with segregation as a threat to social cohesion and political empathy, its apparent growth seems likely to produce socially corrosive patterns of disaffiliation and self-imposed exclusion by the affluent.

A major theme of this chapter is that a growing identification of community sustainability with social diversity via public policy actions will be consistently undermined by social forces relating to social affinity and fear/security operating in a context of increasing social inequalities. Far from producing diverse communities, an analysis of recent policies and housing development suggests that the desire to recapture the affluent in towns and cities is resulting in segregated neighbourhoods in order to promote feelings of safety by the affluent. In this context it seems likely that there will be greater apparent diversity at the city scale as the middle classes re-enter cities, but that there will also be a continuing growth of enclaves and segregation, supporting the social separation of different income groups at the neighbourhood scale. This use of neighbourhood as refuge can be seen as antagonistic to diversity. Meanwhile, the concealed goal of public action has been to create safe and socially homogeneous spaces for housing, consumption and work in order to reverse the socially selective (largely middle-class) loss of population from the UK's urban areas.

This general search for security is driven by a range of factors including the media treatment of deprived areas as well as a broader climate of significant workplace and geopolitical insecurity, in which home and neighbourhood provide increasingly important spaces for social reproduction (Butler with Robson, 2003) and sources of stability in a period of social flux (Forrest, 2004). However, private decisions to maximise safety and the insulation of households with choice are likely to have the public consequence of widening the withdrawal of affluent households while the urban poor is contained in areas of ghettoised social housing and treated with increasingly punitive controls (Damer, 2002). In the context set out here, it would seem likely that these forces will produce defended enclaves rather than the diverse communities publicly aspired to by policy makers.

Today, housing is part of a wider and interlocking mosaic of agencies aiming to provide, but increasingly to control, what are seen as unruly populations. Far from being a distant dystopia these processes are already tangible: zero-tolerance policing, private- and state-sponsored gentrification, market renewal and demolition, Business Improvement Districts (BIDS), punitive antisocial behaviour measures, gated communities and a wider privatisation of public space appearing as responses to a deeper need to 'civilise' and tame urban areas. In conditions of increasing and profound inequality (Palmer et al, 2004) such processes of social separation and revenge (Smith, 1996) are likely to undermine the effectiveness of policy actions attempting to combat segregation.

Building sustainable and diverse communities in the context of current urban and housing policy

The neighbourhood forms a critical junction at which housing and urban policy interventions are now scaled (Forrest, 2004). This section pays particular attention to critical and underlying assumptions in these policy areas which appear to support what can be seen as 'insulated' spaces provided for and desired by those with choice to attain city sustainability by drawing back the affluent (Atkinson, 2006). Key policies, particularly the sustainable communities plan (ODPM, 2003), discuss the need for diversity although it is not clear how such diversity is to be promoted. Policy appears to be publicly in favour of social diversity (Urban Task Force, 2002; ODPM, 2003) even as new development more often favours mono-tenure owner-occupation, spatial separation and the need to provide amenity and the control of disorder. The desirability of encouraging the return of higher-income households to cities in the UK has been critiqued as the kind of 'back to the city' process presaged by gentrification in the past, and which leads to household displacement rather than social diversity (Lees,

2003; Atkinson, 2004). Nevertheless, the idea of an urban 'renaissance' with high-quality design, mixed tenure and land-use functions, remains an attractive vision for our cities even if it might be seen as potentially unrealistic.

Visions of sustainability and development predicated on social diversity are incompatible with the residential aspirations of middle- and upper-income households striving for privacy, safety and predictability, stemming from a need for 'bounded diversity'. In other words, the hallmark of search strategies by middle-class households is one of social diversity but within certain parameters. This desire to live in neighbourhoods in which local identities, values and status are consonant with our own creates segregation since we live in a society of significant inequalities. These social forces would appear to be at least as strong as economic and institutional factors that have often been used to explain segregation (Massey and Denton, 1998).

Regional imbalances in housing supply and affordability have also led to the creation of significant plans for state-sponsored affordable housing provision in the South East. However, it is not clear that social diversity will be promoted, even that this might be counterproductive to such plans if higher-income groups are to be encouraged back to the city given their aversion to locating next to low-income households.

Policies on sustainability and diverse communities talk the talk of inclusivity even as, as argued here, they walk the walk of urban 'pioneers' and 'homesteaders', as saviours of inner-city areas selectively exited by those with choice and averse to the educational, crime and environmental qualities associated with cities. The response to these issues in the North of England, under the sustainable communities plan, has been the promotion of nine housing market renewal pathfinders (see Chapter Five). The militarist discourse of such policy vehicles reflects a strategic use of compulsory purchase, environmental improvement and demolition (around 400,000 dwellings) as well as replacement with significantly greater levels of owner-occupation. While the plans of the pathfinders remain largely private, due to the market sensitivities of their designated geographies through which speculative investment might be promoted, these undemocratic programmes are designed to increase market confidence and boost middle-class occupation, which raises past spectres of community displacement and substitution (Young and Willmott, 1969).

The renewal pathfinders have already been criticised for regeneration activity that may promote homelessness through the demolition of private and social housing in the areas identified (Shelter, 2004), with tenants evicted due to speculation that property will be compulsorily purchased. With little social housing being built, increasing income inequalities (Goodman and Oldfield, 2004) and a lack of strong guidance on affordable housing (Minton, 2004) are creating further spatial polarisation, with emerging increases in ghettoised social housing and affluent gated communities. Taken as a whole there is a convincing single-mindedness about continued calls for the occupation of central city and deprived areas by higher-income groups that may be interpreted as gentrification rather than the kind of deeper revitalisation that many have called for (Cameron, 2003).

Under current housing and urban policies, existing economic and housing market processes are being reinforced to create increasingly visible concentrations of segregated poverty and affluence. While social housing investment is locked into areas of ghettoised poverty (Bramley and Morgan, 2002), private house developers build houses that are targeted away from social housing and in ways that attempt to avoid the inclusion of affordable or social housing to maintain the market viability of such projects in their eyes (Crook et al, 2002). Even in the public sector, subsidies are moving towards the promotion of private housing using traditional sources of social housing income with Social Housing Grant in Glasgow already being used in part to promote owner-occupation in greenbelt releases to attract homeowners back to the city. This suggests that the public promotion of diversity in new neighbourhoods is and will increasingly be shunned in order to make such developments sustainable given existing residential preferences. In a housing system marked primarily by market allocation and widening social inequalities, the prospects for social diversity appear bleak.

Private choices, public consequences

Why does social diversity have such an appeal? What benefits might stem from socially diverse areas for their residents or wider society? The centrality of diversity to housing and community sustainability has been underpinned by little empirical evidence. Nevertheless, the profound social consequences of ghettoised poverty have led to a default position in which diversity is either seen as the answer or inherently preferable. However, assessing the hypothesis that living in areas of concentrated poverty is worse than living in more socially diverse areas remains an area of research riven by debate about what evidence might provide confirmation or rejection of such hypotheses (Ellen and Turner, 1997). Nevertheless, there is a deep intuitive resonance to the idea that living in ghettoised poverty has compounding negative effects on life chances and opportunity structures. The everyday choices of households not taking advantage of cheaper housing in deprived areas attests to this. Even when households make such decisions, the resulting process of gentrification has been shown to be problematic for poorer communities, making clear insight into policy solutions difficult.

Why should we be concerned whether neighbourhoods will or should provide a home for a diverse cross-section of the population? A thought experiment is in order at this point. Academics have often suggested that concentrations of poverty (Massey and Denton, 1998; Musterd and Ostendorf, 2001) have created and compounded problems for the residents of such areas. Does this suggest that part of a mission of wider social reform could be linked to our own housing choices, that a move to a peripheral housing estate might be seen as a positive step? How might we imagine that this could help? The thesis that area effects may have an impact rests on a number of assumptions, including the need for role models by those living in deprived areas as a spur or guide to self-help and goal attainment. In addition, the potential for nearby affluent residents to extract better public services and provide the demand for more substantial private services in combination with a reduced demand on local public infrastructure holds out the possibility that diversity could lead to wider benefits. However, such an 'experiment' presents a range of problems. Why would 'I' move to an area with a poor-quality environment or face the threat of higher crime? Indeed, would 'my' move be interpreted as a kind of colonisation by a higher-income group? How would 'I' be viewed by existing residents, and would they see such a move as inherently patronising?

Consider another thought experiment. How effective might it be to move benefit-dependent households to more affluent areas rather than pursuing the resiting of the affluent in deprived, cheaper areas? What new opportunities might be opened by such a change in the direction of policy? Might the out-migration of deprived households from some of the 'worst', 'sink' and 'no-go' areas of the UK portrayed by our media provide an ameliorative for area effects and the prospect of brighter futures? If we think that this would not or could not work, we should ask ourselves why. Might the territoriality and the community networks of deprived households prevent such moves? Would it in fact be middle-class mobilisation and NIMBYism (not in my backyard) that would be more likely to halt such policies? It is important that we look with honesty at our own fears, aspirations and prejudices to see how these positions arise.

Finally, consider what might happen if economic inequalities were reduced to some acceptable level (a difficult equilibrium to imagine). How might we imagine the social geography of our cities in this context? Perhaps we would find that our occupation, stage in the life course, personal political affiliation and other aspects of social identity might still lead to an identifiable social mosaic based on needs for social affinity. But would such constellations affect the life chances of residents in the negative ways that currently occur? Regardless of how we might explain our own responses to such experiments, they allow us to partially unravel the reasons through which towns and cities take on the kind of social and spatial patterning that we view as problematic, and forces us to confront our own values and choices which make up that context. The following subsections look at the fundamental drivers of such continued spatial segregation.

Homogeneity and safety

Fundamental to an understanding of why segregation and social homogeneity tend to characterise neighbourhood life in the UK and elsewhere is that such social similarity provides a sense of shelter and togetherness. In a context in which the media drives fears of crime, disorder, antisocial behaviour and predatory offending and links these to areas of social rented housing (Brown, 2004) and to cities (Yanich, 2004), the neighbourhood plays an increasingly significant role as a place of sanctuary. Such safety is also found in the relative social homogeneity of neighbourhoods.

It is also possible to find research evidence that supports the possibility that diversity provides an uncomfortable context for many households. Work on neighbourhood satisfaction has demonstrated that this is lower among social renters and owners the more these tenures are mixed together (Parkes et al, 2002). In focus groups conducted on attitudes to urban living, researchers (URBED et al, 1999) found that cities were perceived to be more dangerous than the suburbs or the countryside by all participants across three cities. In addition, proximity to social housing was seen as a particular problem of city living even though many felt that such areas had undeserved reputations.

In research on neighbourhood satisfaction we also consistently find that crime and schooling are closely linked to low satisfaction and subsequent migration. The effect of this has been to drive residential choices with house type and size as important factors, but also important has been the avoidance of crime as a decentralising force (Scottish Executive, 2002). In Glasgow's drive to retain families, moves to create new neighbourhoods were seen as potentially desirable in a survey: (a) where such developments could provide a social 'mix' akin to that of suburban developments; (b) where local schools were of adequate quality; and (c) where the development was secure/crime free (Bramley and Morgan, 2002). All of this suggests that certain constellations of diversity act to lower the perceived quality of life for residents, and that this primarily occurs for those with choice.

Other research in the US (Harris, 2001) has suggested that both White and Black households seek predominantly White neighbours. In the case of White households this was seen as the product of racial preferences and prejudice, and yet the desire by Black households to mirror such preferences was linked to an association between White areas and lower crime rates. Thus the interpretation that Black households have a greater desire for integration may not be supported, but that a desire for safety is desired by both groups, rather than being linked to racial preferences.

In the 2003 citizenship survey, the Home Office (2003) found that levels of civic trust were lower in ethnically diverse areas (Pennant, 2005). Other research evidence from the US has suggested that perceptions of neighbourhood social diversity may lead to feelings of uncertainty in the environment and thereby increased levels of fear (Kennedy and Silverman, 1985). Certainly, in newly emerging property markets like that of Beijing, early research also suggests that movers seek areas with 'good reputations' and concerns for neighbourhood security (Wang and Li, 2004).

The effects of search strategies, for safety and quality, operating in a system of unequal resources, may have profound negative consequences. Important research on schooling in Philadelphia (Saporito, 2003) demonstrated that choice led to white families avoiding schools with higher percentages of non-white students, which went beyond the possible explanations of performance or poverty. The effect of these 'private choices' was to increase segregation in the school system that these students exited, thus creating the potential for a further deterioration in educational standards for those pupils left behind. This pattern of 'out-group avoidance' (Saporito, 2003, p 184) has been viewed as not merely the demarcation between different social groups but also the avoidance of places and social groups of lower perceived 'race' or class status. This led Massey and Denton (1998) to suggest that racial segregation could be interpreted as largely the result of white avoidance of areas populated by non-whites.

Learning the social ecology of the city

A powerful force in dictating residential choices and aspirations is connected to our own experiences and the contexts we grow up in, kinship, friendship and neighbourhood. Wider social and in-group affiliations also construct a sense of reality shaped by the values and locations of those we see as our peers or those who socialise us. From this it is possible to suggest that the process of socialisation helps us to 'learn' segregation. For higher-income groups this is reinforced by spatial separation from 'problem' or poverty areas, but is now increasingly supported by information and transport technologies that allow the relative invisibility of negotiated movement around the city (Graham and Marvin, 2001). Video-gaming, with its increasingly sophisticated urban social ecologies of ghettos, business districts and corrupt/wealthy suburbs, provides a source of imagined and semi-real urban environments from which future locational decisions and risk ecologies are learned in more subtle ways than has yet been researched.

Technology and neighbourhood searches

Residential searches aided by the detailed description of area characteristics by neighbourhood profilers also act to reinforce neighbourhood hierarchies of desirability, circuits of schooling and amenity (Burrows et al, 2005). People may pick where they live on the basis of geo-demographic descriptors, selecting parameters of acceptable school performance, local amenity and crime rates. The implications of this are clear: those who have choice to move do so within a framework which by default excludes options which are perceived to be dangerous, low quality and unsupportive of the social reproduction of the household. In the future, such choices may increasingly act to promote segregation and separation.

Changes in the built environment

The spatial separation of the affluent and choice-limited poor is widening (Musterd and Ostendorf, 2001; Minton, 2004). As the development of enclave-style private housing grows, it supports an increasingly 'nodal' pattern of household movement in which affluent households can effectively manage their contact with areas they see as desirable or risky. The built environment increasingly supports car use by the affluent, with semi-fortified residential spaces providing impenetrable neighbourhoods to maximise perceived safety and privacy

(Atkinson et al, 2003). Gated communities support the residential aspirations of increasingly paranoid high-income strata, but also provide a template for their democratisation, with cheaper copies of this format available to security- and status-conscious middle-income households. Even in open-plan private housing development we find low walls, cul de sacs, spatial separation and architectural distinction from surrounding public housing.

Research on the push for diversity in areas of social housing has also suggested that diversity in tenant composition has been viewed with a strategic use, in terms of reduced management costs rather than a deep-seated commitment to produce a diverse local populace for its own sake (Cole and Goodchild, 2001). We should, then, be wary of calls for diversity and the underlying rationales that sometimes lie behind them.

Of course, all of these processes are to say nothing of the prime sorter of households, the housing system itself, which allocates households according to the relative desirability of neighbourhoods. Outside this market framework social housing is widely viewed as being located in the 'worst' areas. Nevertheless, this system, with the constrained choices of those in social housing and the relatively freer choices of those in private markets, is subtly shaped by values, aspirations and deeply embedded social needs and fears which are often neglected in economic analyses of residential choice. Such social processes are likely to interact with and reinforce existing patterns of social segregation in the future, and threaten the policy goal of producing more equitable access to resources in neighbourhood contexts.

The idea that where we live might significantly affect and reproduce social inequalities is critical to an understanding of the desirability of social heterogeneity at the local level. Even before area effects had become a significant area for research, writers like Sennett (1970) and Gans (1968) were already arguing that diversity provided an important social and planning goal since it promoted political empathy through contact with people with different attitudes, beliefs and experiences which both challenge and educate us. This confrontation with difference has provided commentators with the ammunition required to attack the kinds of rarefied, privatised and fortified developments that have been created in more recent years. In other words, private choices enabled through affluence may have latent or secondary feedback effects on the wider community which lead to its detriment in the longer term. Can policy stem these social as well as economic forces using housing and urban policies without attention to wider inequalities? In a social world of reduced inequalities segregation would not be an issue for concerned policy makers and commentators. What sense would it make to talk of segregation in an 'equal' society? But how far are we on the road to such a future?

Future scenarios of social segregation and sustainability

This section extends preceding comments about social mix, homogeneity and safety by considering future housing developments that may reflect on these social, economic and political tendencies. Referring back to the title of this chapter, the idea is pursued that a split may become increasingly evident between those with choice and those without, and that spatial clustering along these lines will develop in more entrenched ways. In this context it is appropriate to consider the motivations and impacts of what Low has called social 'splitting' (2003), observed in the context of increasing residence in gated communities in the US. This idea refers to the moving out of those with choice and resources to protected spaces in which control over entry allows privacy and safety as well as inevitable social homogeneity. It is this theme of splitting that helps here in describing what might seem plausible housing futures given the increasing strength of such social forces and their facilitation by local and central states.

Rich and poor mobs: gated communities and the incarceration of social renting

In a recent paper (Atkinson, 2006) it was argued that locational choices are primarily driven by a search for relative safety in the neighbourhood context, and these social imperatives can be split into types ranging from insulation, to incubation and incarceration. In other words, the drivers for segregation are as much social pressures as economic, and reflect a desire for safety (insulation), for maintaining the social reproduction of the daily life of the household (incubation) and motivations of ultra-privacy and self- or externally-imposed separation or isolation (incarceration).

In the context of social housing, its geographical concentration and stigmatised reputation, some have argued that it effectively contains and restricts the social world of an urban poor, and that this serves 'respectable' society that seeks to be separated from such 'risky' populations. Growing calls by the government for getting tough on antisocial behaviour have simultaneously condemned and supported communities in areas of social rented housing where it is seen to be a significant problem. Such areas are seen as being ruled by unruly bands of youth, out-of-control tenants and dysfunctional families, who should be subjected to increasing regulation and control (Brown, 2004). This ratcheting-up of punitive regimes to control antisocial behaviour continues to stigmatise those living in such areas, while strengthening the appeal of residential choices that lie outside or are, indeed, protected from such spaces. This is attested to by the growth in new build private housing in adjacent areas, often walled off to allow residents to feel both safe and distinct from their 'non-neighbours'.

It does not seem likely, given the current political capital to be drawn from alarmist and vicious portrayals of life in deprived neighbourhoods, that the stigmatisation and fear associated with social renting will dissipate. It may be that in years to come the possibility of incarcerating deprived populations in areas of concentrated surveillance, regulation and containment is seen to serve as a politically desirable and even a cost-effective means of dealing with emerging social problems. This scenario seems perhaps more plausible than the possibility that root causes of such problems will be addressed.

Far from countering tendencies toward the further residualisation and concentration of deprivation, it is more probable that problems relating to social control and disorder in spaces characterised as the colonies of a 'feckless' underclass will increase, as the ghettoisation of

Photograph 7.1: Spaces of incarceration for the deprived

poverty also grows through the exiting of those able to exercise residential choice. Media sensationalism and accompanying political diatribes feeding off disorder and antisocial behaviour may become increasingly spatialised and directed at areas of concentrated deprivation. In this sense the perception of respectable society being held to ransom by the mob rule of an uncontrollable urban underclass may provoke increasingly vengeful reactions by local and central states, as well as the multiagency partnerships increasingly co-opted to help with such problems (Smith, 1996). With revenue funding for progressive intermediary social programmes like youth training and neighbourhood wardens already waning, such problems may increase.

While recent theories of economic growth in cities have been popularised around notions of creativity and tolerance (Florida, 2002), it may be worthwhile supplementing these ideas with the notion that safety might play a significant role in boosting local economic development. Neither is such protection something that only high-income groups desire; there is reason to believe that gating and security are also at the heart of demands by tenants to achieve a level of security that would enable social life to take place without fear. 'Alley-gating' and attempts to have more control over waiting lists might also be mentioned in this regard. However, such demands are constrained by relative deprivation, while the affluent take increasing advantage of housing and other devices by which security may be assured. A more significant problem in future may be the relative democratisation of such devices, for example, gated communities. Such 'communities' might become more prevalent but with the function of both reducing the victimisation and social control of the poor.

In a recent report (Minton, 2004), gated communities have been seen as divisive and maintaining unbalanced communities that have been immune from the kind of criticism to which areas of concentrated poverty have been treated. Gated communities are therefore more difficult to pin down as 'problems', and yet display more clearly than ever before the increasingly polarised nature of British urban areas and the social fear that has driven this withdrawal. Counter-intuitively, anthropological research has suggested that the result of residing in gated communities is often an exaggerated sense of risk associated with venturing beyond the gates (Low, 2003).

It seems unlikely that the use of gated communities to restore security and reduce fear for poorer communities, called for some time ago by David Blunkett (when Home Secretary), will prove effective. However, gating is likely to lead to imperatives for further fortification for two key reasons. First, an increased sensitivity to issues around security might raise demand for this kind of development. Second, the desire not to be a soft target relative to adjacent target-hardened and gated communities may displace crime and provide an incentive to join such clubs. Like the increase in sales of 4×4 cars with rear-tinted windows, the best way to avoid being run down by one is to be driving your own! Continuing growth in real incomes may also make such privacy, status and security a commodity more easily purchased by a greater number of households, leading to a range of secondary problematic outcomes.

The 'factional' BBC documentary 'If ... things don't get better', considered the effects of a future growth in gated communities. In the programme community relations rapidly deteriorate as a gated community is installed. As residents complain about incursions by neighbouring youths, security is escalated and the boundaries made more secure, with the increasing involvement of local police to supplement the presence of private guards. As the documentary illustrated, such 'communities' may create micro-geographies of segregation where affluent households are 'able' to live side-by-side but are insulated from the perceived risks of living next to deprived areas. The creation of apparent wider neighbourhood diversity may conceal the hyper-segregation of rich and poor, as well as separated daily trajectories of upper- and lower-income groups passing side-by-side without interacting, fuelling the potential for resentment. The likely rise of such 'club goods' in housing development will pose distinctive problems in the future for a number of reasons:

1. The *displacement of crime* and *increasing cost of social services* to other neighbourhoods: a recurrent theme in the literature on gated communities is their push for fiscal autonomy from the local state. If we can imagine their significant growth and political organisation in the future, it is possible to envisage a similar drive to opt out of local state provision for local environmental services and even law enforcement on the basis that residents pay 'twice' for such services. It may be unlikely that such autonomy will be successful, but this will depend on the scale of such development in future, and perhaps also the scale of political capital to be drawn from appealing to the petitions of gated community residents. Critically, the impact of moves in this direction will create further strains on the cost of providing public services to other, more deprived, communities.

2. The socialisation of *generations raised in super-insulated neighbourhoods*: reference has already been made to research which suggests that

residents of gated communities may become more fearful of the area outside their gates. Certainly, attitudes to risk and social difference may become problematic under such residential conditions with, if anything, a drive to withdraw or 'fort-up' even further. Even more importantly we need to consider the long-run impacts where children are socialised in gated conditions and the likely character of social beliefs regarding those outside the gates who apparently provoked the withdrawal of parents to such protected enclaves in the first place.

While these are clearly segregated spaces of *residence*, the extended patterns of *movement* from these protected nodes to other linked spaces provides the possibility of near-'weightless' citizens set free from the concerns generated by local crime and wider disorder (Atkinson and Flint, 2004). Such developments may also increase the mutual invisibility of the affluent and deprived in the city, negotiating protected pathways using cars and sheltering in homes, shopping centres and workspaces increasingly protected from intrusion. If we already view residential (or static) segregation as problematic, gated communities hold out the possibility of dynamic forms in which social groups disengage across institutional and public spaces, posing threats to progressive presumptions in favour of social diversity.

Photograph 7.2: Spaces of insulated seclusion for the affluent

3. Gated communities also present risks to urban sustainability through their *impermeability* to public movement. In the event that gated communities are developed on a significant scale, as with South African cities, increasing congestion on arterial roads with increases in travel times made around gated communities may become a reality.

4. Perhaps most importantly, developers are likely to become key actors in the *promotion of fear* in which nightmare scenarios serve an important function in yielding greater revenues from sales of gated communities and other 'saviour technologies' (for example, CCTV, Sports Utility Vehicles and so on). The portrayal of dangerous urban spaces within which gated communities provide a refuge is already apparent in the marketing literature for such developments. Like public (that is, private) schools, the clubbing together of consumers enables the provision of goods not supplied by the state. Like other private clubs they prevent access to non-members while providing, in this case, access to security on the basis of ability to pay.

Policy makers are likely to be attracted by gated communities in order to allow the protected return and investment of high-income households to UK cities, given the longer history of their withdrawal. It may even be possible that they are argued to help form sustainable forms of living that might reduce pressures on urban sprawl and the promotion of diversity within the wider neighbourhood. The subsequent impact of such changes may be to reduce any political impetus towards reform and greater social inequality, since the traditional costs that feed back to higher-income groups when inequalities rise, crime and fear, may, in future, be avoided.

Gentrification: the middle classes as the saviour of the city

Policy makers have often viewed gentrification, an influx of high-income households to low-income neighbourhoods, as a benign migration to the city by middle-class households. Practitioner theories of the process articulate a connection between a re-colonisation by high-income households and the lifting of flagging city fortunes while boosting local tax bases. In this context the need to provide high-quality, insulated refuges is seen as paramount to regaining middle-class households and corporate decision makers:

There is room for some middle class and affluent enclaves.... Affluent residential enclaves affect business location decisions not only by attracting business owners.... In order to attract the rich, cities must allow and encourage the development of affluent enclaves, the pursuit of income diversity should focus on the gentrification of distressed neighbourhoods rather than the introduction of poverty to middle-class neighbourhoods. (Belmont, 2002, p 339)

In fact, Belmont's theme has been echoed by recent research in the UK in which suburbs have been seen as important to city competitiveness: "Having good places to live for its middle-class professional workers, we would argue, is important if Manchester is to secure its status as a competitive city" (Halfpenny et al, 2004, p 262). It has not proved difficult to locate similar discourses among those policy makers looking to boost the fortunes of low-demand areas and seeking to revitalise city cores in the North. Now and in the future it seems clear that diversity and community are things that low-income households need to do. In the meantime, and if city fortunes are linked to the housing choices of high-income groups, enclaves preserved from the apparent contamination of diversity will need to be maintained.

Who would have thought that cities like Leeds, Newcastle and Glasgow would be capable of producing gentrified neighbourhoods 10 years ago? When I asked one policy maker in Liverpool if an area with several trendy restaurants was now being gentrified he responded: "Can we have some please?". As economic prospects improve in British deindustrialised cities, gentrification seems assured; the gaps between existing low-value uses of areas close to the central city now provide rich investment opportunities. Public policy strategies of insulation are employed to attract the social and economic investment of upper-income households, sought by all cities. In this context, development appears without affordable housing, enclave-styles separated from social housing or gated to 'protect' residents. The justification for this may be made on the grounds that high-income groups are unwilling to mix with other groups, while social housing is prevalent enough to deal with the housing demands of low-income groups. The real flaw in this logic is precisely that social diversity is not being given the opportunity to flourish *within* neighbourhood locations and that existing separation is being reinforced.

The implications of growing numbers of elite and high-income residential areas are similar to those for gated communities. However, processes of gentrification themselves have been argued by some policy makers to be a form of increasing diversity. Nevertheless, gentrification is more likely to continue in ways that displace lower-income households, diminish the political voice of existing residents as well as recasting the neighbourhood in the image and needs of middle-class households. This form of urban 'colonialism' is likely to continue at least insofar as housing developers, private households and city authorities are driven to move to the central areas of cities which were largely emptied industrially and residentially by shifts in their local economies.

Conclusion

Everyday dystopias in public discourse and private imaginations fuel the decisions of households to locate in particular neighbourhoods. Such places are 'chosen', either through social housing systems, or by us in private housing markets in which affinity towards social similarity drives feelings of safety and the subsequent production of wider patterns of segregation. While everyday policy language is suffuse with noble aims of engendering diversity, the reality has been increasingly stark social and income polarisation, which has been transmitted through the housing system to produce areas of pronounced deprivation as well as an entrenched enclavism in which the affluent shelter in gated communities and gentrified neighbourhoods away from areas of social difference and insecurity.

The protection and direction of investment towards ailing cities by neo-liberal city regimes has been linked to increasingly punitive actions directed at poorer groups, politically progressive local politics and the homeless, in a bid to clean up the city to make way for the interests of capital (Smith, 1996; Wyly and Hammel, 2005). As social housing has become a space of last resort, so it has become synonymous with crime, disorder and antisocial behaviour. The possibility of a vengeful urbanism is already manifest and likely to increase as actions are taken to tackle the products of social exclusion rather than their root causes. In such a scenario social housing is increasingly likely to provide the means by which wider fears and problematic populations might be contained, while growing bands of middle- and high-income groups shelter behind gates and walls and in protected modes of transportation.

There are reasons to think these processes will both deepen and become more problematic in the future, but also that the impacts will fall on high-income, as well as poorer, households in the future. For those with choice, the social dividend of reinforced residential segregation is likely to take the form of social unease and fear of crime. Even now firms in cities like London find it difficult to find cleaning staff displaced to the margins of the capital and the housing system, while public service workers, not themselves low paid, struggle in the face of housing costs and to the detriment of those services. However, it seems unlikely that such outcomes may themselves create the political capital needed for public interventions to enforce local social diversity. More likely is the prospect of a downward spiral in a race to the bottom to achieve security, at which point militarised responses to disorder, pronounced social fear and segregation (Davis, 1998) react to the symptoms of inequality rather than their causes, which would require substantially more political will and investment.

The creation and maintenance of sustainable communities has been seen as an issue of neighbourhood social composition and re-sorting in lieu of thinking about the wider economic gaps that exist between social groups. However, diversity itself functions as a distraction from a central issue for those studying housing and urban systems – that diversity and segregation are the products of an unequal social system that plays itself out spatially. Nevertheless, if we accept that where we live affects our life chances, the move towards social diversity remains critically important and immediately necessary to improve the opportunities of deprived groups.

The gathering together of high-income groups, like oil on water, enables security, identity and social sustenance through association with people felt to mirror social identities and values. This has made segregation a highly durable form of socio-spatial patterning in our cities. The role of policy to prevent the further retrenchment of such separated social relationships may be doomed. Even where policy has suggested itself amenable to the production of socially diverse neighbourhoods, we see equally forceful actions by private households, investors and local policy makers towards socially insulated, new build development. In this context, the fundamental challenge to political willingness to create sustainability is not the need for social diversity; rather it is to create a less unequal society and thereby a less stigmatised and spatially concentrated social housing system, in order that the social patchwork of towns and cities does not reflect a map of unequal life chances and disaffiliation between citizens and neighbours. As is often the case, words from the past suggest themselves as guides to the future, as with Jacob Riis's quote from the poetry of James Russel Lowell:

Think ye that building shall endure
Which shelters the noble and crushes the poor?

References

Atkinson, R. (2004) 'The evidence on the impact of gentrification: new lessons for the urban renaissance?', *European Journal of Housing Policy*, vol 4, no 1, pp 107-31.

Atkinson, R. (2006) 'Padding the bunker: strategies for middle class disaffiliation and colonisation in the city', *Urban Studies*, vol 43, no 4.

Atkinson, R. and Flint, J. (2004) 'Fortress UK? Gated communities, the spatial revolt of the elites and time-space trajectories of segregation', *Housing Studies*, vol 19, no 6, pp 875-92.

Atkinson, R., Blandy, S., Flint, J. and Lister, D. (2003) *Gated communities in England*, London: ODPM.

Belmont, S. (2002) *Cities in full: Recognizing and Realizing the great potential of urban America*, Chicago, IL: American Planning Association.

Bramley, G. and Morgan, J. (2002) 'The role of housebuilding in central Scotland's cities', Paper to Housing Studies Association, York, 3 and 4 April.

Brown, A.P. (2004) 'Anti-social behaviour, crime control and social control', *The Howard Journal*, vol 43, no 2, pp 203-11.

Burrows, R., Ellison, N. and Woods, B. (2005) *Neighbourhoods on the net: The nature and impact of internet-based neighbourhood information services*, Bristol: The Policy Press.

Butler, T. with Robson, G. (2003) *London calling: The middle-classes and the remaking of inner London*, Oxford: Berg.

Cameron, S. (2003) 'Gentrification, housing redifferentiation and urban regeneration: "going for growth" in Newcastle upon Tyne', *Urban Studies*, vol 40, no 12, pp 2367-83.

Cole, I. and Goodchild, B. (2001) 'Social mix and the "balanced community" in British housing policy – a tale of two epochs', *GeoJournal*, vol 51, pp 351-60.

Crook, A., Currie, J., Jackson, A., Monk, S., Rowley, S., Smith, K. and Whitehead, C.M.E. (2002) *Planning gain and affordable housing*, York: Joseph Rowntree Foundation.

Damer, S. (2002) '"Engineers of the human machine": the social practice of council housing management in Glasgow, 1895-1939', *Urban Studies*, vol 37, no 11, pp 2207-26.

Davis, M. (1998) *Ecology of fear: Los Angeles and the imagination of disaster*, London: Picador.

Ellen, I. and Turner, M. (1997) 'Does neighbourhood matter? Assessing recent evidence', *Housing Policy Debate*, vol 8, no 1, pp 833-66.

Florida, R.L. (2002) *The rise of the creative class: And how it's transforming work, leisure, community and everyday life*, New York, NY: Basic Books.

Forrest, R. (2004) *Who cares about neighbourhoods?*, CNR Paper 26, Bristol: Centre for Neighbourhood Research.

Gans, H. (1968) *People and plans: Essays on urban problems and solutions*, New York, NY: Basic Books.

Goodman, A. and Oldfield, Z. (2004) *Permanent differences? Income and expenditure inequality in the 1990s and 2000s*, London: Institute for Fiscal Studies.

Graham, S. and Marvin, S. (2001) *Splintering urbanism: Networked infrastructures, technological mobilities and the urban condition*, London: Routledge.

Halfpenny, P., Britton, N.J., Devine, F. and Mellor, R. (2004) 'The "good" surburb as an urban asset in enhancing a city's competitiveness', in M. Boddy and M. Parkinson (eds) *City matters: Competitiveness, cohesion and urban governance*, Bristol: The Policy Press, pp 255-68.

Harris, D. (2001) 'Why are whites and blacks averse to black neighbors?', *Social Science Research*, vol 30, no 1, pp 100-16.

Home Office (2005) *National citizenship survey*, London: Home Office.

Kennedy, L.W. and Silverman, R.A. (1985) 'Perception of social diversity and fear of crime', *Environment and Behavior*, vol 17, no 3, pp 275-95.

Kumar, K. (1978) *Prophecy and progress: The sociology of industrial and post-industrial society*, Harmondsworth: Penguin.

Lees, L. (2003) 'Visions of "urban renaissance": the Urban Task Force and the Urban White Paper', in R. Imrie and M. Raco (eds) *Urban renaissance? New Labour, community and urban policy*, Bristol: The Policy Press, pp 61-82.

Low, S. (2003) *Behind the gates: Life, security, and the pursuit of happiness in Fortress America*, London: Routledge.

Massey, D. and Denton, N. (1998) *American apartheid: Segregation and the making of the underclass*, Boston, MA: Harvard University Press.

Minton, A. (2004) *Mind the gap – Tackling social polarisation through balanced communities*, London: RICS.

Musterd, S. and Ostendorf, W. (eds) (2001) *Urban segregation and the welfare state: Inequality and exclusion in western cities*, London: Routledge.

ODPM (Office of the Deputy Prime Minister) (2003) *Sustainable communities: Building for the future*, London: ODPM.

Palmer, G., Carr, J. and Kenway, P. (2004) *Monitoring poverty and social exclusion in Scotland 2004*, York: Joseph Rowntree Foundation.

Parkes, A., Kearns, A. and Atkinson, R. (2002) 'What makes people dissatisfied with their neighbourhoods?', *Urban Studies*, vol 39, no 13, pp 2413-38.

Ravetz, A. (2001) *Council housing and culture: The history of a social experiment*, London: Routledge.

Riis, J. (1971/1890) *How the other half lives: Studies among the tenements of New York, with 100 photographs from the Jacob A. Riis collection*, New York, NY: Dover.

Saporito, S. (2003) 'Private choices, public consequences: magnet school choice and segregation by race and poverty', *Social Problems*, vol 50, no 2, pp 181-203.

Scottish Executive (2002) *Review of Scotland's cities – The analysis*, Edinburgh: Scottish Executive.

Sennett, R. (1970) *The uses of disorder: Personal identity and city life*, New York, NY: Knopf.

Shelter (2004) *On the up: The housing crisis in the north*, London: Shelter.

Smith, N. (1996) *The new urban frontier: Gentrification and the revanchist city*, London: Routledge.

Urban Task Force (2002) *Towards an urban renaissance – Final report of the Urban Task Force chaired by Lord Rogers of Riverside*, London: The Stationery Office.

URBED et al (1999) *But would you live there? Shaping attitudes to urban living*, London: DETR.

Wang, D. and Li, S. (2004) 'Housing preferences in a transitional housing system: the case of Beijing, China', *Environment and Planning, A*, vol 36, no 1, pp 69-88.

Wyly, E. and Hammel, D. (2005) 'Mapping neo-liberal American urbanism', in R. Atkinson and G. Bridge (eds) *Gentrification in a global context: The new urban colonialism*, London: Routledge.

Yanich, D. (2004) 'Crime creep: urban and suburban crime on local TV news', *Journal of Urban Affairs*, vol 26, no 5, pp 535-63.

Young, M. and Willmott, P. (1969) *Family and kinship in East London*, London: Penguin.

EIGHT

Housing and the ageing population

Moyra Riseborough and Peter Fletcher

Introduction

Understanding about older people and housing[1] has been influenced by pervasive social constructions of ageing that portray older life as a time of disengagement from the workforce, followed by low economic production or consumption, increasing decline, poverty, dependency and death (Phillipson, 1998; Tulle-Winterton, 1999). Today older age is rarely portrayed so narrowly, but negative images are persistent (Age Concern England and ITC, 2000; Audit Commission, 2004), and ageism, described by Bytheway (1995) as prejudice on the grounds of age, is deeply embedded in society and our institutions. The cumulative effects frequently lead to impoverished and narrow views about the relationship between housing and later life, a state of affairs that Means, for example, has strongly contested (see Means, 1999).

The 2001 Census showed that for the first time there are more people aged 60 and over than there are children in Britain. It is part of a shift in the age balance of the population, and the trend is set to continue, but we are not prepared for the changes that have occurred and will come. This chapter looks ahead to 2020, and considers where current policy, patterns of consumption, changes as a result of having more people who are 'older' in the workforce, changes in planning, house production and technology, and the impacts of a shifting age balance will take us. There are some trends we can be relatively certain about, but others are harder to predict, for example, trends indicating that health improvements will continue for most in later life. The chapter also aims to bring the subject of having an ageing society into mainstream housing and planning debates. After all, by 2020, which is not far away, the older population will be swelled by retiring 'baby boomers', and by 2025 the number of people in Britain over 60 years old will outnumber people under 25. By 2050 the ratio of people aged 65 years and older compared to 20- to 64-year-olds will rise from around 27% to 48% (DTI, 2000; GAD, 2003a).

The broad picture

The age shift

The 2001 Census reported population figures for England of just over 48 million, and showed that 27.9% are aged 55 and over. Increases in the older population have been predicted for some time, but the Census also underlined the effects of having a declining younger population as well as an increasing older population and the resulting shift in the age balance of the population.

The shift has come about because we are living longer and fewer children are being born or brought into the population. This is seen as inevitable for the first half of the century as the bulge in the post-Second World War population, the latest wave of 'baby boomers',[2] gradually enter retirement. Government Actuaries predict that until 2040 the number of people under 65 will remain about the same, but the number of people aged between 65 and 84 will increase by about one-and-a-half times while the number of people over 85 will double (cited in Audit Commission, 2004).

The UK has not reached a stage where too few people are being born to 'replace' the population that is dying, a situation occurring in some other European countries, but the shift in the age balance is nonetheless important. There are differences in how this is currently being, and will be, experienced across the UK. For example, Northern Ireland's population is ageing more slowly than other UK countries, and birth rates are not declining as sharply (NISRA, 2003). Wales has the highest proportion of people aged over 50, particularly in coastal areas. Scotland has the lowest fertility rate, and a declining population overall. Projections for Scotland indicate that key changes will occur by 2031, when the percentage of people aged 65 and over will rise from 16% to 26%, and the percentage of people aged 85 years and over will dramatically increase, from 1.7% to 4.1% (ONS, 2004).

Across English regions, the South West is seeing a decrease in the number of 15- to 29-year-olds, and a higher proportion of people aged 30-59 as well as the highest percentage of people over 60 years old, 22%. Norfolk, East and West Sussex and the Isle of Wight have similarly high percentages of older people in their populations. On the other hand, in some areas there will be a decline in the numbers of the older population as a result of health inequalities and people moving to other areas, for example, Liverpool.

There are also rural and urban differences. In England there is a growing older population in rural rather than urban areas. Migration from towns and cities largely accounts for the increase and looks set to continue. The number of people over 65 in English rural areas will rise by 20% compared to England as a whole (ONS, 2004). Table 8.1 shows how the older population is distributed between rural and urban areas by gender and age band.

The composition of the older population is beginning to change. Across the UK black and minority ethnic (BME) communities are showing signs of ageing: 15% of the non-White population is currently over 50 years old compared to 33% of the White population. However, some communities already contain more older people, and there are sub-regional and highly local differences, and these are important for understanding the make-up of the older population in local areas. For example, people from an African-Caribbean background have the oldest age structure compared to other BME communities, reflecting earlier migration patterns to the UK in the 1950s. At sub-regional levels some areas currently have significant BME older populations, for example, parts of the East and West Midlands, the North West and London.

Tenure change

A major change has occurred in the housing tenure of older people. Approximately 70% of older people own their homes across the UK, although there are variations in rates of ownership across countries and regions. In England 56% of owner-occupiers are aged 65 and over, and the number of older owner-occupiers will increase as people in middle age, predominantly owner-occupiers, retire (for a discussion on this, see King, 2001). Of the remaining 30% of older people who are not owner-occupiers, most rent properties from housing associations or local authorities (ONS, 2004).

There are significant rural–urban differences in the tenure older people occupy (see Table 8.2). In England only 16.6% of people aged 75-84 in rural areas live in social rented housing, compared to 27.4% in urban areas. Of people aged 85 and over in rural areas, only 18.6% live in social housing compared to 30.8% in urban areas. More very old people (85 and over) are owner-occupiers in rural compared to urban areas.

Shifts in the distribution of the older population across tenures mark

Table 8.1: England: older people as a proportion of all people by gender and by age band

	55-59 (%)	60-64 (%)	65-69 (%)	70-74 (%)	75-79 (%)	80-84 (%)	85-89 (%)	90+ (%)	All 55+ (%)	All people (n)
Men										
% of all people										
Rural	3.6	3.0	2.6	2.2	1.7	1.0	0.5	0.2	14.7	12,133,162
Urban	2.7	2.3	2.0	1.7	1.3	0.8	0.3	0.1	11.4	36,114,414
All	3.1	2.6	2.3	2.0	1.5	0.9	0.4	0.1	12.8	48,247,576
% of all men										
Rural	7.3	6.1	5.4	4.6	3.5	2.0	0.9	0.3	30.1	5,928,275
Urban	5.6	4.8	4.2	3.6	2.8	1.6	0.7	0.2	23.4	17,581,204
All	6.3	5.3	4.7	4.0	3.1	1.8	0.8	0.3	26.3	23,509,479
Women										
% of all people										
Rural	3.6	3.0	2.7	2.5	2.2	1.5	0.9	0.4	16.7	12,133,162
Urban	2.8	2.4	2.2	2.1	1.9	1.3	0.8	0.3	13.8	36,114,414
All	3.1	2.7	2.4	2.3	2.0	1.4	0.8	0.4	15.1	48,247,576
% of all women										
Rural	7.1	5.9	5.3	4.9	4.2	2.9	1.7	0.8	32.7	6,204,887
Urban	5.4	4.7	4.4	4.1	3.7	2.5	1.5	0.6	26.9	18,533,210
All	6.1	5.2	4.8	4.4	3.9	2.7	1.6	0.7	29.4	24,738,097
Total										
% of all people										
Rural	7.2	6.0	5.3	4.7	3.9	2.5	1.3	0.5	31.5	12,133,162
Urban	5.5	4.7	4.3	3.9	3.2	2.1	1.1	0.4	25.2	36,114,414
All	6.2	5.2	4.7	4.2	3.5	2.3	1.2	0.5	27.9	48,247,576

Source: 2001 Census; Bevan et al (forthcoming)

Table 8.2: England: tenure of older people by rural/urban areas

Tenure	55-59 (%)	60-64 (%)	65-74 (%)	75-84 (%)	85+ (%)	All 55+ (%)
Owner-occupied						
Rural	85.6	84.4	81.3	74.1	68.6	80.8
Urban	78.8	77.2	73.9	65.2	58.1	72.9
All	81.7	80.3	77.1	69.0	62.6	76.3
Social rented						
Rural	6.7	8.4	11.9	16.6	18.6	11.3
Urban	15.5	17.4	21.0	27.4	30.8	21.0
All	11.7	13.5	17.1	22.7	25.5	16.8
Private rented						
Rural	7.7	7.2	6.8	9.3	12.8	7.9
Urban	5.8	5.4	5.1	7.4	11.1	6.1
All	6.6	6.1	5.8	8.2	11.8	6.9
Total						
Rural/urban/all	100	100	100	100	100	100
n	2,769,675	2,378,132	4,059,956	2,632,067	763,935	12,603,765

Base: all people aged 55+.

a significant change in older people's relationships with housing in older age. However, the implications are only beginning to be taken on board by local authorities and other partners when it comes to planning and charging for services that enable people to continue to live in their homes in older age. For example, considerable financial resources are tied up in subsidies for rented housing, particularly social rented housing, either to reduce rents or help low-income tenants pay for rents. In contrast, low-income older owner-occupiers receive less financial support. Some support services are similarly subsidised, for example, in rented sheltered housing, and this is being increasingly challenged as inequitable (see, for example, Durham and Districts Supporting People Partnership, 2005; Kent Supporting People, 2005). We return to this theme later in the chapter.

The implications

There are implications from having an ageing population and a decreasing younger population for just about every aspect of social and economic policy and civil life. They include:

- A longer period of 'active' and healthy life for most people, although this experience is not evenly spread. Older people in deprived areas,

BME elders and older people from lower-income groups have more health problems and long-term limiting illnesses than the majority.

- Increased demands on the state to fund additional services, provide pensions and welfare income.
- How an ageing population will change the nature of the population requiring and providing care with more focus on mutual elder care and care across older cohort groups.
- Shortages of labour as a result of a decline in numbers of younger people joining the paid workforce. There are already knock-on effects for many areas of work, including caring professions, where we are becoming increasingly reliant on economic migrants from Africa, Asia and Eastern Europe to fill the gap.
- More opportunities, and pressure, for older people to contribute to the paid labour market.
- More demands on older people to provide informal care.
- Higher demands for housing in locations older people want to be and increasing demands for adaptations and related infrastructure issues linked to transport and access to public and private facilities.
- More opportunities to engage older people in civil life, voluntary and community organisations and draw on their experience and expertise.
- Opportunities for economic development linked to the purchasing requirements of older individuals.

Changes in the workforce age balance

The number of people continuing in the paid workforce over the age they would be eligible to receive the state pension has been increasing and is expected to rise. In 2004 around 8.4% of men over 65 and almost 10% of women over 60 years old were in paid employment across the UK (DWP, 2005). This figure will change as a result of a change in the age at which women and men will be eligible to receive the state retirement pension – often called 'equivalising' the eligibility age. In effect, there will be more 'older workers' (people over 50 but under 65) as well as more people working beyond the age they can claim the state retirement pension.

When it comes to unpaid work, older people are heavy participants. A central aspect of older people's lives that is frequently overlooked is the extent to which they provide informal care to others, including care for spouses and partners, care for adult children with learning disabilities, childcare for grandchildren, support and practical help for adult children experiencing ill health, divorce or other events in their lives and peer support for friends and neighbours. Research by Pickard (2002) and the Foundation for People with Learning Disabilities (FPLD, 2003), for example, show that much of this support continues to be provided by people aged over 70.

The policy response

We look at the policy response at two levels: first, trends in policy making towards older age across a broad canvas and, second, particular aspects of housing and related policies that affect older people and how the future will look.

Broad policy trends and directions

Modern public policy in the UK aspires to be coherent, to join up previously dislocated streams of policy making and to create a sustainable environment for all that balances the needs of rural communities and urban areas (ODPM, 2003; DEFRA, 2004). Until recently, policy makers tended to focus on older people in a very partial way, primarily in terms of their need for services or benefits. The tendency to link older people and the experience of age in society with policies to deal with social problems led to older age being seen as a problem and hence to a narrow vision. However, as can be seen from our description of policy change, a broader holistic approach is emerging.

Since 1999, a consistent policy trend has emerged that aims to join up areas of policy affecting older people. Older people's contributions to society are also increasingly acknowledged. Two White Papers signalled the change. *Modernising social services* (DH, 1998) confirmed the government's commitment to promoting independence, improving protection and raising standards in social services. Next, the *NHS Plan* (DH, 2000) stated that health policy should help older people enjoy rather than endure the prospect of living longer. It also mentioned flexible services that enable older people to receive care 'close to home', and recognised that older people want to stay in their own homes, living independently, for as long as they can.

Signs of a coherent approach for older citizens can also be seen in closer integration between policies affecting welfare and pensions reform, programmes to tackle poverty and social exclusion, health, social care, housing and transport. Collaborative arrangements between government departments and other stakeholders are part of the change. Collaborative arrangements occurred, for example, in developing the

Supporting People policy (announced in 1998 and enacted in 2003), and housing policy for older people (DTLR and DH, 2001). In addition, the concept of 'age proofing', a method to check the appropriateness of policies and proposals to ensure they acknowledge the diversity of older people's experience, has come to the fore in public policy (The Housing Corporation, 2002; Audit Commission, 2004).

The Social Exclusion Unit has also begun to focus on older people. Its interim report, *Excluded older people* (SEU, 2005), highlights three key ways in which respondents to the consultation say provision needs to improve if older people are to enjoy a better quality of life:

- joined-up services are key;
- intervening early is important, and investment in low-level prevention can reduce costlier interventions later; and
- older people generally know what they need and want, and they should be involved in the design and – where practicable – the delivery of services.

A recent Green Paper takes things further (DH, 2005). The starting point "is the principle that everyone in society has a positive contribution to make to that society and that they should have a right to control their own lives". Key recommendations include:

- Individual budgets for people with care brokers to help people assess their needs, and manage their own budget. The aim is to give older people rather than professionals control over resources and hopefully help drive changes in the pattern of services available to reflect what older people want.
- New responsive models of care including extra-care housing and telecare. The Green Paper recognises the importance of suitable housing and related services as fundamental to the well-being of older people.
- Strengthening arrangements for cooperation and collaboration between the NHS and voluntary and community sector.
- New directors of adult social services who will provide strategic leadership, not just in social care but also across all adult services. Potentially this could also include housing policy in the future.
- Streamlining assessments between agencies including local authorities and across government, again including housing.
- Engaging the whole of local government to make sure all services are accessible for those with the greatest need and to encourage a shift to more preventative universal services.

Policy formulation has also opened up. Policy makers refer frequently to listening to and including stakeholders of all ages, including older people (ODPM and DH, 2003; DWP, 2005). Their help is sought to identify solutions to perennial problems as well as solutions to deal with changing expectations and needs. For example, the Better Government for Older People programme, established in the 1990s, informs the Older People's Advisory Group (and advises the Department for Work and Pensions). There is also the Housing and Older People's Advisory Group, established in 2002, which sits between the Office of the Deputy Prime Minister and the Department of Health and takes a strategic overview of all key areas of policy affecting older people, particularly housing, care and support. In addition, there is a Cabinet sub-committee on older people, all local authorities are required to have an Older People's Champion, and numerous regional and sub-regional consultative and service user groups are in operation.

Opportunity age: Meeting the challenges of age in the 21st century (DWP, 2005) sets out the government's strategy for older age. It does this by knitting together a number of policy themes and bringing together principles and targets. *Opportunity age* also announces the government's intentions to introduce legislation in 2006 to prevent age discrimination in employment and training, and to appoint a Commission for Equality and Human Rights. While *Opportunity age* is arguably the bones of an older age policy for England for the first time, England is still lagging behind Wales. Wales is the only country in the UK that has an overall vision and framework for an ageing society (Welsh Assembly, 2003). The rest of the UK is moving more slowly.

Pensions and staying in the workforce for longer

Policies on pensions and employment are integral parts of policy planning for an older society. However, policies are often inconsistent. To some extent it depends on what we mean by 'older'. There are two main discourses and they do not always work together. One concerns tackling unemployment rates among people aged over 50 but under the age at which they could receive the state retirement pension (this is also linked to a drive to reduce the number of people in this age group receiving long-term sick and disability benefits). The other concerns encouraging people to remain in the workforce even though they could afford to retire with early occupational pensions and other income, and encouraging people to stay in occupations after the age they could claim the state retirement pension.

Between 2010 and 2020 the age at which women and men can

become eligible to receive the state retirement pension will be the same. As a result more women will be retained in the workforce. At the same time government policy is encouraging more people of both genders to remain in the workforce for longer. Welfare and pension reforms to encourage people to remain in the workforce for longer, while drawing on their occupational retirement income but deferring their entitlement to state pensions, are among the outcomes announced so far. Raising the retirement age has implications for everyone in paid work now and for those who are or were intending to retire, but the change in eligibility for state pensions is still some way off. In fact the main changes in retirement ages for pensions are occurring elsewhere largely in occupational-based pension schemes, including those for civil servants and local government officers. For baby boomers this means that a proportion of them are going to have to wait longer to retire if they rely on final salary schemes (Pensions Commission, 2004).

Cynics would argue that pension reforms are stimulated as much by a desire to save on welfare as they are to redress skill shortfalls and the lack of younger people in the workforce. They would not be far wrong in our view since, as we explain, the changes are motivated by a mix of factors.

Yet there also seem to be efforts to understand, to gather evidence and plan future policies on the basis of known facts. Perhaps for the first time there is no shortage of knowledge on the older population available to the government. For example, the Foresight Ageing Population Panel was set up in 1993. The government is able to draw on the wealth of information that the Ageing Population Panel has produced, and has commissioned (DTI, 2000), as well as numerous other research reports and studies on key issues including work by the authors of this chapter.

So far we have looked at the broad policy response to a shift in the population's age balance and some implications. How are these broad tendencies in policy being translated into more specific policies that affect housing and neighbourhoods and what are the impacts?

How housing and related policies are responding

Unravelling policies that affect the accommodation and neighbourhoods older people live in is far from straightforward. For example, policies for 'social' housing are linked to regeneration and improving local communities, and regeneration policies have links to crime reduction and policies to improve health and educational attainment levels, and to reduce the number of homes in disrepair including the number of non-'decent' privately owner-occupied and rented homes. In addition, policies to improve social and personal services for older people (and the rest of the population) emphasise the importance of community rather than residential care and enabling people to continue to live in 'ordinary' housing.

The content and direction of current policy has been affected by older people's expectations and aspirations and by the realisation that what we mean by older age has changed. For example, people experience ageing differently and poor health and loss of mobility are not defining characteristics of older age. Most importantly the general sweep of government policy is aimed at enabling people to continue to live in ordinary housing. However, services that may help them to do this are almost always means tested or linked to living in particular kinds of housing. They are usually rationed, hard to find out about, are often split in inexplicable ways between different departments and agencies, can be inappropriate and are never sufficiently resourced.

New policies introduced in the spirit of community care include *Supporting People*, implemented in 2003 (www.odpm.gov.uk/index), and a number of government initiatives to increase spending and capacity on grants for repairs and adaptations, other services and to expand the range of housing options for older people, including extra-care housing. They are arguably producing good service changes but they also introduce new complications, and, as a result, services are just as rationed, uneven and uncertain as before.

Interestingly, much of the current drive to ensure that housing is seen as an essential aspect in planning for, and supporting independence in, older age has come from the social care and health sector, and from the Department of Health. The Department of Health is encouraging health and social services at a local level to adopt a prevention approach in order to support more older people at home, or in a supported housing setting, through: reducing unnecessary hospital and care home admissions by developing intermediate care services to provide intensive support at times of ill health or crisis; strengthening primary and community care services; and working with the housing sector to provide a wider range of housing options and services for older people. These include specific Department of Health funding for:

- developing the role of Home Improvement Agencies to address property-related issues for older people – adaptations, repair and improvements, energy efficiency and fuel poverty – at the time of hospital discharge, to enable older people to return home rather than go to a care home;

- a capital funding programme to develop extra-care housing as an alternative to residential care (£87 million for 2004-05 and 2005-06), and now extended in the 2004 Comprehensive Spending Review for a further two years with £60 million additional capital funding; and
- £80 million new funding also announced in the 2004 Comprehensive Spending Review – for introduction in 2006 – for telecare and social alarms to support older and vulnerable people in their homes.

Prevention is one of the themes that engages policy makers, and housing is seen as one of the levers that could be used to prevent people from entering residential care or hospital and to save the Department of Health money. The Association of Directors of Social Services (ADSS) and Local Government Association (LGA) picked up the prevention theme in a highly publicised discussion paper, *All our tomorrows: Inverting the triangle of care* (ADSS and LGA, 2003). They argued that services should switch from focusing on acute care and the frailest older people (see Figure 8.1). Future services need to reverse this trend by inverting the triangle so that the community strategy and promotion of well-being is at the top of the triangle and the extension of universal services for all older people is seen as crucial to all agencies (see Figure 8.2).

The inverted triangle suggests that there are ways to rethink housing for older people up to 2020. Instead of the current tendency to focus only on residential and nursing home care, sheltered housing, or extra-care housing when older people are mentioned, all kinds of housing and related services could be planned for. For example, by having the right type of accessible housing, property services (handyperson, equipment and adaptations) and flexible practical help (gardening, cleaning, shopping), all older people across all tenures could be enabled to remain living in ordinary housing rather than communal or institutional types of living. The idea is that services would be linked to good accessible information and financial products such as equity release to enable older people to fund the services they need, with state support if they are income poor.

None of these messages is new. *Quality and choice for older people's housing: A strategic framework* (DTLR and DH, 2001), for example, referred to similar things. The main change is that the messages seem to be accepted by social care professionals.

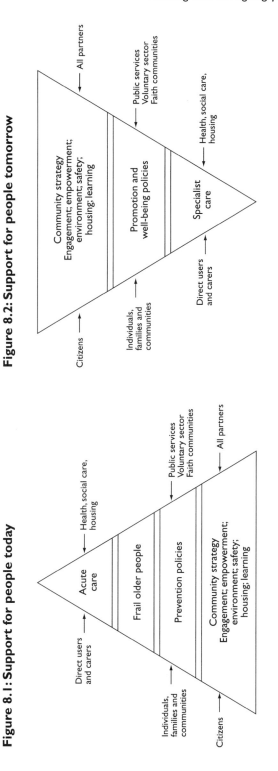

Figure 8.1: Support for people today

Figure 8.2: Support for people tomorrow

Overall then, broad trends towards joining up policies for older people at a central government level across departments show that there is a much greater understanding about the way people live their lives and make decisions. Attempts to join up policy and service planning reflect the fact that services that compartmentalise people have a bad effect on people trying to plan their lives and keep control over them. The aspirations are well intentioned and no one would argue with them. However, the reality is more fragmented.

Housing policy increasingly appears to have no direction of its own because it is shaped by other policies. In the case of older people (and other groups that are seen as somehow different) this means that health and social care agendas are increasingly influencing their housing futures, but the same groups may well be ignored in a host of other national policies that relate to housing and neighbourhoods. For example, the *Sustainable Communities* plan (ODPM, 2003) makes hardly any reference to the implications of a shift in the age balance of the population, and refers to the older population only in terms of the need for specialist housing despite abundant evidence that the majority of the older population do not, and will never, live in specialist housing or residential care settings of any kind.

There is no doubt that policy can never be entirely rational or always proceed in a straightforward direction. However, the absence of consistent age awareness in policy has led to divided opinions on how far the government's vision stretches (see Joseph Rowntree Foundation, 2004a, the forerunner to *Opportunity Age*).

Policy intent then is one thing and implementation is something else. Nowhere is this clearer than at regional and local levels where the broad brush of government policies are being worked out and enacted. For example, the implications of having an older population are barely referred to in emerging regional strategies including regional housing strategies, spatial strategies and rural strategies (see Joseph Rowntree Foundation, 2004b). Likewise the development of regional and sub-regional housing strategies has no connection with health strategies at a strategic health authority level despite the fact that the Department of Health is de facto leading most of the policy thinking and change on older age and housing.

The government is aware that there are problems and has responded. For example, the Office of the Deputy Prime Minister and the Department of Health, through the Housing for Older People Development Group, commissioned guidance on *Developing older people's strategies: Linking housing to health, social care and other local strategies* (ODPM and DH, 2003). The guidance promotes a broad whole systems approach which links housing into other aspects of older people's lives. It also addresses all older people, active as well as more vulnerable, across tenure and housing type rather than the traditional approach of focusing only on special needs. A whole systems approach (see Fletcher et al, 1999, for a discussion) can help plan for the whole older population and replaces approaches that focus on the minority, those who need significant levels of health and or social care services. Unfortunately, the guidance is permissive and the Office of the Deputy Prime Minister does not intend to make it compulsory.

To some extent the lack of compulsion is understandable given the pace of policy and regulatory change local authorities and other agencies have had to deal with, but slow changes are happening in any case. For example, a growing number of local authorities have commissioned specific housing strategies for older people based on the guidance. Some local authorities and their partners (usually local strategic partnerships) have gone further and are starting to overhaul their thinking and planning on older age and the implications for all policies. In some cases the catalyst is older people themselves, for example, Newcastle upon Tyne Elders Council produced an agenda for the future called *The way ahead* (Elders Council of Newcastle, 2003). The principles of the agenda, shown in Table 8.3, encapsulate what most of these strategic plans are aiming to reflect.

There are also good examples where older people are included in planning the future of their neighbourhoods.

Table 8.3: Principles and issues that are important to older people

Principles
• Being valued for their lives and experiences
• Being able to put forward their views and contribute
• Interdependence – older people as a resource working in partnership
• Addressing discrimination
• Having the choices and control to feel independent
• Having information and services that are accessible and joined up

Issues
• Lifelong learning
• Arts and culture
• Health and social care
• Housing
• Transport
• Finance and income
• Crime and community safety
• Environment
• Regeneration and building communities
• Equality and diversity

Strategies like the one being pursued in Newcastle upon Tyne show that there are good reasons why housing should not be considered as a policy strand on its own. Yet there is a long way to go to make the aspirations they contain come to fruition. Our work with local strategic partnerships to help them develop integrated older people's strategies has revealed deep cultural and practical problems that get in the way.

One of the problems is affordability. In general, affordability is applied to rented social housing and tends to be construed in terms of people of working age – housing costs are considered affordable in relation to earned income. There are also formulas that are applied to assess the affordability of housing for sale or part rent by younger low-income groups and key workers. However, housing affordability by older groups rarely comes into the equation at local levels and is not mentioned in national guidance and policies. There is no reason why local partnerships cannot apply imaginative approaches that meet the needs of their local populations, and some have done so, but lack of affordability criteria for older people tends to be used as an excuse to do nothing or apply inappropriate approaches. The imagination gap possibly stems from a tendency to concentrate service planning only on the poorest because this is how services have traditionally been planned. The assumption is that those who are not poor can afford to purchase what they need from the marketplace. Home ownership was traditionally out of the reach of most people in the UK so not surprisingly there is a close link between tenure and income in ideas about who services are for. In general, rented housing was assumed to be occupied by poorer people and services were planned around tenure. Yet older people are now owner-occupiers and many are not in receipt of high incomes, especially in advanced older age. Even if they are it does not necessarily follow that there are appropriate housing options and services that can be purchased. Affordability when applied as narrowly as it often is completely overlooks the older population and their diverse circumstances and needs.

Looking back, government policy from 1996 until now is often encouraging. However, departmentalism and a selective approach to older age are still dominant. No single department takes responsibility on its own for many of the services older people require or want. The fact that the policy direction is increasingly being driven by the Department of Health rather than the Office of the Deputy Prime Minister means that policy is not being formulated on a shared basis as much as we might be led to believe. Meanwhile, the Department for Work and Pensions, which is leading the strategy for older people (DWP, 2005), does not have any reason to lead on services that it does not have a duty to oversee. The cross-cutting issues that affect people's lives, such as transport that enables people to get about and see family and friends, go to the shops and reach services, are as important as housing and care. Yet cross-cutting issues somehow get left out of the mix by all departments.

Where are we going? Housing and services, consumption and lifestyles

Consumer studies indicate very clearly that an ageing population represents an economic opportunity for commerce, and new marketing approaches have appeared as a result (Szmigan and Carrigan, 2001). Lifestyle is important to people who are 'younger older', while care services and help with maintaining the home and obtaining other services are only a small part of the interests of those who are very old. The home is a source of wealth and the way many people express their identity. Studies by Warnes (1993), King et al (2000) and Heywood et al (2002) show that the home plays a range of roles in pre- and post-retirement strategies and aspirations. People make decisions linked to their lifestyles, dreams of a different life and desire to be closer to families. Decisions to move in younger old age can be, but are not always, different to those made in advanced age. The differences come with health status, security and safety and ability to continue to drive. Affluence and the means to make housing decisions linked to lifestyle are obviously integral to decision making but affluence does not guarantee a good outcome. Older people regularly report that it is difficult to find information on housing options, and there is a lack of a sufficiently wide range of types of housing and access to flexible services when they are needed in most if not all local areas. Having the means to pay has not increased supply or choice to the extent that is needed.

Low-income older groups also have dreams and aspirations. In a study of moves to social rented housing in seaside and rural areas by older people (Riseborough et al, 2001), we found that the same aspirations were expressed through these moves although it was difficult for people to realise them because moves were harder to achieve through social renting.

So far the housing market is responding only partially to the growing demands and desires of the older population. We have not yet grasped the heterogeneity of the older population in terms of developing future housing strategies and related planning requirements to support them. Blocks of flats are still being built without lifts, thereby excluding a key group – older people with a chronic condition – from living in them above the ground floor, even though they may well be able to care for themselves in other ways. Some older people are still moving into sheltered housing with traditional warden services – and having to pay for such services – because this is the only choice, not because they want such accommodation. For example, the recently published Older People's Housing Strategy for Hounslow identified a need to rebalance the tenure mix of sheltered housing available in the borough with more leasehold and shared ownership housing. The need was confirmed by sheltered housing for sale providers who identified a high demand among owner-occupiers, while local social landlords providing sheltered housing for rent reported that some homeowners were applying for rented sheltered housing because there were no suitable leasehold schemes in their area.

Diversity

There is a persistent tendency to overlook the kinds of needs and services that BME communities require, particularly where numbers of people from different BME groups are small. There are signs that BME communities are becoming better involved in planning services, but progress has been painfully slow. A discussion with a range of local authorities hosted by the Office of the Deputy Prime Minister and Department of Health-sponsored Housing and Older People Development Group (HOPDEV) in 2002 (see www.odpm.gov.uk/index) found that there had been little real progress in 15 years. There are lots of good practice examples and projects but BME elders and BME communities still tend to be on the edge. There are not enough services that respond to their needs and wishes appropriately. For example, in many local areas older people from BME communities do not know about the services that are available to older people in the area. Even when they do know about services, people often find the services are insensitive and inappropriate, for example, vegetarian meals are not routinely made available and not enough effort is made by commissioners to purchase services from suitable contractors.

It is doubtful whether the situation will improve to the extent that it needs to in the next 15 years. Starting from such a low base the outlook is very poor. It is unlikely that the supply will meet the needs and aspirations of the next cohort due to retire. Studies by MORI (Worcester, 2000), for example, indicate that the baby boomer generation, people approaching retirement now and in the next decade, have high lifestyle aspirations, and intend to pursue them provided they can afford to.

Yet the idea that older people might be significant in the housing market is still under-acknowledged and undeveloped. The first round of regional housing strategies said very little about them. Housing needs studies still tend to concentrate on frail older people rather than the older population as a whole. However, the growing realisation of the importance of older people in the workforce, and their importance to families as carers for grandchildren and others, is beginning to produce some changes.

A different approach to planning and conceptualising accommodation

Planning for the future needs to consider a different housing and age mix. It is not just about tenure or income groups – it should also be about facilitating the market to respond appropriately and balancing and mixing age groups. Older people are going to be the majority in many locations and they cannot be overlooked. In future planners may have to consider a mix of types of properties that explicitly enable people of all ages, regardless of disability or reduced mobility, to live there. This would make housing more flexible and suitable for everyone.

Planners need to be thinking about specifying a percentage of accessible housing – flats, cottages and bungalows, as well as houses. In rural and urban areas this is necessary to enable older people to stay in the areas they want or to be able to move to suitable properties if they wish. At the moment there is a distinct lack of suitable property that meets people's needs and aspirations. There are more single-person households and this trend will continue, but we also know that people want and need larger properties than those that are available now.

The Royal Town Planning Institute (RTPI) (2002) suggests that one of the difficulties lies in traditional conceptions of housing careers and how they inform what is built and for whom. It is also suggested that fewer people in future will want the starter homes that are planned for many of the 'growth areas', while regeneration plans that focus on city living are unlikely to appeal to the growing older population. We believe that the RTPI's predictions are in keeping with trends noted so far for urban to rural migration, although our work suggests that some groups of older people *would* be interested in city and town living. For example, people want to be closer to facilities and services in advanced older age and/or want to enjoy the cultural and other aspects of urban life including work. At the moment regeneration plans for cities and towns pay little attention to them.

There are strong views in some quarters that if enough accessible housing was developed, with flexible practical and support services available, then almost all older people would opt to remain living in ordinary housing until they die. However, there are equally strong views that other factors, such as pressures on the availability of care workers and the costs of providing practical and care services to older people in general needs housing, make the above scenario unattainable, even if it was the first choice option. This means that there is a continuing role for specialist accommodation.

The future for specialist accommodation

Movements in the commercial specialist accommodation market suggest that investors and care home owners believe that care homes and nursing homes will still be important in the future. As a result, while the number of residential care homes is declining overall, private care home providers are still building new care homes despite governmental preferences for extra-care provision. There are several reasons for this. Commercial providers believe that care and nursing homes are cheaper to run and affordability arguments are understood by consumers, relatives and the state (which often 'buys' places in these homes). There is also a sense of caution because extra-care is relatively untested in commercial terms. On the other hand, commercial providers are aware of changes in consumer preferences and some are hedging their bets by developing residential care homes with extra-care 'wings' (Laing & Buisson, 2004). Others are building flats or bungalows in the grounds of existing care homes. These are sold on the basis that care and support from staff in care homes can be provided flexibly to people purchasing units. This model is often called 'assisted living' or 'close care'.

The costs question is a vexed issue. The drive from government and some local authorities to develop extra-care housing has arisen partly because it is seen as a cheaper option. The commercial sector obviously thinks differently. Our experience suggests that costs are often higher in extra-care compared to residential care (see Fletcher et al, 1999). The main difference is a cost shunt. Where costs would fall on the state the responsibility for paying costs for housing and support can be shifted from a social services department to Housing Benefit and *Supporting People*.

As far as demand is concerned, there is plenty of evidence that older people are opting for extra-care. However, interviews with extra-care residents (Fletcher et al, 1999) show that it is a compromise rather than a first choice housing option. There are also indications that extra-care does not attract many active older people and this affects the fundamental proposition that extra-care offers a livelier, less 'care'-oriented setting.

Extra-care is only one example of quite new specialist accommodation types and another is the retirement village. There is a lack of knowledge about their role in promoting a good older age and their sustainability. We also do not know if older people are moving to them as a housing option – 'pull' factors – or whether they are moving because they feel vulnerable and need support – 'push' factors. Despite the absence of good knowledge there are plans in many regions to build retirement villages and some are very large in scale, for example, Reeve Court Retirement Village in St Helens developed by St Helens and Arena Housing Associations and run by the Extra-Care Charitable Trust, or the planned village in Hartlepool being developed by the Joseph Rowntree Housing Trust.

In addition to these models, there is also sheltered housing of various types and supported housing developed along the lines of assisted living units or small domestic scale homes where occupants have their own flat with a live-in support staff. Putting them all together, there is a growing menu of choice but consumers, the government or the commercial sector favour certain options even when the evidence is not established.

What seems to be emerging is that some specialist housing options are being colonised by health and social care as substitutes for residential care. We think that this trend will continue not only because housing interests are being overtaken by those of health and social care planners, but also because older people tend to see such housing as an accommodation *and* care option. As a result there is no doubt that there will be increased growth in extra-care and retirement villages, and we are currently estimating the level of expected growth. There are dangers associated with this growth largely because there is not enough evidence to suggest that future cohorts of older people will be attracted to them. At the same time if choice over housing expands in the mainstream it is unlikely that sufficient people would choose this provision.

Housing is not the only thing that planners and others need to address. The environment, transport and access to shops and facilities are just as important as having a good range of housing. Research on moves to other areas by older people (Riseborough et al, 2001) showed that these other factors were as important as, if not more than, the housing itself in making decisions about staying put or moving in older age. Older people compromise over the housing or accommodation they select, from a narrow range of choices, in order to be in the locations they want.

The most important findings coming out of consumer research on moving decisions are that older people want more choice, do not want to be labelled and need good information to be able to make the right decision at the right time for them. Good housing, on its own, without the right environment and services around it, is not enough. Nor is more choice likely to be a reality if older people do not know what options are available. It is difficult to foretell in detail what the market will look like in 2020 but we can be certain that, since expectations and aspirations have risen in the present older generation, future older cohorts will want more choice and flexibility in terms of housing and tenure options and how to pay.

Retirement pathways

Housing is linked to changing experiences of moving into retirement from the paid workforce. There are strong indications now that retirement pathways are changing. More people are already working beyond state retirement age, more are entering self-employment and these trends will continue. We think there will be impacts on life and home preferences and needs. However, we do not know what these will be or how they will translate into housing, and research on these topics is needed.

Money, housing and future age

Looking at people who are retired now, one of the clearest trends is that people tend to get poorer as they get older because they erode the assets they have accumulated or their incomes are worth less. Women, particularly single women, amass less wealth, assets and pensions in their working years, which affects them in later life. However, women born in the 1960s are participating more in the labour force compared to previous generations, and we might expect the outlook for women to be better (Evandrou and Falkingham, 2004). Unfortunately women still tend to accumulate less. Research by Rowlingson et al (1999) showed that in 1995/96, working-age women had saved an average of £2,000 compared with men's £13,000. Women also had slightly more assets in state rather than in occupational pensions.

Older people from BME groups feature strongly in the poorest groups, while people who never participated in the paid labour force, had broken job histories and poor health, or lost their place in the labour market also tend to have very low incomes in older age. Current trends suggest that men in particular tend to leave the labour market before retirement. The New Deal has been extended to include 'older' workers as a result. One of the theories put forward by the government and some economists is that if the right conditions are in place to encourage people to work for longer, people would not only be able to add to their retirement income but some low-income problems could be overcome as well (DWP, 2004). Proposals along these lines include more private sector style arrangements, such as protected annuity schemes that could pay out a lump sum to another beneficiary if the holder dies before the annuity matures. In addition, there are proposals to make membership of occupational pensions compulsory.

In the 1980s and 1990s, older people's share of income and wealth improved, but it is unclear if the general trend will continue in the same way. Some of the cohort immediately in front of the baby boomers did very well out of the state earnings related pension scheme (SERPS), occupational and private pensions, property investments and savings schemes, largely because of stable employment and a thriving economy including an overheated housing market. Current trends for baby boomers suggest that more people have assets to draw on, largely as a result of home ownership. However, there are many demands on the incomes of the baby boomer generation, including maintaining children in further and higher education. In addition, baby boomers owe more and levels of debt are higher among people getting closer to retirement than in the past (Huber and Skidmore, 2003).

Home ownership increased rapidly in the 1980s and then grew more slowly between the 1990s and the first two years of this century (68% of all households in 1991 to 71% in 2002-03 in England and Wales). Estimates on the value of property vary. For example, research by the Council of Mortgage Lenders (2001) suggested that older homeowners have more than £400 billion worth of equity in property. Older homeowners currently draw on little more than 1% of equity. Will baby boomers be any different?

A lack of trusted products, along with lack of awareness, are thought to be key reasons why current older homeowners have been unwilling to use equity release to buy services they want or to fund essential repairs and adaptations. Other reasons are linked to a strong belief that they should not have to draw on an asset they worked hard for and a desire to pass on the benefits to kin. In contrast, baby boomers report that they intend to be less cautious than previous generations (Huber and Skidmore, 2003). MORI calls baby boomers the SKIN (Spend the Kids' Inheritance Now) generation (Worcester, 2000). Baby boomers actually seem to be accumulating assets in order to *enjoy* them. Far from expecting to have to accumulate more in order to provide for a longer period in retirement because we are living longer, the idea seems to be to retire early if possible and to spend the money on activities people want do (Martin, 2003; Metz and Underwood, 2004).

Second home ownership is on the increase. Housing statistics for England in 2003-04 show that 298,000 households had a second home in England (excluding those held solely as an investment) and 178,000 had second homes outside Britain (ODPM, 2005). The most common reasons for a second home were a holiday or retirement home (38%), having an investment (40%) or working away from home (10%) (ODPM, 2002). Parents of students are also among the groups that have retained an interest. This is partly because purchases can be made to yield an income through house and flat sharing with other students and partly because parents want to protect their children from the worst experiences of student lets (*The Guardian*, 21 September 2002). Baby boomers are doing all of these things and there are likely to be complicated effects on incomes in older age.

Consumer research across Europe suggests that hedonism is on the rise. Worcester (2000) characterises the changes as the move from saving to *savouring* time. Baby boomers are said to have less respect for authority, traditional institutions or organisations. They are more articulate and are quick to voice dissent or dissatisfaction. They have highly developed networks, enjoy a variety of different leisure and cultural activities, consume more and travel further afield than previous generations. Above all many do not see the point in saving for the future if it involves not being able to enjoy it when they get there because of ill health or even death.

Predictions for the generation behind the baby boomers, people aged 21-42, indicate that the gaps we are seeing now between the affluent and less affluent are likely to deepen in later age in future. There will be effects on people who are older in 2020, but it will most dramatically affect people who are in or approaching middle age. Meanwhile the youngest adults on modest to low incomes seem to be facing a very insecure future. Research by the National Consumer Council (NCC, 2002) showed that very few of the younger generation are saving or contributing to pensions of any kind. Few younger people on modest to low incomes had any disposable income left over to contribute to their future retirement, they did not regard saving for retirement as a high priority, and had few expectations that the state would help in the future.

Housing, technology and future age

It is often said that technology does not mean much to older people and technology tends to be seen as an interesting but not essential subject. For example, in discussions about the impact of call centres on older people, one often hears that older people really want a personal relationship or a person to respond rather than a machine. Yet, there is no evidence that all older people think like this. Instead there is evidence that people are getting used to technologies of all kinds. People who own or have access to PCs, for example, are likely to want to continue to use them in later age. Over 30% of people who are now older own or have access to a PC and use the Internet (Age Concern England, 2004). Education and health status, particularly the ability to see the screen or keyboard, response time and levels of manual dexterity, make a difference to how people perceive this kind of technology and their willingness to learn/use it.

Internet shopping, chat rooms, hobby exchange and e-mail communications can also be facilitated through PCs, and cheap systems linked to wireless technology and broadband are being installed in many private sector and social extra-care housing schemes and ordinary housing for sale. They are also being installed in village halls and rural settings across England and Wales.

There is an exploding market of new products and services, particularly in the US and Japan. In the UK interest in technological solutions has tended to be confined to younger and middle-aged and baby boomer groups, but this is changing. Among the many products and services coming onto the market are new diagnostic tools (Viacom), wireless technology-aided services that can support passive monitoring of lifestyles, provide cheap communication, facilitate door, window and curtain opening, burglar and smoke control and sense if domestic equipment and appliances are being used safely. Sensors can also prevent gas escapes, domestic floods caused by water overflows and monitor 'wandering'. These products are increasingly being used as part of the range of community equipment, telecare or telehealth options to enable people to self-care for longer. Many are still being worked into mainstream services, for example, pilots in Kent and County Durham will be integrated into long-term plans and services by local strategic partnerships, but the potential for growth can be seen.

There is a great interest among policy makers to encourage technological solutions that enable people to self-manage and self-care. For example, the Department of Health has established a Policy Collaborative on Assistive Technology and a fund of £80 million for 2006-08. The Department of Health will be giving all social services authorities a grant from the fund in 2006 to help stimulate thinking and good practice on assistive technology and telecare. This aims to benefit the whole population, not just older people. Interest includes developing some of the products and 'solutions' described earlier. PC-driven and stand-alone computer diagnostic and health monitoring aids have been developed and are being used widely in the US. They are currently being examined in UK pilots (for example, Kent Telemedicine Project).

Technological advances can be seen as part of one's lifestyle, health and well-being, they help people to maintain their home and keep it accessible and manageable, but they can also be seen as part of attempts by the state to fill the gap left by a lack of personal care, health and support staff. A mix of all factors is actually at work. There is little doubt that in future more will be expected from people to self-care and there will be fewer face-to-face contacts. However, it also seems reasonable to say that older people will expect to have an array of products, services and gadgets to help them lead their lives, and technology will be integral to this.

Work and future age

It is likely that over time the age at which people are expected to retire (currently linked to eligibility for the state pension in most instances) and due to increase between 2010 and 2020 across the UK will increase again. The Confederation of British Industry recently floated the idea that the state retirement pension age should be raised to 70 by 2030 (BBC News, 30 November 2004). Government actuarial predictions on the percentage of GDP (Gross Domestic Product) that will have to be transferred to support state retirement incomes and keep pensioners well-off relative to average net incomes indicate that retirement ages would have to rise to 69.8 years (GAD, 2003b).

Whatever the outcome is, in the future it is clear that some people, particularly those on the lowest incomes, will have no choice but to work into older age. Unpaid work will also increase since the rise of older people caring for the even older will increase, as will demands from younger members of families for help with childcare. There are knock-on effects for other unpaid work including contributions to voluntary and community activities. Older people contribute substantially to volunteering but their participation is decreasing and further decreases are likely.

A changing experience of older age

Whatever being older means it does not mean that there is a process everyone goes through which defines a person internally and externally as old. There are huge debates between older groups about what old means and research among different cohorts in the older population conclusively demonstrates that one label, one experience, does not fit. As the younger population declines there are signs that middle-aged and younger old people (for example, people under 70) want to hang on to youth and are actively rejecting notions of ageing and behaviours that may stereotypically be associated with becoming mature (see Metz and Underwood, 2004).

Does this mean that 60 will be the new 50, or 70 the new 60? Morbidity trends so far indicate that most ill health, disability and needs for intensive support and care occur in the 'fourth age', the last years of life. We do not know if this will continue or if morbidity in older age will be compressed even further. What we do know is that there are distinct differences in people's experience of, and attitude towards, older age, but there are few signs that this is acknowledged and taken seriously by planners. The real challenge will come from the growing majority, and the market will have to respond. This is already happening in terms of insurance products, leisure, holidays, beauty products, sport and fitness and other areas, but there will be significant changes ahead.

Challenges

Policy, practice and housing theory

This chapter illustrates that we know a lot about some things and we can say with some certainty where current trends will take us, but there are also many unknowns.

One of the really striking things is how long it has taken policy makers to make slow and unremarkable changes. Having an aging population is something that is happening now and was predicted. It will take far too long at the rate we are going to adjust to meet the needs and aspirations of the population as it continues to age. Will more exhortation do the trick? Are any radical policies on the horizon that will dramatically seek to redress imbalances in incomes and wealth, the choice to retire or work and to ensure that housing and services will appear to meet the needs and aspirations for the whole and increasingly diverse older population? Although there has been a lot of policy change, and much of this is in the right direction, a radical approach of the kind we describe is not on the agenda in the near future. The importance of the older vote and the influence of a growing older majority in the population could bring further changes, but a highly organised campaign would be needed to do this.

It is crystal clear that the experience of being older and what it means has changed and will continue to change. There is no excuse for formulating or implementing policies on the basis that older people will not be concerned or affected. Yet this chapter illustrates the persistence of myths and social constructions of older age, and how they get in the way of planning for the future in every sense. We described how they blinker approaches to housing and communities, and how out-of-step such approaches are in the face of a changing population and all that this implies. There is no doubt that life experiences and opportunities in younger life have a direct bearing on the health, housing and incomes people have in later life. In reality the vast majority of older people now live independent, active lives, in their own homes and contribute to life around them. This is not to say that we should forget that low income and poverty is still a feature of older life for many, as is bereavement, isolation and poor health, but none of these experiences are rounded ways to describe people. They are not the salient characteristics we would use to describe another age group in the population.

What needs to change

The baby boomer generation challenges current policy thinking and responses to older age and this chapter has described some of the impacts and implications.

Ageism is deeply embedded in policy, practice and academic research and has to be challenged. There are conceptual and equality issues that need to be tackled. There are shortcomings in concepts, such as tenure, commonly used to draw distinctions and to describe the relationships between different housing ownership and rental arrangements. Tenure in itself does not tell us very much about the role that housing plays in older people's lives, nor does it capture anything of the changing relationship people have with housing and their lifestyles. The notion of housing careers as a way of expressing how people move through housing in their lifetimes prevents policy makers and professional practitioners from including the older population with a range of housing demands in plans for the present and the future.

Housing, accommodation and older age has close links with a welfare approach devised as part of the advent of the welfare state in the UK. Enabling people to retire with a state-funded pension rather than having to work in order to survive, and giving them access to decent affordable housing, were key tenets of the post-Second World War welfare settlement. The same principles are still worth pursuing, but as this chapter shows, there are many shifts and changes that need to be taken into account to plan for a changing older population.

A summary of key challenges

- There is a need to address ageism and the inequalities that it masks.
- Mechanisms and policies need to be developed that can integrate policy planning and implementation across departmental and functional boundaries.
- Traditional assumptions in planning for older age that focus on the most dependent, the poorest but actively disable and abandon the majority need to be replaced. Instead policy and planning should be informed by good research that pays attention to older people in the housing market and wider accommodation system including extra-care, residential care and retirement villages.
- Policy makers, practitioners and students should be encouraged to understand the poverty of current concepts and thinking. We are just beginning to understand the importance of lifestyles and transitions in the third and fourth age and we need these concepts and understanding to be part of mainstream thinking, planning and education.
- The place housing occupies in policy is changing. Whatever housing policy was it is not now. Housing practitioners and researchers need to understand and participate in these changes.

Questions and issues

Wealth and poverty

Present trends suggest that there will be extremes of affluence and poverty among future older cohorts but they will affect people at the tail end of the baby boomer generation and cohorts behind them, particularly after 2040. We do not know how many people could be affected and we cannot predict how baby boomers will actually behave as opposed to what they say they will do later. Their actions and their willingness to force changes in economic policy, welfare and taxation will affect the future. Will this be an opportunity to achieve a new social and economic contract across the generations? We do not know, but we do know that the coming of the baby boomers into older age has the potential to overturn conventional thinking and practice.

Public services

So far neither public services nor the not-for-profit sector have responded by providing or commissioning the diverse services that older people want. The market has responded in some ways but not others, and there are huge implications from this. There are indications that many people who are in the oldest groups now have an enduring belief in the reliability of public-run services. However, the vast majority of older people rarely come into contact with public services and there is strong evidence that younger older people do not think public services are attractive or relevant.

Will public services respond to a changing older population? Will we see public services facilitating and brokering arrangements so that the majority as well as the minority can have accommodation, care, health, support and housing arrangements that will be a good standard, reliable, secure and trustworthy? Will public services change their stance and practice and acknowledge that older people often know what is best? Will public services influence the market and work with it so that there are better and more appropriate services to meet the needs of a diverse older population? Some of the trends we have described, where authorities and partners are taking a lead role to strategically intervene and plan services, including encouraging the private sector to provide services that would be useful, indicate that public services can have a beneficial role. However, the high-level strategic planning that this kind of intervention demands is very new, and implementing plans depends on complex agreements and a common vision and culture with many agencies. Public services could and arguably should hold the ring, but will they have the capacity to do this and the resources?

The labour market

Older people will form a significant part of the labour force but how will they fare? Resistance to employing older workers is already high so what are the implications from current policies to ensure that there are more? Employment practice tends to negate the skills and contributions that older workers can contribute, but will the shortages of younger recruits make a difference? So far some employers are responding to the ageing of the workforce and to initiatives such as New Deal to encourage people over the age of 50 back into the workforce. However, progress is slow. We do not know how much this will change, but we do know that there are already more older people in the paid workforce, and we need to know much more about their reasons for continuing to stay in the workforce and their experience given other demands on their time, and how people combine paid and unpaid work with getting older.

Shortages of labour and a lack of skills in certain trades and occupations are already causing major problems. Lack of people willing to fill care, nursing and support jobs poses real challenges for the future. Immigrant labour is filling some of the gaps but there are tensions of all kinds as a result.

The government is currently pinning its hopes on a formula for creating a range of opportunities and services for people in older age, which is only partly developed and unlikely to have all the answers. The formula depends on people continuing to be healthy, taking appropriate decisions about their own older age that will enable them to self-care and manage for as long as possible, and on most people being able to pay for accommodation and suitable services. Technology and design are also expected to fulfil different roles in older people's lives, enabling them to carry out certain everyday tasks that would otherwise be labour-intensive. We have described some of these things earlier. However, there is a long way to go before technology, equipment and aids and adaptations, housing and accommodation design and so on will be widely available to people who are older. The investment needed to develop products and services is also a problem. The market is responding to some extent, and there are likely to be big developments over the next 10 years but it could be much longer before major changes are seen. There are challenges as a result for many of the assisted living, extra-care, supported housing and support services that have been part of the continued evolution of community care. Will we go back to a kind of volume-based residential care model as a result because they are less labour-intensive and the costs are lower and easier to understand?

Will we see older people caring for other older people and being paid for it? This is one scenario that policy makers have tackled but only indirectly. Informal care is heavily relied on currently and the intention to extend Direct Payments to older people who are assessed as needing social care services so they can purchase the services they want rather than those they are offered means that we could see older workers in formal caring jobs. However, we could also see older people entering or continuing in the labour force in other jobs with severe impacts on informal care and family support.

Notes

[1] The chapter avoids defining the older population because this is well rehearsed elsewhere. On the other hand, concepts such as ageing as part of the life course, transitions, life stages and the emergence of the third age are pivotal because they contest normative definitions derived largely from the medical model of older age (see, for example, Phillipson, 1998 and Reed et al, 2004 for discussions). We also dispute normative definitions and acknowledge that there are many ways to describe older people, but the chapter draws attention to the ways older people are actually described and categorised in policy, practice and research. While we do this in order to make their usage explicit, we do not necessarily agree with their application.

[2] There have been several waves of baby boomers. In this chapter we are describing people born in the UK between 1945 and 1965.

References

ADSS (Association of Directors of Social Services) and LGA (Local Government Association) (2003) *All our tomorrows: Inverting the triangle of care*, London: ADSS.

Age Concern England (2004) *Older people in the UK: General statistics: Leisure, learning and computers. Fact card*, London: Age Concern England.

Age Concern England and ITC (2000) *Television and the over 50s: A study of portrayal, representation and viewing*, London: Age Concern England.

Audit Commission (2004) *Older people, independence and well-being: The challenge for public services*, London: Audit Commission.

Bevan, M., Crouch, K., Fletcher, P. and Riseborough, M. (forthcoming) *The housing needs of older people in the countryside*, London: Countryside Agency/DEFRA.

Bytheway, B. (1995) *Ageism*, Buckingham: Open University Press.

CML (Council of Mortgage Lenders) (2001) 'The time is right to develop equity release', Press release, 5 November.

DEFRA (Department for Environment, Food and Rural Affairs) (2004) *Rural strategy*, London: DEFRA.

DH (Department of Health) (1998) *Modernising social services: Promoting independence, improving protection, raising standards*, Cm 4169, London: The Stationery Office.

DH (2000) *The NHS Plan: A plan for investment, a plan for reform*, Cm 4818-1, London: Crown Copyright.

DH (2005) *Independence, well being and choice: Our vision for the future of social care for adults in England*, London: Crown Copyright.

DTI (Department of Trade and Industry) (2000) *Ageing population panel report*, London: DTI.

DTLR (Department for Transport, Local Government and the Regions) and DH (Department of Health) (2001) *Quality and choice for older people's housing: A strategic framework*, London: The Stationery Office.

Durham and Districts Supporting People Partnership (2005) *Five-Year Supporting People Strategy 2005–2010* (www.spkweb.org.uk).

DWP (Department for Work and Pensions) (2004) *Pensions Green Paper: Simplicity, security and choice: Informed choices for working, saving and choice*. London: DWP.

DWP (2005) *Opportunity age: Meeting the challenges of age in the 21st century*, London: Crown Copyright, March.

Elders Council of Newcastle (2003) *The way ahead: Elders Council of Newcastle action plan*, Newcastle upon Tyne: Newcastle Health Cities Project.

Evandrou, M. and Falkingham, J. (2004) 'How will tomorrow's elders differ from today's differentials in socio-economic characteristics between and within birth cohorts?', Presentation at the British Society for Population Studies 'Planning Data Needs for an Aging Society' Conference, London, 26 April.

Fletcher, P., Riseborough, M., Humphries, J., Jenkins, C. and Whittingham, P. (1999) *Citizenship and services in older age: The strategic role of very sheltered housing*, Beaconsfield: Housing 21.

FPLD (Foundation for People with Learning Disabilities) (2003) *Planning for tomorrow*, London: FPLD.

GAD (Government Actuary's Department) (2003a) *Principal projections*, London: GAD.

GAD (2003b) *Impact of the 2003-based population projections*, London: GAD.

Guardian, The (2002) 'When it's home from home', 21 September.

Heywood, F., Oldman, C. and Means, R. (2002) *Housing and home in later life*, Buckingham: Open University Press.

Housing Corporation, The (2002) *Housing policy for older people*, London: The Housing Corporation.

Huber, J. and Skidmore, P. (2003) *The new old: Why baby boomers won't be pensioned off*, London: DEMOS.

Joseph Rowntree Foundation (2004a) *Consultation response to 'DWP: Link age'*, York: Joseph Rowntree Foundation, November.

Joseph Rowntree Foundation (2004b) *From welfare to well-being: Planning for an ageing society. Report from the Task Group on Housing, Money and Care for Older People*, York: Joseph Rowntree Foundation.

Kent Supporting People (2005) *Five-Year Strategy 2005-2010* (www.spkweb.org.uk).

King, D. (ed) (2001) *Changing households, changing housing markets*, London: Council of Mortgage Lenders.

King, R., Warnes, T. and Williams, A. (2000) *Sunset lives: British retirement migration to the Mediterranean*, Oxford: Berg Publishers.

Laing & Buisson (2004) *Care of elderly people – UK market survey 2004*, London: Laing & Buisson.

Martin, A. (2003) *Grey power/The grey ahead*, London: MORI.

Means, R. (1999) 'Housing and housing organisations: a review of their contribution to alternative models of care for older people', in Royal Commission, *Research Volume 2 of the Report on Long Term Care*, London: The Stationery Office.

Metz, D. and Underwood, M. (2004) *Older, richer, fitter*, London: Age Concern Books.

NCC (National Consumer Council) (2002) *No nest egg: Research into attitudes of younger consumers to saving for retirement*, London: NCC.

NISRA (Northern Ireland Statistics and Research Agency) (2003) *Mid-year population estimates*, Belfast: NISRA.

ODPM (Office of the Deputy Prime Minister) (2002) *Survey of English housing 2002/3*, London: ODPM.

ODPM (2003) *Sustainable Communities: Building for the future*, London: ODPM.

ODPM (2005) *Housing in England 2003/4. Part 2: Owner occupiers and second homes*, London: ODPM.

ODPM and DH (2003) *Developing older people's strategies: Linking housing to health, social care and other local strategies*, London: DH.

ONS (Office for National Statistics) (2004) *Housing in England 2002/03. A report principally from the 2002/03 Survey of English Housing*, London: Crown Copyright.

Pensions Commission (2004) *Pensions: Challenges and choices, The first report of the Pensions Commission*, London: The Stationery Office, October.

Phillipson, C. (1998) *Reconstructing old age: New agendas in social theory and social practice*, London: Sage Publications.

Pickard, S. (2002) 'Involvement of family carers in the personal care of older people', *Research Findings Register*, London: DH.

Reed, J., Cook, G., Childs, S. and Hall, A. (2004) *Getting old is not for cowards: Comfortable, healthy ageing*, York: Joseph Rowntree Foundation.

Riseborough, M., Fletcher, P. and Mullins, D. (2001) *What future for category one sheltered housing? Updating policy and practice*, Birmingham: CURS, University of Birmingham and The Housing Corporation.

Rowlingson, K., Whyly, C. and Warren, T. (1999) *Wealth in Britain: A life cycle perspective*, London: Policy Studies Institute.

RTPI (2002) *Planning for an ageing population*, London: RTPI.

SEU (Social Exclusion Unit) (2005) *Excluded older people: Social Exclusion Unit interim report*, London: ODPM.

Szmigan, I. and Carrigan, M. (2001) 'Learning to love the older consumer', *Journal of Consumer Behaviour: An International Research Review*, vol 21, no 13, pp 22-35.

Tulle Winterton, E. (1999) 'Growing old and resistance to a new cultural economy of old age?', *Ageing and Society*, vol 19, no 3, pp 281-300.

Warnes, A.M. (1993) 'The development of retirement migration in Great Britain', *Espace, Populations, Societies*, vol 3, pp 431-55.

Welsh Assembly (2003) *A strategy for older people in Wales*, Cardiff: Welsh Assembly.

Worcester, R.M. (2000) *Challenges of the demographic shift. Foresight Ageing Population Panel*, London: MORI.

NINE

Tenant futures: the future of tenants in social housing

Phil Morgan

Introduction

This chapter looks at the role of tenants in social housing in 2025. It seeks to explore trends that are already apparent and to ask some uncomfortable questions about the housing futures of both tenants and landlords. The chapter aims to be, in equal parts, predictive, aspirational and provocative. It is not, however, a solo effort, and thanks go to a number of TPAS (Tenant Participation Advisory Service) staff and activists for their earlier commentary. The responsibility for the chapter is, however, mine alone.

Tenants in 2025 will not be the same as tenants today, and so this chapter sets out opportunities which, if realised, would show that social housing has the ability to broaden its appeal. As a result 'tenants' will become a more diverse group. The name 'tenant' will become increasingly anachronistic as social housing creates new types of 'ownership'. Tenants will also have the ability to choose between different types of tenancies depending on their circumstances, and, in certain circumstances, be able to choose different landlords. Finally, tenants will see two types of social landlord services: first, the delivery of direct services, which will include a range of rents, services and equity; and, second, the ability to be part of successful communities through the social landlord's advocacy role, currently articulated through the National Housing Federation's 'In Business' campaign.

Who will be the tenants?

In order to discuss 'tenants', we need to understand who the tenants will be. An obvious trend is the increasing concentration of the most socially excluded into social housing. As the Right to Buy and increasing affluence take more tenants away from social housing, the remaining stock inevitably becomes focused on those for whom home ownership is unattainable. This results in social housing becoming the tenure of no choice, which makes it harder to sustain an attractive product for social housing as 'why bother, they've got no choice anyway' takes hold in the mindset of politicians and housing providers. Social housing should not be about having no choice, it does not have to be about having no choice, and it can have a clear future.

Younger tenants

There is a group of younger, middle-class, aspirational people who cannot afford to buy (and who will define their 'poverty' by that lack of ability to buy). The current housing market does not fulfil the demands of those who aspire to home ownership but who cannot, because of the currently inflated housing market, afford to buy. This group are also not in sufficient need to access social housing and their aspirations would tend to make them reluctant applicants in any case because of the perceived stigma attached. Although the house price bubble may burst, student debt is likely to be higher in future, further restricting home ownership immediately post-university.

For graduates, the ability to either work off student debt and/or to raise a deposit for a future property is important and could be a normal part of a young person's life between the ages of 22 and 26 or later. This points to a different product than what is currently offered, and one aimed at a short-term lease, of, say, three to five years, including elements of rent, minimal services and the conversion of some of that rent into equity at the end of a lease. That equity would be the most obvious attraction, allowing accumulation of a deposit for home ownership. In addition, the minimal services would be an introduction to the world of taking responsibility for the well-being of property. It would also allow a degree of flexibility in people's lives during a time, at the start of their careers, when they may want to move around more. Social housing is well placed to offer such an arrangement – it is able to provide a bridge between student renting and home ownership, and could be trusted to provide good-quality accommodation.

Older tenants

As discussed in Chapter Eight, older people are an increasingly numerous and diverse group. Among them is a set of people with limited pensions and substantial capital assets in their homes, for whom a social landlord with the ability to release equity and maintain the fabric of their home would be a viable option. Over the past five years there have been sharp reductions in the stock market and annuity rates, with a profound knock-on effect on the ability of pensions to keep pace with expectations. This has come at the same time as sharp rises in the housing market, leaving two groups of people: those who got on the property ladder early and are comparatively well-off in terms of capital, and those who did not and are not. Thus we have, in the first group, people who are approaching old age with limited pensions and lots of tied-up capital who will want to release that capital to enjoy a good standard of life without it all going to their children. There are already lifetime mortgages and home reversion schemes. However, social landlords have the unique ability to create opportunities for older homeowners who wish to release equity and relieve themselves of the burden of looking after their property. It is possible to envisage a market that would see larger proportions of capital realised, rent paid, maintenance of the property taken care of, all at minimal risk as the landlord would have the capital value of the property to fall back on. The selling points are the care of the property, which could tie into rent or further release of equity, and that social landlords are not tainted with the uneven reputation of the private financial market.

Rewards and incentives

One of the points made by tenants is that a disproportionate amount of attention is devoted to difficult and undeserving tenants, and nothing positive happens to 'good' tenants. However, links can be made between successful tenants and various rewards – either individual or collective – building on elements of the approach pioneered by Irwell Valley Housing Association (Hembrow and Wadhams, 2003; ODPM, 2003). It is worth making the point that there is a subtle but important difference between incentives and rewards for what landlords want from tenants, and the volunteer ethos that still drives a substantial proportion of vital community activity.

There is also the possibility of incentivising involvement in the local community such as school governors, local boards, youth groups, environmental groups and religious activities, which could also tie into both the demand for such people and their interest in accruing capital as a reward for such engagement. TPAS work on rewards for volunteers points to an increasing interest by landlords in rewards and incentives. We could see the creation of rewards schemes tying in with short-term (three to five year) leases aimed at recent graduates and young people. These will be connected with building up an asset base for those young people and rewarding their involvement in that local community. At the end of the lease (and not before) a guaranteed amount will be available as equity, plus a proportion of the increase in the value of the property.

New approach, not just new products

While this chapter identifies two new groups of potential tenants in younger and older people, it is also about creating a new approach to social housing. Simply creating two new products and ignoring issues for the no-choice tenants does not really solve another problem. TPAS have long believed that the lack of 'ownership' status of tenants results in poorer services and they have wanted to blur the edges of home ownership (which in many cases means you own a small part of your home) and renting (which means you still live somewhere you call home but without the same view of 'ownership'). The idea of a future where existing tenure categories become less clear-cut connects to the argument developed by Alan Murie (see Chapter Two).

This is also an issue for the persistently poor who find it increasingly difficult to get on the cycle of home (or any other kind of) ownership, as prices reflect the legacy of homeowners passing on their assets to their homeowning children. It is now becoming harder, not easier, for children born in poverty to escape from it as wealth becomes increasingly concentrated among those who own property. Therefore the government should have an interest in supporting even comparatively small amounts of ownership.

Future changes would be summarised as:

- The creation of a new market for homeowners reaching old age to liquidise their capital asset into cash for spending. This new market will require both financial capacity and the ability for someone to manage the resulting split asset. The current restrictions on both type and amount that can be borrowed need to be relaxed as housing associations take on both the funding and management role in exchange for rental stream within their not-for-profit ethos.
- The creation of short-term (three to five year) leases aimed at recent graduates and young people.
- The introduction of equity stakes for four purposes:
  – to create opportunities for home ownership by helping form a deposit;

    – to break down the barriers of 'ownership' in terms of services;
    – to create a capital resource, able to borrowed against, for small
      enterprises; and
    – to incentivise good behaviour.

It is plausible to foresee three types of 'tenant' emerging:

• 'mature' owners with a relationship with a social landlord;
• 'aspiring' owners with a relationship with a social landlord; and
• 'tenants' with no choice.

Strictly speaking they are all tenants of some kind, but it is unlikely that the phrase 'tenant' would be used for either of the first or second groupings. In fact, forward thinking social landlords would start marketing themselves as 'cradle-to-grave' partners, able to fit into people's complex lives and allowing staircasing up and down of assets and repairs, much in the same ways as leading financial institutions do. Some may go even further and align themselves to those financial institutions to create a menu of services for a far wider range of customers than is currently the case.

If the product was sufficiently flexible it could help to create a different ethos around social housing. Flexibility could include the possibility of different combinations of rent, service, equity and wider issues around empowerment and community. It is not just about creating two new types of tenant – it is about creating a new approach to tenants that includes those two types.

Choice and customers

All political parties now talk the language of choice. The most recent symbol is choice-based lettings, although it is too early to tell what impact this will have. In the late 1990s declining numbers in some areas of social housing meant talk of reluctant customers and social housing needing to make itself more attractive to retain its viability. Now the increase in demand and house prices mean that, with the exception of a few areas of long-term decline, social housing does not need to be 'attractive' to anyone – it just waits for the queues to form of those in need and those unable to buy. Although there has been a North–South divide, expressed crudely as low-demand North and high-demand South, many parts of the 'North' now have rising demand. There will remain some areas in the North (currently known as market renewal pathfinders, see Chapter Five, this volume) where both discontinuity in the labour and housing markets, combined with lack of demand for some types of housing, will result in low demand, although these remain exceptions.

Although macro-economic policies and the slow increase in house building will eventually dampen demand for social housing across most of England, the good news for social housing providers is that demand will mean they do not have to worry about choice.

Or will they?

Even where there is a limited supply of housing, people will exercise choice, and creating no-choice housing simply means that as soon as people can exercise a choice then they will move, or they will resent their no-choice housing and express this in negative ways.

Choice over landlord product

One of the distinctive features of social housing has been that there is, to all intents and purposes, a single tenancy. The differences between the current types of tenancy agreements are diminishing and, apart from the Right to Buy, they effectively act as one tenancy. The single tenancy is a long-held ambition of the tenants' movement in England, and largely a worthwhile achievement in preventing two-tier tenants.

Yet the legal judgment that effectively separated social housing provision from supported housing provision started the process of splitting up tenants into two groups – those in supported housing and those not. For the former group, it is clear that they require a higher level of care (and money) than other tenants. There is beginning to be a debate about whether some tenants can carry out minor repairs (some already do so) – if so, should they not get a lower rent?

Earlier parts of this chapter explored the importance both of responding to new markets and better meeting the existing one. This suggests that social landlords will need to develop new products to respond to differing situations. The one-size-fits-all model is already cracking at the edges as some tenants clearly want different services than others. The creation of *Supporting People* is perhaps the most overt sign, but it is increasingly hard to argue for a monolithic rent/ services approach. Equity stakes and shared ownership are the next steps in a process that will result in a number of different products aimed at attracting and retaining new and existing tenants.

These products would include those mentioned earlier for young professional and older people, but should also include the following:

- different levels of rent related to different levels of service;
- opportunities to gain equity;
- opportunities for shared ownership;
- negotiated levels of service;
- negotiated tenant contribution;
- how antisocial behaviour (ASB) would be tackled;
- opportunities for involvement; and
- successful communities.

This also ties in with earlier comments about incentives and rewards – is a lower rent a reward for requiring fewer services? Would equity shares be linked to good behaviour? Again we could see a blurring of the current divides between rent–service, rent–equity, behaviour–reward to create a single framework that connected all these issues.

Choice over landlord

More arguably there is a case for tenants, in certain circumstances, being able to choose between landlords. Currently a landlord is a fixed item for a tenant. Apart from stock options/transfer there is no ability for a tenant of a property to choose their landlord. However, why would anyone want to stay with a 'bad' landlord – either as shown through external evaluation or through their own experience? We can choose lenders, supermarkets, cars and increasingly schools and hospitals – why not landlords?

It is not just an issue for tenants. Government, too, has an interest in ensuring value for money, and effective social landlords subsidised through the public purse. With an emphasis on choice, it would be attractive to governments of whatever political colour to offer tenants of bad landlords the opportunity to move to a better landlord.

There are obvious limits to any such choice, as recently recognised by the House of Commons Public Administration Select Committee (2005). It would be difficult to sustain lending from the financial market if there were frequent changes of landlord, and stability is also important in terms of staffing and structures. However, there are three scenarios where choice over landlord would be appropriate:

- where tenant management was appropriate (as now for local authorities);
- where social landlords were delivering a poor level of service, say equivalent to 1 star or less. This would be through a collective process where tenants choose a new landlord, much as through the

stock options process now where different landlords can compete; and

• for individuals with a sustained individual complaint about consistently poor levels of service that are reported through the Ombudsman.

What is interesting about this proposal is that it reinforces the need for landlords to behave as good landlords, which is of benefit to everyone.

What do I want as a tenant?

There are certain core standards that could be expected to be in place for all tenants and would form part of the new 'product'.

"I want to be free of antisocial behaviour (ASB)"

TPAS has long argued that crime and ASB are now the defining feature of failing communities and housing – far more so than poverty or ill health or illiteracy (although there are connections) (Morgan, 2002; Warrington, 2005). The government is slowly responding through various initiatives that either deal with crime/ASB generically (such as the ASB Academy) or specifically through legal requirements on social landlords (although see earlier in this chapter for trends about enforcement by government). Generally, there is a climate for action for both prevention and enforcement.

Landlords already face a clear demand from tenants for action to combat ASB and, in many cases, are doing something about it. A clear line needs to be drawn around the landlord role, about tackling tenants who commit ASB, and the wider advocate role, which is more about working with other agencies who can assist both with their tenants and other people who harass tenants.

Thus, future landlord roles will break into four parts:

Prevention by landlord
• More activity around the commencement of a tenancy.
• Pre-tenancy checks for drug and alcohol abuse.
• Working with tenants who are creating ASB.

Prevention advocacy by landlord
• Preventative work on parenting skills, illiteracy, drug and alcohol abuse with other agencies.

- Partnership approach with police, council, social services and Crime and Disorder Reduction Partnerships.
- Backed up by tenancy clauses (attend and you keep your tenancy).
- Social landlords leading the creation of local crime and grime groups with police forces.

Enforcement by landlord
- Power for landlords to instantly terminate tenancies for ASB.
- Key staff available at short notice to deal with any cases of ASB.

Enforcement advocacy by landlord
- The growth of zero tolerance areas – backed up by local tenant and resident ballots.
- Access to instant ASBOs (Anti-Social Behaviour Orders) at less than 24 hours notice.

There is also a case for a tenant role:

- agreement not to commit ASB;
- contributing to ASB strategies;
- reporting ASB;
- providing feedback on the effectiveness of ASB strategies;
- attending local groups;
- working with the police; and
- voting for zero tolerance zones.

It is arguable that ASB now poses the biggest single threat to social housing. What will put off anyone about social housing is the concern, perceived or real, that it is synonymous with ASB and crime. Social housing will reduce costs, provide better services and have happier tenants if they can break ASB and its baleful impact on tenants' lives.

"I want a good service ... but it's not just about my housing, it's also my community"

It is reasonable for tenants to want a good level of service. One of TPAS's predictions for Tenant Compacts was that they would become a model not just for resident involvement, but also for linking service delivery between providers and customers. What attracted us to that idea of service delivery was not only the ability of tenants as customers to influence standards of service, but also that the government, as with Public Service Agreements, could increasingly promote value for money. Neighbourhood Charters and Local Area Agreements are now being mooted. Again, there is a dual role for landlords: to create their own direct agreements with tenants over service delivery, and to promote similar agreements with other service providers within local communities.

England differs from other European countries such as Sweden in that there is a lack of any kind of regular dialogue about rents and services in England. Rents have increasingly followed a national pattern and the level of services has simply followed that pattern.

First, there could be an annual process of review of rents and services – either the current single product or the wider range of products proposed in this chapter. This would allow for a real dialogue about what matters, and what does not, create accountability of the landlord to tenants and allow the tenants to understand why certain decisions are proposed.

Second, that process could also allow for dialogue about wider community issues where the landlord is unlikely to have any direct control but is in a position to be able to influence other public service providers about the quality and quantity of their service provision. Again this creates a different role for the landlord about being an advocate for their tenants and the opportunity for a good reputation to talk up their tenants. It also creates a very clear divide between private rented housing and social housing as products. There is a case to be made for private rented housing offering a type of service in return for rent. The community advocate role would be distinctive for social landlords and part of why the government continued to subsidise rents.

The creation of these direct service delivery agreements should not be viewed as a one-way process. It is quite reasonable for this to be part of an annual cycle that also tests tenants' willingness to contribute, be it through not committing ASB, or by assisting activity within either housing or their local community. Some of the early work on Community Service Agreements points in this direction. Again there are links with the rewards/incentives agenda as tenants' behaviour shapes both individual and collective relationships with the landlord.

"I want to be involved"

One of the marked changes over the past few years has been the decline of traditional representative structures for tenants. While neither terminal nor simple, that decline has been marked by a number of different trends. The representative model itself has come into question.

Landlords are less likely to rely on a single point of contact and tenants themselves are far more discerning about what they do with their time. In addition, other factors have driven the breakdown of the single point of contact – modernisation of local government, neighbourhood renewal, Best Value and Tenant Compacts have all led to a more complex situation and one ill suited to tenant representative structures (Morgan, 2000). That is not all bad news. Some of those structures have shown themselves ill equipped to meet three key tests – are they democratic, representative and inclusive? – preferring to remain small and exclusive. Some tenants have demonstrated an understanding of the situation and many 'newer' tenant groups now work closely with their landlords, the police and local authorities as a key stakeholder. Unfortunately some landlords have taken this as an open invitation to simply close down their dialogue with tenants, replacing often 'difficult' tenant groups with 'tame' tenant sounding boards that cause less problems.

However, the main driver has been cultural – tenants are now far less homogeneous, far less likely to go to formal meetings and far less likely to be part of traditional structures. Informal routes have proved to be successful in many cases at engaging with a wider group of tenants.

Along with growing cultural diversity, changes in working patterns and the dismissal of 'process' in tenant involvement, it would be easy to predict a future bereft of tenant representative structures. That would be a mistake. Recent government publications, such as *Citizen engagement and public services* (ODPM/Home Office, 2005), point out the importance of communities being involved in local decision making and service delivery. Strong communities require more, not fewer, people to be involved. Tenant representatives have the ability to play a leading role within their communities and can help shape the wider engagement. We need to embrace the valuable commitment and contribution by many thousands of tenant activists who act as the lifeblood of their local communities – and find ways to support and deepen it, not throw it aside.

Good structures and processes strengthen, not weaken, that involvement – as backed up by the Landlord–Tenant Dispute Toolkit (Morgan, 2005). Indeed, as The Housing Corporation found when outlining its *Involvement policy* (2004), landlords still need to talk with someone about how to talk to tenants.

- The end of a single point of contact between tenants and landlords.
- The acceptance of many different ways to involve tenants – both formal and informal.
- Leading tenants and tenant groups having an important and enduring role in helping shape tenant involvement.
- Contact being more about delivery of services.

As stated earlier, TPAS also has predicted that rewards will grow. This will be driven by one of the two forces in tenant involvement – the landlord wanting to engage, and tenants wanting to engage. Landlords will increasingly look to encourage and reward tenants when they, the landlords, want or need tenant involvement.

Although related to the above points about old versus new ways of engagement, there is also another point about engagement through traditional and non-traditional structures. There is a long-term trend about how people want to be engaged. We are all far less likely to take part in the 'traditional' structures – be it the Church of England, political parties, or scouting – but does that show a lack of interest? Perhaps not – there is evidence to suggest that it is not apathy but those institutions that drive down interest. Younger people do take part in single-issue campaigns and express their interest in issues that drive them – such as the environment – that do not fit easily into left–right politics or traditional structures for engagement.

One of the distinctive features of Thatcherism was the exaltation of the individual over the collective. Margaret Thatcher's claim that "There is no such thing as society" brutally defined the explosion of individualism as people bought their own homes and left restrictive social structures. One of the objectives of Blairism was to stress the communitarian approach as a reaction to what were seen as the excesses of individualism. Parts of that approach can be seen in the civic renewal agenda and most closely personified in David Blunkett's time at the Home Office.

We believe that the collective approach will continue to have a role, but will not again be of the same scale or type as, say, 20 years ago. People relish their ability to be different – or, in current terminology, diverse – but still appreciate their ability to interact with others in communities of interest. These can be both geographically or non-geographically based:

- That landlords will need to respond both to a strong individualist streak in tenants – wanting good individual services.

- However, landlords will still want to respond to collective approaches from tenants in particular areas and in communities of interest.
- Landlords will want to encourage those groupings both as good landlords and in their wider community role.
- Those groupings will be far more fluid.

"I want to be connected (mostly)"

There is no doubting the transformation that new technology has made to our lives. Be it work, play or education, many of us spend hours fixed to our computer screens, satellite TVs, DVDs and i-pods. There have already been some successful and innovative ways in which new technology has helped the delivery of services. It is not difficult to imagine how that might continue with Internet broadband connections for every tenant allowing them free access to repair or other landlord services, and wider access to the Internet and virtual communities. In many ways this is admirable. For those who cannot leave their homes easily, through disability, age or rural isolation, there will be a free and easy link to landlords, friends and the outside world. The technology becomes increasingly cheap and available. It will help landlords provide better services, be very time responsive and allow them to canvass tenants' views quickly. Tenants, too, will become more IT literate, as young people become older. We are already seeing the use of text messaging by landlords – expect more not less, especially for the purpose of engaging groups that do not respond to traditional approaches.

Yet there is a nagging doubt that IT alone is the answer. For many it is an addition rather than a substitute for human interaction. When you rely on it and it stops working it can drive you nuts!

Therefore we may see the growth of a new breed of locally based officers who provide some of that human jam in the sandwich. They will help link with isolated people and ensure that small human communities exist to lend support. This may not just be a landlord service either – local authorities and other neighbourhood service providers may find similar pressures on them 'to be seen':

- IT broadband for all tenants.
- Support for non-IT literate tenants to use IT.
- All repairs reporting through IT.
- Landlords to use virtual panels of tenants for consultation.
- Dedicated staff to provide 'human' link to tenants and residents.

"I want my landlord to be nearby"

The number of landlords is in the process of reducing very sharply. Although the government's original intention was for arm's length management organisations (ALMOs) to be restricted to a maximum of 6,000 units and some stock transfers were similarly capped at 6,000 units, it is now obvious that the dislike of large-scale and allegedly bureaucratic landlords has ebbed. This stands in contrast to the argument put forward by writers such as Anne Power (1987), that there were no economies of scale in housing management. Although the efficiency agenda has crystallised the need to reduce procurement costs through partnering, merger and group structures, the reality is that The Housing Corporation, now explicitly supported by Housing Ministers, has been actively encouraging this for several years. There is hardly a single housing association in England that has not considered a merger or group structure over the past five years.

That will accelerate – both the efficiency agenda and the desire of any business to maintain its market position will create yet more interest in driving down the costs of procurement. This will continue through the three models of partnering, merger and group structures. The Housing Corporation and, implicitly, the government, will continue to support this change to landlord provision.

In the US it has been estimated that as few as five private landlords control the rented housing sector. While that would be an extreme prediction for England, the number of landlords will fall sharply and be restricted more by the exhaustion brought about by previous mergers than by any other factor.

For tenants the results will be very mixed. There will be reductions in costs of procurement as the Wal-Mart principle takes hold. Whether this will be sucked into government saving or passed onto tenants in terms of lower rents/better services is more debateable.

The Audit Commission report into mergers and group structures cast doubt into the ability of tenants to get into the heart of decision making in the new structures (Audit Commission, 2001). As the new mega-landlords take shape it is easy to see housing association boards being increasingly driven by the need to run a billion pound business successfully and being less concerned about tenants, except in their role as customers of their service.

It is hard to see, in an environment of mega-landlords and decreased reliance on formal tenant structures, how tenants will influence the major decisions. Instead we see two trends of mega-landlords branding themselves as being efficient/deliverers and local versions of those landlords (which may include the names of former housing associations). It is these local brands that will focus on their relationship with tenants within the parameters set by the mega-landlord and regulators:

- Under 500 landlords in total.
- Of these a comparatively small number holding 50% of all stock.
- Social housing rebranded as efficient and delivery housing.
- Local brands of larger landlords having the closer relationship with tenants.

"I want rights ... but accept I have responsibilities"

For many years the tenant activist agenda was about securing more rights for tenants – over their tenancy agreements, rents, repairs and ability to manage their own housing. This chapter has argued for further increases in what tenants can expect, although this needs to link in with an agenda around personal responsibility. The onward march of tenants' rights is also under challenge as it becomes clear that someone's 'right' conflicts with someone else's 'rights'.

The first challenge has been from tenants themselves over the ASB agenda. Put simply, tenants are fed up with ASB wrecking their lives and their communities. They want to see 'something' done about it and do not particularly care what it is. They are fed up with delay and support being given to the perpetrators of crime, rather than the victims of crime. As a consequence they already support introductory tenancies and demotion (although not withdrawal of benefits). Some tenant activists still argue the case for retaining rights for all tenants and that the actions of a small minority should not result in the weakening of rights for all.

We believe that the challenge has been successful, and, as indicated earlier, tenants, as a body, will support more immediate and draconian action against ASB perpetrators through local Judge Judy style courts able to take remedial action against those perpetrators and the causes of their actions.

The second challenge has been about repairs. Landlords are uneasy about the explosion of repairs cases triggered by sleazy firms preying on tenants. Although the Disrepair Protocol has helped, there remains evidence of continuing abuse by firms of housing disrepair rights for their own ends. Landlords would love to remove these rights and move to a less enforceable regime. We foresee reluctance by both government and tenants to such moves. Instead, we foresee the diversion of such cases to local tribunals with considerable saving to the public purse for solicitors' fees:

- The creation of local housing tribunals with power to direct remedial action for ASB perpetrators and deal with disrepair cases.

However, these are just symbols of a tension that needs to be drawn out between 'rights' and 'responsibilities'. The acceptance of personal responsibility is a key issue for all of us as individuals. Just as the lack of ownership leads to poorer services there is a case for considering how tenants would view their home if they 'owned' it in some way. It is debatable whether this needs to be personal and financial or whether some other looser form of collective ownership might work, such as we all have, say, with our local park or school. Certainly the equity models referred to earlier would create a clear 'ownership' and it would be reasonable to tie that into certain responsibilities for that tenant. However, it would be useful to create a wider sense of ownership of both landlord and community – part of that means that tenants would take some responsibility (as many do already) for their homes and community.

Conclusion

As stated at the beginning of this chapter this is an attempt to link the aspirational, predictive and provocative. This chapter has set out a test for thinkers in social housing about how the future might look. Although landlords will change, tenants are likely to change as well. If the more ambitious statements in this chapter are realised, then tenants are likely to be responsible for more than now, from different types of rent/services product to part-equity to tackling ASB and finally to involvement in their homes. It is that responsibility that will carry out the most ambitious aim of blurring the distinction between home ownership and renting, and has the ability to transform how people view their homes and communities.

References

Audit Commission (2001) *Group dynamics: Group structures and registered social landlords*, London: Audit Commission.

Hembrow, I. and Wadhams, C. (2003) *Rewards for volunteers: Report of TPAS's Innovation and Good Practice Project*, Salford: TPAS, September.

House of Commons Public Administration Select Committee (2005) *Choice, voice and public services: Fourth report of session 2004-2005*, London: The Stationery Office.

Housing Corporation, The (2004) *Involvement policy for the housing association sector*, London: The Housing Corporation.

Morgan, P. (2000) *TPAS national strategy for neighbourhood renewal response*, Manchester: TPAS.

Morgan, P. (2002) *TPAS tackling anti social tenants response*, Manchester: TPAS.

Morgan, P. (2005) *Landlord–tenant dispute tookit*, Manchester: TPAS.

ODPM (Office of the Deputy Prime Minister) (2003) *Incentives and beyond? The transferability of the Irwell Valley Gold Service to other landlords*, London: ODPM.

ODPM and Home Office (2005) *Citizen engagement and public services: Why neighbourhoods matter*, London: ODPM.

Power, A (1987) *Property before people: The management of twentieth century council housing*, London: Allen and Unwin.

Warrington, R. (2005) *TPAS response to building communities, beating crime*, Manchester: TPAS, January.

TEN

Democracy and development

Stephen Platt and Ian Cooper

Introduction

Earlier chapters have explored a range of factors – affordability, market forces, demographic change and policy action – that affect or are likely to affect housing futures. In this chapter we develop the discussion of consumer preferences begun by Phil Morgan (Chapter Nine), looking at their likely impact in future years. The aim is to report a number of innovative studies that have explored the potential for stakeholders to discuss how towns and cities might develop over time. The chapter outlines novel methodologies for investigating stakeholder views, and reports the findings of studies in different parts of England. An important outcome of the research was the demonstration that consumers of housing and urban environments not only have views but are able to express them in ways that could lead to better policies.

In England, London and the South East are prospering while manufacturing towns in the Midlands and the North have declined. Imbalances of growth and decline mean that there is a shortage of housing in the South and an excess in the North. What is to be done? And how can citizens be involved in decision making? In particular, how can an effective voice be given to the very broad range of stakeholders involved in and affected by the development and regeneration of our towns and cities?

This chapter draws lessons from three housing futures studies conducted by Cambridge Architectural Research (CAR) and Eclipse Research Consultants. The aim of each of them was to create a platform to enable stakeholders to discuss meaningfully the future of their particular neighbourhoods, towns and regions. The first of these studies looked at Cambridge, where housing demand and supply problems are acute as a result of strong economic growth. Cambridge is located in one of the designated growth areas in the South East, and as such it experiences quite different housing market pressures from those in northern cities, as discussed by Brendan Nevin and Philip Leather in Chapter Five.

Cambridge Futures

Cambridge Futures was a unique example of the marriage of applied research and public policy. Its aim was to provide a forum for considering options that could engage with and gain the support of a wide coalition of interests in the Cambridge region. This forum was used to develop a range of options addressing the concerns of a large consortium of different interests including university academics, councillors and planning officers from the city, district and county council, business people, social landlords, developers, house builders and representatives of community and resident groups.

Prior to the mid-1990s growth and development in the Cambridge region was highly constrained by planning policy dating back to 1950 (Holford and Wright, 1950). In 1993, concerned about the constraints on growth in Cambridge, Peter Carolin, then Head of the Department of Architecture, University of Cambridge, invited six people from the university, the city council and the business community to talk about the problem. This grouping was subsequently enlarged and went on to form Cambridge Futures. It produced seven options for the development of the Cambridge region (www.cambridgefutures.org). The intention was not to make specific recommendations but rather to demonstrate the possibilities, and, in so doing, to generate informed debate and aid the formal planning process.

In 1999, as our contribution to the consortium, CAR surveyed public opinion. A central feature of the survey was to offer resident and non-resident stakeholders a range of options for the development of the Cambridge region, to describe their likely outcomes simply and clearly and to invite members of the general public to express their opinions. The findings have had a significant influence on planning policy in the region (Cambridge Futures, 1999).

The study's main finding was that there was little support for the status quo: 67% of those who completed the survey disliked the minimum growth option and only 18% agreed that "Cambridge and its surroundings should be kept just as they are". The options that won the least support were close to the then current policies of minimum growth in the city and necklace development of surrounding villages that had distorted the growth of the region since 1950.

There was a small effect of people voting according to where they lived. So marginally more people living in the city preferred selected extension into the green belt, while people living outside the city preferred densification. But this effect was much less than we expected.

People were very concerned about high house prices and their impact on the social balance of the city: 81% of people agreed, "It would be a bad thing if only wealthy people could afford to live in Cambridge". People were also concerned about traffic congestion and favoured options that minimised car use: 59% of people supported some form of road pricing.

Overall the main message was that there was solid support for growth: 78% of people agreed that "The region's high-tech businesses must be allowed to grow". People favoured a balanced mix of development with some growth of the city through densification and selected expansion into the green belt, and growth outside Cambridge based on good public transport links.

The findings also indicated that public opinion responds to balanced and clearly presented information about urban development. As Professor Peter Carolin observed, "The public consultation exercise was a most amazing piece of research, it proved to politicians that the general public is not as stupid as the tabloid press would have us believe" (personal communication).

Cambridge Futures was very influential. As well as having a major impact on development in the Cambridge area and the rest of the eastern region, the study also influenced thinking about how to engage stakeholders in planning the future. Prior to 1996, the four local authorities responsible for planning in the city – East Cambridgeshire, South Cambridgeshire, the City Council and the County Council – refused to confront the issue. The Futures study overcame local politicians' anxiety that the public were opposed to growth, and demonstrated that it was possible to engage a wide range of stakeholders in thinking strategically about the future. It also overcame the initial caution of planning officers who found the independence of Cambridge Futures was useful in rehearsing options before getting locked into the planning process.

By 2000, the logjam that had stifled growth in the region was broken. Peter Studdert, then Director of Environment and Planning at Cambridge City Council, said, "Cambridge Futures convinced people that if options were explained clearly then the general public were much less intransigent about change than might have been supposed.... Although there are still matters of dispute, there is general agreement about the need for new land for housing and about development in the green belt" (personal communication).

The Cambridge Futures approach to enrolling stakeholders in local democratic decision making represented a significant advance in engaging citizens, both opinion formers and the general public, in the planning process at a strategic level. A similar approach might usefully be adopted in other towns and cities and could be very useful in helping people think positively about change, in overcoming fear and opposition to development and in reaching a consensus about the way forward.

Housing Futures in South East England

Two ideas came out of Cambridge Futures. The first is that the public respond positively to clear options for change. The second is that a consortium of interest groups, if broadly based, working together can be a very powerful agent of change. The significant lesson to be drawn from Cambridge Futures is that, over the four years that the consortium met, the prevailing mindset about future development in the region completely swung from constraint to managed growth.

As a direct result of the success of Cambridge Futures, the Joseph Rowntree Foundation supported a wider survey of public opinion in the South East by CAR to canvass public reaction to building new houses in the region. Called Housing Futures, this study also found that the public were less opposed to growth than had been supposed. The study, published in 2004, tested the public's reaction to new housing in three towns in the South East: Aylesbury, Maidenhead and Medway (JRF, 2004). It attempted to answer two questions. First, if the consequences are explained clearly, what are people's reactions to different development options such as densification or extension into open land? And, second, what preferences do people have for different housing types and densities?

CAR developed the content of the survey with planners, housing providers and other interested parties in each of the three towns, together with a number of national experts in housing and planning. The main effort went into public exhibitions in shopping centres, libraries and hospitals. The survey was computer based and described the likely outcomes of each option in terms of housing supply, house prices, traffic congestion, loss of open land and access to services. There was a paper version for people who did not want to use one of the laptops. In total, over 1,400 people completed the survey and the pattern of age, employment and tenure of respondents in each town was similar to the 2001 Census.

The findings show that no single development option was favoured. Three development options were marginally more liked than disliked.

These were new town, urban extension and densification. Two options – village growth and new settlement – were less liked. The difference between new town and new settlement is one of size. New towns were defined as having at least 20,000 homes and new settlements as having 4,000 or less. Because the new town, urban extension and densification options were almost equally favoured, there seemed to be no blanket opposition to land being used for development, nor was there a strong preference for the use of brownfield over open land. The survey suggests that a balanced pattern of settlement for new housing in the South East would meet with most approval. The appropriate form of development would depend on the specific locality, but, overall, it was suggested spreading new development by building 25% of new homes in each of the three favoured options: infill, urban extension and new town and the remaining 25% in existing villages and new settlements.

The survey also asked about house type and density. Lower-density detached and semi-detached houses were the preferred house type. Although most people were opposed to high-density flats being built in their area, a substantial proportion (47%) found medium-density terraces acceptable and higher-density flats were acceptable to a minority (21%). Like the general population, most first-time buyers would like to live in a detached or semi-detached house. But a significant proportion would be prepared to live in higher-density flats (30%). The survey suggested a mix of new housing, with about 45% lower-density detached and semi-detached, 35% medium-density terraces and only about 20% higher-density flats. This mix of density would still meet the government's target of 30-50 dwellings per hectare.

The survey also tested people's general attitudes to growth and change. Respondents were almost evenly divided about whether they liked or disliked a policy of minimum growth and 31% were undecided. The evidence suggests that people would support new development in the South East if they were convinced that growth could be achieved without sacrificing quality of life. But people perceived the main problem to be affordability, not housing shortage. This is interesting given the evidence in the Barker Report (2004), which shows that the rate of housing completions has been declining steadily since 1967. This is almost entirely due to the demise of local authority housing. The rate of private sector new build has remained steady but the supply of social housing has dropped steadily, from about 50% of total completions up to the mid- to late 1970s to about 12% in 2002. The Barker Report makes a strong case for increasing the supply of housing in the South East, but the message from Housing Futures is that the public still need to be convinced.

From talking to hundreds of people in the three towns, we know that people realise the negative effects of high house prices. The majority of us have a home and we are all 'nimbys' (Not-In-My-Backyard') to some extent. But high house prices affect everyone and people realise this. If we have children and their school cannot recruit good teachers, or if our local police force cannot retain experienced officers, then we are all affected. People make trade-offs between the benefits of growth and the impact on quality of life. In particular they favour options that reduce the distance to services. Although approval for new town development may, to some extent, be motivated by 'nimbyism', people also value the infrastructure that comes with larger-scale, planned development. Overall, marginally more people were in favour of change than were opposed to it. Only a third of people agreed that their town and surroundings should be kept the same and 40% agreed that their region must be allowed to grow. But over two thirds of respondents thought that, "Quality of housing is more important than quantity". This raises questions about what people mean by quality.

In summary there is opposition to housing development, but less than policy makers may have imagined. The public would, however, prefer housing development to be spread. They want some densification on brownfield sites but would like to see the majority of new housing on new open land. They also want a mix of house types, with about half of them detached or semi-detached with family gardens.

In conclusion, getting the public to engage with problems at a strategic level through proactive consultation was highly effective. When presented with information about a range of options, people made reasoned choices and compromises. Watching people rapt in thought, considering their answers carefully, one could not

Photograph 10.1:
Housing Futures survey

help conclude that they took the process seriously and that their answers were significant.

Urban Futures in Burnley and Luton

The final study was undertaken for Building Futures, a joint venture between the Commission for Architecture and the Built Environment (CABE) and the Royal Institute of British Architects (RIBA). Called Urban Futures, it was conducted by CAR in collaboration with Eclipse Research Consultants (CABE and RIBA, 2005).

Over the next 20 years, many towns and cities will undergo considerable change, growing or declining, whether planned or unplanned. Government initiatives like the Sustainable Communities plan and housing market renewal are accelerating the rate of change in particular areas. Physical change in towns and cities is driven by a wide range of factors. And urban areas in different regions are being affected in different ways. In these circumstances, the capacity of decision makers and other stakeholders to anticipate and implement change is of crucial importance.

The study looked 10-20 years ahead and tried to envisage how urban regeneration might be achieved by focusing on two neighbourhoods – one in Luton in the growing South East, the other in Burnley in the North West with a declining population and struggling economy. Both towns are recipients of government regeneration funding and both are scenes of intense local government activity. The study reports people's aspirations and concerns. It describes the current regeneration initiatives and explores options for the future of the two neighbourhoods and towns. Most importantly it draws lessons from these two types of places – one with a buoyant economy and increasing population, the other with a struggling economy and declining population – about how to plan and implement urban futures more effectively.

The approach adopted was simple. Rather than try to quantify the factors that contribute to regeneration, the study set out to tell the 'story' about change in these two towns and neighbourhoods. Both towns were visited and the officers responsible for regeneration were interviewed. In each town, two or three neighbourhoods were suggested for study. In Burnley, Burnley Wood was chosen and in Luton, High Town was selected. Both are inner-city neighbourhoods with Victorian terraced housing and low-value commercial property.

In each town, people were carefully chosen to represent the three target audiences: policy makers, service providers and community

Photograph 10.2: Burnley town centre and Arndale Centre, Luton

members. From these selected interviewees, a broad range of stakeholder aspirations and concerns were identified. All the people that had been interviewed were invited to events billed as blue-skies workshops to explore the future of places like Burnley and Luton. It quickly became apparent that some way was required to make the wealth of material captured accessible to people coming to the workshops. An Urban Futures game was devised to provide a framework to help them think constructively about the future.

Photograph 10.3: Comparison of the two towns

Before thinking about the future, it is important to understand the contexts occupied by the two sets of workshop participants. Burnley became a centre of weaving in the 18th century and, along with many other towns in the North of England, grew rapidly in the 19th century. By 1886 there were 100,000 looms in the town, together with several coal pits and factories producing machinery and steam engines, and Burnley was the biggest producer of cotton cloth in the world. Burnley Wood is just over the canal from the Weaver's Triangle, next to the town centre. The new light engineering industries attracted to the town since the 1930s have nearly all gone. Since 1920 Burnley's population has steadily declined, at 2-3% a year, and in 2005 it was about 90,000. Luton was the centre of the hat industry located in Platters Lea and High Town, and as this declined the automotive industry took over. Recently Vauxhall closed down, but the economy, based on the airport and high-tech industry, is still buoyant. High Town is just over the railway line from the town centre. Luton saw an increase in population above national average between 1880-1980. And since 1980, population growth has been similar to the rest of the country and in 2005 it was 185,000, twice as big as Burnley.

The two towns are situated in very different regions. Burnley is in North East Lancashire, a region that has seen a steady decline in its population since 1920. Luton is in the prosperous South East and lies between two of the main growth areas in the country – the South

Midlands/Milton Keynes area and the M11 corridor. Most significantly Luton has excellent rail connections to London while in Burnley travellers have to change in Preston or Hebden Bridge to get to Manchester. Both neighbourhoods are 10 minutes' walk from their town centres but, because of geography and infrastructure, both feel isolated. Burnley Wood is to the south of the Leeds–Liverpool canal while High Town is to the north of the railway line.

At first sight Burnley and Luton seem quite different. Yet in both towns there are neighbourhoods, including Burnley Wood and High Town, among the 10% most deprived in the country. Both towns have areas of derelict commercial property and poor housing. And in both there are rundown areas of inner-city Victorian terraces and outer suburbs of 1960s council housing in desperate need of maintenance or renewal. Both towns have a poor image. Luton was voted the 'Worst Town in Britain' in an online poll of 20,000 people in 2004. Both towns also look gritty and rough. Both have the working-class feel of manufacturing towns in decline. Although unemployment is low in Burnley, there is a lot of 'make-work' – part-time, low-paid jobs – and that is reflected in average earnings. And, despite Burnley's notoriety, its Asian population is smaller than in Luton. In summary, the two towns have things in common. They both have similar small town inferiority complexes. They have similar low educational attainment and similar low aspirations and expectations. But they each have very different economic prospects.

What sets the two neighbourhoods of Burnley Wood and High Town in Luton apart is the state of the housing market. In Burnley there has been a significant fall in house prices. A standard 'two–up two–down' terraced house in Burnley Wood fetched about £25,000 in 1989. But when Philip Chew, the vicar at St Stephens, came to live

Table 10.1: The two towns compared (2005)

	Burnley	Luton	National
Population size	90,000	185,000	60 million
Population growth per year	declining 2-3%	national average	increasing 0.5%
Young people under 15 (%)	21	22	19
Asian minority (%)	7	18	4
Manufacturing employment (%)	30	20	14
Unemployment (%)	3.1	3.8	3.4
Annual earnings	£15,312	£24,970	£22,248
Burglary per 1,000 households	14	10	6
	(crime trend up)	(crime trend down)	(crime trend down)
Educational attainment	low	low	average

Table 10.2: Housing prices in the two towns compared (2005)

	Burnley Wood	High Town
2-3 bed terrace	£20,000	£135,000
3 bed semi	£94,000	£160,000
4 bed Edwardian	£150,000	£170,000
5 bed detached	£225,000	£250,000

there in 2002 you could buy a terraced house on a credit card. Currently compulsory purchase has fixed the going price at about £20,000. Yet within five minutes' walk there are houses on sale for a £250,000 and there are new infill terraces on Todmorden Road, on the edge of the neighbourhood, being built by a private developer that will sell for £200,000. In sharp contrast, in High Town the average price of a terraced house is £135,000. But the difference in the average price of semi-detached and larger houses is not nearly so marked. In a weak housing market, with a large excess supply, the least desirable housing can sink to very low values. As the market strengthens, previously undesirable housing can of course become desirable. In summary the two neighbourhoods have a lot in common. They have similar patterns of Victorian terraces and mixed uses. They both feel 'cut off' from the town centre. In both the occupants are a mix of 'transient' incomers and the remnants of a more stable community. But each has very different regeneration prospects.

Current initiatives

Given their 'deprived' status, there are wide-ranging government initiatives in the two towns. Only those related directly to regeneration of the selected neighbourhoods are described here. In Burnley, Burnley Wood is one of three Neighbourhood Action Areas sharing £15 million Elevate pathfinder funding from the Office of the Deputy Prime Minister. Regeneration is being tackled through direct intervention in the housing market. In the short term, this will involve significant demolition and clearance. Whether it will produce benefits in the longer term is not clear, especially to the inhabitants of the neighbourhood. In Luton, High Town is one of five priority areas also sharing £15 million of Single Regeneration Budget and Objective 2 funding. The money is going into a new community centre and upgrading the high street. It is hoped that proximity to London and regional growth will deliver further regeneration. These sums look large. But to put them in perspective, £22 billion is earmarked for the Thames Gateway compared with £500 million for all nine pathfinders in the North and Midlands. Admittedly, the growth area figure covers the provision of infrastructure, not just housing. But the comparison does indicate a different order of magnitude.

The thinking behind regeneration in both towns is to stimulate private investment. But the regeneration process is led by council officers whose main aim has been to win government funding. Once they have got it, they have to meet the often short-term milestones attached to it. Another problem is continuity. Regeneration takes a long while, perhaps as long as 20 years, but funding is time-limited and this can breed short-term thinking. There is also the issue of effective community engagement. There has been lots of consultation. In fact both communities speak of consultation fatigue. But, in both towns, decision making rests with the council whose main concern is, quite naturally, for the needs of the whole town, not just these two neighbourhoods.

The Urban Futures game

A novel feature of the study was the development of the Urban Futures game. The game was used to explore the aspirations and concerns of the inhabitants of both towns and to rehearse options for the future of the neighbourhoods selected as case studies.

The Urban Futures game confronted stakeholders with their aspirations, concerns, options and their criteria for measuring the success of regeneration. Sets of playing cards were devised on which the aspirations and concerns voiced by interviewees were transcribed. Since people in Burnley and Luton have different aspirations and concerns, separate packs were made for each town. At the workshops, participants were asked to make choices by prioritising the cards. To record people's answers wall charts were designed in which the aspiration and concern choices were arranged in eight-by-six matrices. The column headings were labelled: people, housing, community, infrastructure, economy, education, process and leadership.

Neighbourhood regeneration in both towns is constrained by a need to meet short-term goals. So it was decided to devise options or scenarios to raise people's horizons. Our immersion in the two towns was used to develop four broad and generic options for how the case study neighbourhoods could be regenerated over the next 10-20 years. At the workshops, these options were used to promote a dialogue between stakeholders about what might be done. We drew on the interviews to identify a wide range of criteria that people thought should be used to judge whether regeneration had been successful

Photograph 10.4: People's priorities
People's priorities and preferences are recorded on wall charts

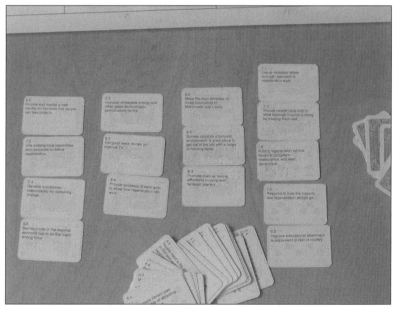

Photograph 10.5: Two sets of cards
Two sets of cards are used in the Urban Futures game, one for aspirations, the other for concerns

over this timescale. At the workshops, participants were asked to prioritise which criteria should be used to measure whether change had been successful in their neighbourhood. The game made the wealth of material collected and collated accessible to people coming to the workshop. It also made the process more enjoyable.

Aspirations

At first glance the spread of aspirations in the two towns looked similar. There are dots in all the columns of the wall chart that meant that there was a wide range of priorities in both towns. This complexity reflects what we learnt from the interviews – there are many ideas about regenerating these places and different people value different things. Nevertheless there were differences between the two towns. In Burnley the focus was on the economy and education columns, while in Luton it was on community, infrastructure and process. There were also clear areas of agreement and disagreement between different interest groups. In Burnley everyone agreed that regeneration depended on the regional economy. Policy makers/providers then chose aspirations that described current policy initiatives, while residents of Burnley Wood seemed to be thinking more holistically. In contrast, in Luton policy makers/providers were thinking more broadly in choosing to focus on the neighbourhood–town link and on continuity, while the community members chose issues closer to home that would improve the prospects of High Town.

Concerns

As one might expect from the diversity of aspirations given priority, there were widespread concerns about regeneration. In Burnley the overriding concern was about the economy while in Luton the primary focus was on infrastructure and the environment. This is not surprising. Burnley has a long history of false dawns and Luton has a tradition of poor architecture. In Burnley, as one might expect, both sides were concerned that the town will still be struggling in 20 years' time. In sharp contrast, however, policy makers/providers were more concerned about introducing aspiring households into the neighbourhood and raising the expectations of those who already live there, while community members were more concerned about the lack of vision and whether the current pathfinder programme, with its focus on housing market renewal, stood any chance of working. In Luton, policy makers/providers were most concerned about High Town's physical

Figure 10.1: Exercise 1 – aspirations

People	Housing	Community	Infrastructure	Economy	Education	Process	Leadership
1.1 Attract and retain dynamic young people	2.1 Have fewer but broader range of houses	3.1 Don't demolish, refurbish	4.1 Restore old mills and streets sympathetically and encourage conversion of mills into modern apartments	5.1 Establish the town as a major service centre for the area	6.1 Manage the transition from manufacturing to higher skilled service economy	7.1 Use an inclusive 'whole borough' approach to regeneration work	8.1 Get good news stories on regional TV
1.2 Create a more balanced community with a larger middle class	2.2 Push up house prices	3.2 Get rid of absentee private landlords	4.2 Make gateways into town attractive	5.2 Create more vibrant town centre capable of attracting department stores	6.2 Develop skilled service industry activities and small-scale creative industries	7.2 Use existing local capabilities and resources to deliver regeneration	8.2 Provide and market a new identity for the town that people can take pride in
1.3 Give existing residents first choice of new homes	2.3 Insist on adaptable high-quality housing using renewable energy	3.3 Upgrade communities by reducing crime, improving facilities and providing better transport	4.3 Maintain and preserve Victorian heritage and built environment	5.3 Increase renewable energy and other green technologies, permaculture centre	6.3 Deliver greater levels of educational choice	7.3 Ensure people have faith in what Borough Council is doing by treating them well	8.3 Promote town as having affordable housing and fantastic scenery
1.4 Provide houses and facilities to attract young families	2.4 Demolish areas of decline and return them to woodland	3.4 Regain the urban village feel where people care about each other	4.4 Regenerate neighbourhoods to benefit whole town, not just existing residents	5.4 Provide jobs to attract families into the area	6.4 Develop workforce skills through training programme with local colleges	7.4 Develop a collective responsibility for delivering change	8.4 Provide evidence of early wins to show how regeneration can work
1.5 Encourage gentrification of the housing stock	2.5 There will be a market for sandblasted oversized lofts for people who can't afford to live in Manchester	3.5 Deliver mixed communities with greater breakdown in inter-area tensions	4.5 People need to be able to live in BW and walk down to the rapid transit station and be in Manchester in half an hour	5.5 Tackle poverty to reduce racism	6.5 Improve educational attainment to equivalent in rest of country	7.5 Respond to how the majority feel regeneration should go	8.5 Burnley could be a fantastic environment. A great place to get out of the city with a range of housing types
1.6 We will attract people by providing the sort of housing people want to live in and good schools	2.6 I know all the current thinking is about city living but people with kids want more space	3.6 Employ facilitators and residents for community building activities	4.6 The canal is the key to regenerating not only Burnley, but the surrounding area as well	5.6 Burnley's role in the regional economy has to be the major driving force	6.6 Greater university provision to attract and retain university students	7.6 Build a regeneration vehicle based on long-term relationships with lead developers	8.6 Make the town attractive to those commuting to Manchester and Leeds

and social isolation. They thought that people harked back to the past rather than looking positively to the future. People in the community put a more positive spin on this. They wanted a thriving neighbourhood with local shops where people took an active role in the community. Residents were also more concerned about the quality of life and worried about increasing density, which they saw as cramming people in.

In summary, in terms of aspirations and concerns, there were areas of agreement in both towns. The differences revolved around the balance between the needs of existing residents and the future of the town as a whole.

Options

A set of generic options was developed that, with some minor differences, we were able to use in both Burnley and Luton and which might be developed for use elsewhere. Figure 10.2 shows the set of options devised for High Town and Luton. We used the same options in Burnley, but the key features varied slightly. People were asked how much they liked or disliked each option individually and then to rank them as first, second and third choices.

At the workshops people were asked to assess the options for regenerating towns and neighbourhoods like theirs over the next 10–20 years. Despite the abstract nature of the options on offer, none of the participants had problems doing so. What was immediately striking is that no single option is favoured in either town. This means that the preferred solution is likely to be a package of measures. The danger of course is that the plan ends up as a mishmash of ideas trying to satisfy everyone.

In both towns all interest groups clearly preferred Option 3 *Small business incubator*. This obviously reflects their focus on education and the economy. They also liked Option 1 *Commuter village* that would exploit each town's relatively cheap housing and proximity to a major conurbation. Beyond this there are some differences. In Burnley, policy makers/providers preferred Option 4 *Design-led regeneration* while the community was prepared to consider Option 2 *Urban wood*. In Luton, perhaps because of the town's poor record in this area, both community members also prioritised Option 4 *Design-led regeneration*. At both workshops, the consultants responsible for the, as yet unfinished, master plans for each neighbourhood were very interested in and drew on these outcomes.

Figure 10.2: The set of options

Option 1: Commuter village

This option seeks to give opportunities to aspiring and dynamic young families to renovate existing terrace houses. It needs to be kick-started by public sector intervention but renovation is left to the private housing market supported by improvement grants.

This option provides a form of housing attractive to families while not presuming significant changes in local employment opportunities.

Key features

- Gentrification of existing terraces to provide affordable housing with 2 to 3 bedrooms with residential parking provision.
- Houses privately renovated and extended.
- Families with young children move into the area.
- Effective crime and antisocial behaviour initiatives undertaken.
- Households typically involved in commuting to London or within Milton Keynes/South Midlands

Option 2: Urban wood

This option tries to address the current lack of green space close to the town centre directly by providing outdoor leisure amenities to the rest of the town while holding the neighbourhood in abeyance as a public asset against future development.

This option also promotes the town as a leisure destination.

Key features

- Removal of existing commercial development and extension of existing town park to the town centre.
- Demolition returns area to pre-industrialisation status.
- Outdoor leisure pursuits promoted in conjunction with new community centre.
- Green lifestyles promoted through recycling facilities.
- Town promotes itself as a centre for sustainable lifestyles.

Continued

Figure 10.2: The set of options (continued)

Option 3: Small business incubator

This option tries to address the current imbalance in residential and commercial land values. It seeks to stimulate the regeneration of the neighbourhood's commercial area through attracting a more highly skilled workforce.

This option attempts to manage the transition from a low-skill, low-wage industrial economy to a high-skill, high-wage knowledge economy to support regeneration of the high street with specialist shops, cafés and bars.

Key features

- Reinvention of the image and purpose of the area by development of an attractive location for small-scale businesses.
- Adjoining innovation incubator supported by outpost university teaching and research facilities.
- Aligned with a skills training programme in local colleges.
- Incentives for new businesses and developers.
- Rise in skill levels and average wages.

Option 4: Design-led regeneration

This option recognises the value of good design and its role in regeneration. It places high-quality design and innovation at the heart of thinking and action and involves the creativity of the local community in its planning.

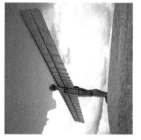

Key features

- Regeneration led by an iconic building, structure or work of art.
- Emphasis on the use of high-quality design as a social and economic generator.
- Focus on liveable environment with street designs to encourage social contact and usable green space.
- Draws on contributions across the mixed community integrating inputs from all ages, social and ethnic groups.
- Mixture of innovative new design and enhanced local heritage and distinctiveness.

Success criteria

The final exercise at the workshops considered the success factors people would use to measure whether change has been effective in 10 or 20 years' time. Although there were differences between the two towns, strikingly there was much more consensus about success criteria, in other words, about where people want to get to, than about aspirations and concerns. In Burnley the focus was on the education, economy and process columns, while in Luton the focus was on community and the economy. In Burnley both interest groups focused on educational attainment and the socioeconomic status of future inhabitants. In Luton both groups chose quality of life issues and pride in the town. The game identified real opportunities here for consensus building. From this it would be possible to build an agreed platform about the way forward and also to identify areas of conflict that needed to be harnessed positively to bring about successful regeneration.

Using options to manage change

Futures methods are largely absent from the toolbox currently being used for urban regeneration and neighbourhood renewal. Yet their effective use could help to mitigate many of the shortcomings identified in the Urban Futures study. The use of cards to represent stakeholders' aspirations and concerns makes sorting and prioritising them fun. But the cards are also democratic. They mean that everybody's voice is brought to the table, anonymously, for joint consideration. Displaying participants' individual choices via wall charts is a good way of making opinions transparent, and aggregating these helps to identify shared and unshared preferences. This aids consensus building as well as signposting areas of conflict that have to be managed positively.

Options are a powerful way of engaging policy makers/providers and the community in thinking about the longer-term future of neighbourhoods and towns. They offer an early opportunity to explore possible futures and to help people to make leaps of the imagination. Options can be employed to clarify the range of hard choices available that confront a community. They can be selected to give voice to all the types of stakeholder involved and to illustrate the underlying motives and intentions, fears and aspirations of each of these groups, regardless of their current power to impose their own preferred solutions. For instance, options can be chosen so that they make explicit what is cherished in a locality and what is seen as expendable.

Options should be based on realistic but aspirational assumptions and tested against economic, social and environmental criteria to identify the option that performs robustly against all three criteria. Any option that performs well on some, but badly on others, should be viewed with suspicion. Options can be used to test the viability of proposals over an extended period of time – for example, beyond the current generation handing over to the next. They can also be employed to expand the scale and the scope of what might be done. Any option preferred by stakeholders can be treated as a desired end state. Backcasting techniques can then be employed to identify what needs to happen for this desired future to be brought about successfully. Finally, stakeholders can use their judgement to make an impact assessment of the options. The key issues are: what timescale does the option operate over? Can its implementation be phased? What are the costs and benefits? Who bears these? What might stop the option happening? In this way a probability ranking might be assigned to each option.

Using a range of options prevents participants rushing to a 'lowest common denominator' shared vision. Options help keep the choices available open for longer. They can also clarify the goals that lie behind these choices and the means of achieving them. And this can happen before goals become buried beneath physical proposals in master plans and before funding begins. Options can also help stakeholders to break free of short-termism and grapple with a longer-term view of what could happen. They can help untangle the complexity of choices and delivery mechanisms – holding them up for comparison, weighing them against each other. As a result, options are a useful mechanism for building consensus and for harnessing conflicts so that they can be exploited positively. If this clarity is absent and plans push ahead without stakeholder support, then there is a strong chance that a regeneration programme will fail. If carefully selected, options can be used to explore innovative solutions and the front-end contribution from developers currently absent in both towns. And finally, in line with Building Futures' remit, options can be used to raise awareness of the issue of design quality that has yet to become part of the general currency for negotiating urban futures.

Taken together, the aspirations, concerns, options and success criteria provided workshop participants with a framework within which to explore possible futures for their town and neighbourhood. Playing the Urban Futures game in Burnley and Luton showed that people from different sides of the process – policy makers, service providers and members of the community – are able to talk about their aspirations and concerns and discuss options for the future in a constructive way.

This experience provides lessons for elsewhere about how to manage both growth and downsizing. The workshops clearly demonstrated how a broader shared platform for managing change could be built for urban regeneration and neighbourhood renewal in both of the case study towns.

There is an apocryphal tale about Burnley Alderman Tony Gallagher taking a deputation to London in the 1960s to demand government investment in jobs. Harold Macmillan said that towns have disappeared throughout history and it was not the government's job to try and stem the tide. Gallagher said that 100,000 people cannot just disappear and that Burnley demanded the same investment as people in the South. Burnley gained a new shopping centre, an inner ring road and new industry, industry that has now all gone.

Towns like Burnley and Luton have to start from where they are now. Other places have shown that the damage of the 1960s can be repaired and these studies demonstrate that enlightened leadership, that is prepared to engage with different interest groups, can develop a joint vision of the future.

Conclusion

A number of principles involved in deliberative decision making underlie all three studies reported in this chapter (Institute for Global Ethics, 2005). In each case, they work by providing people with a framework for thinking about the future. They do this, principally, by offering a range of options for consideration. They also attempt to involve stakeholders from a wide variety of interest groups in discussing issues at a strategic level. The frameworks provided promote clarity by offering a strong but sensitive structure within which to discuss complex issues.

The process has the following steps:

- establish a *forum:* that brings stakeholders from different interest groups together;
- devise a *framework:* that clarifies and provides a structure for effective discussion and testing of the issues raised by these stakeholders;
- devise *options:* that map out solutions and promote dialogue and negotiation pointing to a shared platform for moving forward; and
- report *preferences* and *priorities:* that help create a positive and proactive climate of opinion about the future.

There is a democratic impulse underlying this approach. The Urban Futures game, for instance, temporarily suspends the normal distribution of power between stakeholders that exists outside the context of the workshop. The cards that summarise people's aspirations and concerns help bring everyone's voice to the table. The engagement process creates a common platform that can be built on by stakeholders and used to identify, and if necessary to isolate, those areas of disagreement that need to be dealt with further.

Similar lessons can be drawn from all three of the studies. What they each show is that, provided with a well-structured discussion space, constructive dialogue between stakeholders can be influential in altering the climate of opinion about change and development. There is currently a huge amount of public consultation about urban development and regeneration in the UK, but there is little effective engagement with citizens at a strategic level. These studies show that, if presented with well-grounded information about a range of options, people are quite capable of making reasoned choices and trade-offs and are often far less negative about change and redevelopment than politicians and council officers assume.

Democracy, we think, means engaging citizens in deciding strategy and having a voice in making hard choices. And democracy, we believe, is an essential ingredient in the genius necessary for dealing with change and for a town to reinvent itself.

Acknowledgements

We would like to thank all of the council staff and citizens of Aylesbury, Burnley, Cambridge, Luton, Maidenhead and Medway who gave their time and effort, experience and expertise, to provide the material drawn on in this chapter. We would also like to thank Cambridge Futures, the Joseph Rowntree Foundation, South East England Regional Assembly and Building Futures (CABE and the RIBA) for funding the studies reported here.

References

Barker, K. (2004) *Review of housing supply: Delivering stability: Securing our future housing needs: Final report: Recommendations*, London: HM Treasury/ODPM.

CABE (Commission for Architecture and the Built Environment) and RIBA (Royal Institute of British Architects) (2005) *Urban Futures: Embracing change*, London: CABE and RIBA (available at www.carltd.com/downloads/UrbanFutures.pdf).

Cambridge Futures (1999) *Survey report*, Cambridge: Cambridge Architectural Research Ltd (www.carltd.com/downloads/CambFutures1.pdf).

Holford, W. and Wright, H.M. (1950) *Cambridge planning proposals,* Cambridge: Cambridgeshire Country Council.

Institute for Global Ethics (2005) 'Deliberative public decision-making' (available at www.globalethics.org).

Joseph Rowntree Foundation (2004) *Housing futures: Informed public opinion* (available at www.jrf.org.uk/bookshop/publications.asp and www.carltd.com/downloads/HousingFutures.pdf).

ELEVEN

Conclusion

Liz Cairncross and Peter Malpass

The chapters in this book were originally commissioned for the spring 2005 conference of the Housing Studies Association to mark the anniversaries of two major milestones in housing policy in the UK: the 20th anniversary of the publication of the *Inquiry into British housing*, chaired by the Duke of Edinburgh (NFHA, 1985), and the 25th anniversary of the introduction of the Right to Buy. Both of these events have had a significant impact on the development of housing policy in Britain since 1980, influencing the pattern of tenure and subsidy in existence today.

Looking at the way the housing world has changed in the past 25 years, as Alan Murie, Richard Best and other contributors have done in this book, one may wonder how much of what has occurred in that time could have been predicted in 1980. As Mark Stephens and colleagues observe in their review of housing policy between 1975 and 2000 (ODPM, 2005a), many policies have had unintended consequences, for example, the Right to Buy and homelessness legislation contributed to the residualisation of social rented housing; while other policies may also present trade-offs, such as the growth of financial risk for borrowers alongside increased choice as a result of the liberalisation of the mortgage market. Moreover, new forces and unexpected drivers of change may emerge over time. Economic collapse, climate change and new patterns of migration could all impact in unanticipated ways on the UK housing system. Predicting or speculating about future developments in the next 15-20 years is a challenging exercise. While there appears to be consensus about some aspects of the context and overall trends, there are many areas about which we can only guess. The chapters in this book have presented a variety of visions and possible scenarios of how the future might be. On the whole, the possible futures have tended to be dystopian, and there seems little cause for optimism.

Although coming from a range of backgrounds, academic, policy and practitioner, our contributors demonstrate considerable agreement on some key aspects of the future. While there may be differences of focus and detail, it seems that all our contributors agree on the continuing importance of social, economic and demographic factors, and the interaction between them, as the key drivers of change. Where there is debate, it is around the relative importance of these forces over time, *and* about outcomes.

While the housing situation in Britain and other advanced economies today is a lot better than it was 50 or 60 years ago with improvements in conditions, amenities and overcrowding, it cannot be taken for granted that this is sustainable. This is because it is unclear to what extent the present situation is the result of postwar investment and policies, rather than more recent trends when housing completion rates in both the public and private sectors have fallen to historically low levels. In housing terms, we could be living on borrowed time.

Current trends

We can be reasonably confident that most of the housing stock of 2020 is already built. Although a 'step-change' in supply is part of the government's plans for housing (ODPM, 2003), bolstered by the recommendations of the Barker Review (Barker, 2004), any new building over the next 15 years will represent only a small proportion of the total stock in 2020, around 10% assuming no losses. As a consequence of this, future housing policies need to address the continuing problem of an ageing housing stock. The Decent Homes target may well become a moving one in order to accommodate the continuous process of decline and disrepair affecting both private, local authority and housing association homes. At present 5% of the whole housing stock in England is unfit (ODPM, 2005b), and 21% of the stock was built before 1919 (ODPM, 2005c).

A second area of certainty is the profile of the population and a continuing trend in household formation. Although there is uncertainty about the absolute total, the age profile and the increase in households is part of a long-term trend, particularly of single-person households. It is projected that additional single-person households will represent 71% of the total 3.8 million increase in households anticipated between 1996 and 2021 (DETR, 1999). This has obvious consequences for levels of demand. What is less certain is how this growing number of single-person households will use the available stock. Elderly single-person households left alone in the family home may choose to trade down to smaller homes, or to convert their homes into flats as a way of releasing equity and saving on running costs, or they may continue to consume as much housing as they can afford to pay for. Policy makers may seek to develop mechanisms to encourage more effective use of the existing stock and ways to reduce 'under-occupation' not just in the social housing sector, but also among owner-occupiers where 45% of homeowners are currently 'under-occupying' (ODPM, 2000c).

As Richard Best points out in Chapter Three, increased longevity in the 20th century meant, in effect, that there was an additional generation of people to be housed. In Chapter Eight, Moyra Riseborough and Peter Fletcher address the future growth of the ageing population, making the powerful point that older people in the next generation will be different from those of the past, and that we can expect them to be more affluent, more independent and more determined to secure a satisfactory standard of living in retirement. They will also have considerable voting power, and they can be expected to use it. Many of the additional households in 2020 will be elderly: the government estimates that between 2003 and 2031, the proportion of people aged 65 and above will increase by 23%, while the number of people aged 85 and above will nearly quadruple, to approximately 4 million between 2003 and 2051 (DWP, 2005). A higher percentage of the older population will be owner-occupiers: in 2030, 75% of people aged 45 and above are expected to be owner-occupiers and to remain so throughout the rest of their lives (ONS, 2004).

The coincidence of an ageing housing stock alongside an ageing population will present a growing problem of disrepair. Today's elderly homeowners are people who enjoyed the fruits of full employment, but the next generation will, in an increasing number of cases, be people who have experienced periods of unemployment, and consequently will have experienced greater difficulties keeping their homes in good order. Some of them will be carrying mortgage debts into old age that previous generations would have cleared before retirement. The poor and elderly homeowners of the future will struggle to pay for and organise the work needed to maintain their homes adequately. In addition, as they become increasingly infirm and disabled, there will be a need for increased funding for aids and adaptations to enable them to live independently in their homes. It seems unlikely that future governments will be willing or able to provide significant funding for repairs and adaptations of privately owned homes. The private sector may develop financial products and services which will enable owner-occupiers to extract some of the equity in their homes to enable them to remain decently housed in them. However, hitherto there has been little sign of such products that are seen as good value for money and trusted by consumers, although the government appears to be more enthusiastic.

We can also be confident that this future generation of older people will have higher expectations and different patterns of housing consumption from previous ones. Retirement pathways will become more varied in the coming years as people's experience of old age varies and there is greater opportunity (or financial necessity) to continue working past the statutory retirement age. The growth of Buy to Let in recent times has been partly fuelled by a move by some investors into rented property as a substitute for or supplement to private pension provision. How these factors will impact on housing and the housing market in the longer run is not clear.

Another trend that is largely the result of government policy is also predicted to continue. This is the erosion of the boundaries between tenures. Both in legal and financial terms, the clear fault lines between different types of tenure appear to be blurring. Phil Morgan (Chapter Nine) foresees an increasing variety in forms of tenure, while Alan Murie (Chapter Two) questions the usefulness of the concept of tenure as a framework for the analysis of housing now and in the future, as the old rigid divisions of tenure have declining significance. For example, conventional tenure categories do not allow for shared equity – which is both renting and owning – but this seems set to become a rapidly expanding part of the British housing scene. Murie predicts an increasingly stratified housing market and new fault lines within tenures. People can already move from discretionary tenancies as new council tenants, to a secure council or assured housing association tenancy to various forms of shared and full ownership. The new Homebuy scheme (ODPM, 2005d) provides an additional option based on the concept of equity stakeholding and a belief that this will contribute to the stability and sustainability of communities. In the future, it seems clear that poverty and social exclusion will be less tenure-specific and more related to locational factors.

A final trend which a number of contributors expect to continue over the coming 15-20 years is the decline of local forms of governance and organisation. Government offices and regional housing and planning bodies are manifestations of this development, reducing the role of local authorities in planning and enabling the provision of both affordable and open-market housing. Arm's length management organisations (ALMOs) may be locally based and controlled organisations, but their long-term future is uncertain (and it seems likely that, as their critics predict, they will be merely a staging post on the road to becoming a form of transfer housing association). The housing association movement is witnessing a considerable degree of organisational change with mergers and the formation of group structures taking place on an ever more frequent basis. Pawson and Fancy (2003) cite Housing Corporation data that shows that 60% of all English transfer landlords in existence in 2001 were involved in group structures. New technology facilitates these kinds of development, and the continuing drive for reduced costs and economies of scale provide a further impetus. As housing associations become increasingly reliant on private finance, the search for efficiency savings to satisfy the demands of investors will become more insistent and more mergers are to be expected. The recent history of the building society movement provides an interesting comparator that indicates that the process of mergers and acquisitions may have a long way to run before it reaches exhaustion.

Cleavages

A number of our contributors, Rowland Atkinson (Chapter Seven) and Moyra Riseborough and Peter Fletcher (Chapter Eight) in particular, identify future tensions and conflicts around two main cleavages: socio-spatial segregation and intergenerational issues. Both are the result of powerful and deep-rooted drivers of change that will test the ingenuity of government. However, the way in which these two phenomena evolve and impact on housing, and how politicians and policy makers respond to the challenges they present, will be critical to the maintenance of an equitable society over the longer term.

The growing spatial segregation of the affluent from the poor is a theme that has run through this book, highlighting the tension between the trajectory of market forces and the sustainable mixed community objectives of policy makers. Whether through the very visible, physical form of the gated community where the affluent can insulate themselves from 'sink' estates and antisocial neighbours, discussed by Rowland Atkinson (Chapter Seven), or the less obvious concentration of the well-off in particular parts of post-industrial cities discussed by Brendan Nevin and Philip Leather in their chapter (Chapter Five) on housing market renewal in Manchester, or the flow of the more mobile and better qualified to London and the South East from other regions and other countries presented by Christine Whitehead (Chapter Four), there is a clear trend towards growing spatial segregation in terms of who lives where. Other authors have identified similar patterns in rural–urban flows with the growth of a 'socially exclusive countryside' (Hoggart, cited in Gallent et al, 2003). This development should come as no surprise, reflecting the increased role of the market in sorting and allocating housing in the UK, paralleling the growth of owner-occupation and the deregulation of financial markets.

The growth of spatial segregation (and its companion inequality) is one of the most worrying trends affecting housing in the UK. In his introduction to *Homes for all* (ODPM, 2005d, p 2) John Prescott states that the government's plan is "based on promoting choice". In a period where choice appears to be assigned greater importance than tackling inequality by many politicians and policy makers, it seems likely that the growing spatial separation of rich and poor will prove an increasingly 'wicked' issue. Not only does it appear to threaten the objective of equality so central to the traditional welfare state, but it would seem likely also to undermine other objectives, such as those of mixed and sustainable communities. If rich and poor are to be increasingly spatially concentrated, this is likely to reinforce social exclusion and adversely affect the quality of neighbourhoods, community cohesion and access to public services, with the better-off abandoning failing areas and withdrawing from the consumption of public goods, weakening their commitment to collective, social provision.

The trend in spatial segregation and the elevation of choice as a policy goal also appear to conflict with the concept of urban renaissance and high-density living. The desire to increase densities in order to preserve the green belt and prevent suburban sprawl contradicts the work of futures researchers like Stephen Platt and his colleagues at Cambridge Architectural Research (Chapter Ten), who found strong preferences among first-time buyers for detached and semi-detached homes, that is, low-density housing forms (Platt et al, 2004).

The second major cleavage that can be expected to deepen over the coming years is between the generations. Housing already represents the largest single category of privately held wealth in the UK. There is widespread consensus among our contributors that government sees this wealth as an as yet untapped resource on which individuals should be called to draw, whether to pay for their long-term care, their pensions, or some other aspect of welfare. Governments are loath to tax housing wealth directly, and forcing elderly owner-occupiers to sell their homes to pay for residential care is politically unpopular. However, it seems highly plausible that the further stretching of owner-occupation through the expansion of shared equity schemes is but a necessary preliminary to a widening of the asset base, prior to the introduction of some mechanism for releasing housing equity to contribute to the costs of the welfare state. To the extent that people draw down their housing wealth, they cannot leave it to their children, but it will be their children's generation who will have to buy the houses to allow the equity release: a group that is already facing high levels of personal debt. People in the 25-44 age group have debt to income ratios of 20% (May et al, 2004). If effective demand begins to fail, the question arises of whether property values in the longer term will remain high enough for older people to be able to use their housing wealth to provide for themselves in old age.

If property is to become the basis for paying for individual welfare needs, especially in old age, as appears likely, this has serious implications. First, for those who do not have any housing wealth on which to draw, it may affect their access to services; and, second, it changes the whole basis on which the welfare state was built, potentially making the capacity to pay, rather than need, the criterion for access. Presumably some kind of two-tier system would emerge: a first tier for those with sufficient resources to pay for their care, and a second tier providing a residual, safety-net role for those lacking an equity stake in their home.

Continuing themes

Just as we can be reasonably confident about the key trends and emerging cleavages over the next 15-20 years, there can also be considerable certainty about some of the problems that they will raise. Affordability is and will continue to be a serious barrier to decent housing, affecting a significant proportion of the population, particularly the young and those living in the South of England. In Chapter Six, Glen Bramley identifies the critical constraints on affordability as the lack of new build and inadequate levels of public subsidy. Neither of these is likely to change significantly in the foreseeable future. Access to wealth is already becoming increasingly important for first-time buyers, especially in the South of England. Many of tomorrow's future first-time buyers will come to the market with large student loans and increasing pressure to start saving for their pensions at an early age. The continuing failure of supply, especially in London and the South of England irrespective of a 'step-change' in the production of new homes in the Thames Gateway and other growth areas, the steady and continuing increase in the number of households and high levels of personal indebtedness will all ensure that affordability in the South of England remains a problem in the years to come as a result of shortages and excess demand. If anything, it seems likely that problems of affordability will increase.

Choice in housing, as in health and education, has become a goal shared by the main political parties, and it seems reasonably safe to predict that this will continue for the foreseeable future. However, if greater choice is available, the consequence will be greater inequality as the wealthy move to the suburbs, or the country, or the South of England, leaving the poor to become ever more concentrated in socially excluded neighbourhoods. As a tool for addressing inequality, choice is singularly ineffective. Greater choice may also have a trade-off in terms of greater risk. It seems unavoidable that the consequence of more and more people being given the opportunity of home ownership or some form of stakeholding in property, will be an increase in risk, and their vulnerability to a change in their personal financial circumstances or the wider economy. A sudden downturn in the economy or increase in interest rates in the future could have a serious impact on the housing system, leaving many home owners unable to pay their mortgages and becoming homeless.

Although tenure is predicted to decline in importance, the continued residualisation and stigmatisation of social housing must be a concern for future housing policy makers. It appears already to have become a polarised tenure composed of poor younger households with children, and elderly long-term tenants. At present 23% of older people live in social housing in England (ODPM, 2005c). As this group dwindles, it seems likely that those living in social housing will become ever more marginalised and excluded from wider social and economic opportunities. Phil Morgan (Chapter Nine) identifies antisocial behaviour as the biggest single threat faced by social housing, while Alan Murie (Chapter Two) notes that social housing is acquiring a more transitional role. Both of these developments may affect the stability of neighbourhoods with high concentrations of social housing. Here also it appears that the government objectives of mixed and sustainable communities are in tension with the developments on the ground.

The development of ever larger organisations responsible for the provision and governance of housing appears to contradict the policy objective of widening participation and empowerment of individuals and local communities. But, as Stephen Platt and Ian Cooper (Chapter Ten) remind us, people are able to make reasoned choices – all that is required is a willingness to engage with public opinion in a meaningful way. While forms of governance look set to become more remote from the grass roots, the sorts of methodologies outlined in Chapter

Ten offer a fruitful alternative to established ways of pursuing wider participation. With the decline of the role of local authorities and local housing associations, politicians and policy makers appear concerned to promote greater participation at the local level. There is a question mark about how, for example, tenant board members can play a meaningful role on the boards of large housing associations. Phil Morgan makes the point in Chapter Nine that the emergence of 'mega-landlords' will reduce the opportunities for tenants to be at the heart of decision making. The growing tension between empowerment and managerialism that has developed in housing, as in other areas of social policy, is unlikely to be resolved over the next 15–20 years. It seems predictable that the more distant and professionalised the form of governance becomes, the less likely it will be that people will wish to invest time in what may be perceived as merely symbolic participation.

What we do not know

So far, we have discussed what we think we do know in terms of trends and the problems to be faced in the next 15–20 years. Apart from the global uncertainties such as climate change, disease and migration patterns, there are more local unknowns that could equally have significant effects on the direction of housing and housing policy in the future. The most obvious of these is the economy; housing policy has been developed in the past decade in the context of a growing economy with low inflation, low interest rates and low unemployment. But these cannot be taken for granted in the future. A housing market collapse has happened before, could happen again and has been predicted for 2010 (Harrison, 2005).

Peering into the future, the likelihood of different scenarios becomes more difficult the further we get from the present. In the short term, we can be reasonably confident that the number of houses, the people in them and the systems and processes in operation will be very similar to what exists today, with changes coming from housing market instability and unexpected policy initiatives. Looking further ahead, say 25 years or more, the operation of the cleavages discussed above will be impacting on the housing system in ways that we can only struggle to anticipate.

Owner-occupation is now at 80% for the 45–64 age group in England. How much further can it be extended? If it becomes a 'milch cow' for the welfare state, will other forms of tenure become more attractive? How attractive will the new forms of tenure be? Shared ownership was first introduced in the 1980s and shared owners total just under 80,000 households in England or 0.4% of all households (ODPM and WAG, 2002). Tenure change takes time, and it may still be many years before everyone has a stake in their home, in the way that the government wishes to see.

How will older people use their housing wealth? Will they spend for today or withdraw equity to transfer it to the next generation? Will young people live at home for longer? Will there be more three-generation households as a response to problems of affordability? The response of households to the changing demographic profile and the consequences of increased longevity is one of the most difficult to predict. This is not just a foreign country, but an undiscovered one too.

How will the population change in terms of size and structure over the coming years? The flows of people (mainly of working age) from the European accession states and elsewhere are significant and could reduce the impact of the ageing population on the housing system. Equally, little reliable data is available on the level of emigration from the UK, to southern Europe in particular. More research is needed to assess the long-term impact of these flows about which relatively little is currently known.

Much of today's housing policy is predicated on a growing role for the private sector. Historically, the private sector has shown little interest in meeting the need for affordable housing. How willing will the private sector be to contribute to the 'step-change' in housing supply which is needed to tackle the shortfall in affordable housing in the South of England? Anecdotal evidence from the Thames Gateway indicates that the private sector on its own cannot meet the challenge.

What needs to happen

As we stated at the outset, while this book is not a manifesto, the chapters represent the views of a range of academics, policy makers and practitioners about what can be learnt from the past, and the likely direction of housing and housing policy in the future. While there is considerable consensus on broad trends, there is much more scope for disagreement over the detail and the appropriate policy response to the problems which are anticipated. A key lesson to emerge from the work of Mark Stephens and colleagues (ODPM, 2005a) is that policies work best where they follow the grain of economic and social change. This presents a challenge for any policy maker who seeks to tackle many of the continuing and emerging problems that have been identified in this book.

As we said in our introduction, it seems reasonable to assume that future governments will want to protect and preserve the housing market, not only to maintain economic stability but also as a potential resource to be tapped for the provision of pensions and care in old age. The central problem here is a tension between rational housing policy on the one hand, and the expectations of both consumers and the government on the other. From a housing policy point of view it would be better to place much more emphasis on the use value of homes (seeing them as consumption rather than investment), thereby challenging the apparently widely held expectation that owning a home is a virtually guaranteed route to untaxed wealth accumulation. However, as we have suggested, housing wealth appears to be seen within government as a major part of the solution to the problem of paying for public services in the future. The market contributes, and will continue to contribute, to many of the obstructions to meeting the goal of a decent home for all at a price they can afford: creating a barrier to affordability, growing spatial segregation, intergenerational tensions and regional disparities, constraining the supply of new homes, and contributing to the residualisation of social housing. If policy makers are successfully to tackle these obstacles, major new investment in both new and existing affordable housing is necessary. Housing needs to return to the top of the policy agenda.

References

Barker, K. (2004) *Review of housing supply: Delivering stability: Securing our future housing needs: Final report: Recommendations*, London: HM Treasury/ODPM.

DETR (Department of the Environment, Transport and the Regions) (1999) *Projection of households in England 2021*, London: The Stationery Office.

DWP (Department for Work and Pensions) (2005) *Opportunity age: Vol 2, A social portrait of ageing in the UK*, London: The Stationery Office.

Gallent, N., Shucksmith, M. and Tewdwr-Jones, M. (eds) (2003) *Housing in the European countryside*, London: Routledge.

Harrison, F. (2005) *Boom bust: House prices, banking and the depression of 2010*, London: Shepheard-Walwyn.

Hoggert, K. (2003) in N. Gallent, M. Shucksmith and M. Tewdwr-Jones (eds) *Housing in the European countryside: rural pressure and policy in western Europe*, London: Routledge, pp 153-67.

May, O., Tudela, M. and Young, G. (2004) 'British household indebtedness and financial stress: a household picture', *Bank of England Quarterly Bulletin*, Winter, pp 414-28, London: Bank of England.

NFHA (National Federation of Housing Associations) (1985) *Inquiry into British housing*, London: NFHA.

ODPM (Office of the Deputy Prime Minister) (2003) *Sustainable communities – Building for the future*, London: ODPM.

ODPM (2005a) *Lessons from the past, challenges for the future for housing policy: An evaluation of English housing policy, 1975-2000*, London: ODPM.

ODPM (2005b) *English House Condition Survey, Key findings for 2003: Decent homes and decent places*, London: ODPM.

ODPM (2005c) *Survey of English Housing 2003-04 part one: Trends in tenure and cross tenure topics*, London: ODPM.

ODPM (2005d) *Homes for all: Expanding opportunities for home ownership*, London: ODPM.

ODPM and WAG (Welsh Assembly Government) (2002) *Evaluation of the low-cost home ownership programme*, London: ODPM.

ONS (Office for National Statistics) (2004) *Living in Britain: Results from the General Household Survey, 2002*, London: The Stationery Office.

Pawson, H. and Fancy, C. (2003) *Maturing assets: The evolution of stock transfer housing associations*, Bristol/York: The Policy Press/Joseph Rowntree Foundation.

Platt, S., Fawcett, W. and de Carteret, R. (2004) *Housing Futures: Informed public opinion*, York: York Publishing Services.

Index

Locators shown in *italics* refer to Figures, Photographs and Tables.